The Breaking of the Bread

The Development of the Eucharist
according to the Acts of the Apostles

Eugene LaVerdiere, sss

LTP

LITURGY
TRAINING
PUBLICATIONS

Acknowledgments

Copyright © 1998, Archdiocese of Chicago: Liturgy Training Publications, 1800 North Hermitage Avenue, Chicago IL 60622-1101; 1-800-933-1800; fax 1-800-933-7094; e-mail orders@ltp.org. All rights reserved.

This book was edited by Martin F. Connell. Audrey Novak Riley was the production editor. Anna Manhart created the design, which was executed by production artist Mark Hollopeter in Futura and Sabon. The cover art is by Carolina Arentsen. The map icons on pages 6, 36, 66, 104, 162 and 192 are by Carolina Arentsen and on page 8, by Mary Bowers and Anna Manhart. Printed by Quebecor Printing Book Group in the United States of America.

05 04 03 02 01 00 99 98   6 5 4 3 2 1

Library of Congress Cataloging-in-Publication Data
LaVerdiere, Eugene.
    The breaking of the bread: the development of the Eucharist according to the Acts of the Apostles/Eugene Laverdiere; edited by Martin F. Connell.
        p.   cm.
    Includes index.
    ISBN 1-56854-148-1
    1. Lord's Supper — Biblical teaching. 2. Bible. N.T. Acts — Criticism, interpretation, etc. I. Connell, Martin, 1960 – .
    II. Title.
    BV832.L329   1998
    234'.163'09015 – dc21   98-9770
                                                                    CIP

ISBN 1-56854-148-1
ACTS

Contents

List of Tables

To my sister
Claudette LaVerdiere, MM
A woman of Maryknoll

Preface

If you are lucky enough to have lived in Paris as a young man, then wherever you go for the rest of your life, it stays with you, for Paris is a moveable feast.

Writing to a friend, Ernest Hemingway was describing his early years in Paris. Later, in his book *A Moveable Feast* he invited everyone to join him in the feast.

Paris, a moveable feast. Everyone who has even visited Paris would agree.

But Jerusalem is also a moveable feast. And so is Rome. Paraphrasing Hemingway, if you are blessed enough to have lived in Jerusalem and in Rome during your formative years, then wherever you go for the rest of your life, they stay with you, for Jerusalem is a moveable feast, and so is Rome.

Jerusalem is the city where Jesus celebrated his Last Supper, the city of his passion, resurrection and ascension (Luke 22:1 — 24:53). Jerusalem is also where the apostles gathered in prayer, "together with some women, and Mary the mother of Jesus, and his brothers" (Acts 1:13 – 14). Jerusalem is the city of Pentecost, the city of the primitive community, where they assembled for the breaking of the bread (2:42).

Rome is the city where Paul, after a long, very difficult journey, spent two years. There "he received all who came to him, and with complete assurance and without hindrance he proclaimed the kingdom of God and taught about the Lord Jesus Christ" (28:31 – 32).

Seeing Jerusalem and Rome through Luke's eyes, dining with Jesus and breaking bread with the early communities, we live the feast wherever we go for the rest of our lives. No place is too remote. The moveable feast of Jerusalem and Rome stays with us even "to the ends of the earth" (1:8).

I realized this a few years ago in conversation with an old friend in my parents' home town. Our conversation began with small talk:

health, family, work, happenings around town. Then Clayton, a journalist, said, "Tell me about your trip to China."

"I looked into the face of the early church!" I answered, to my own surprise. At the time I had no idea where the words came from.

Clayton replied, "How wonderful."

I looked into the face of the early church at a shrine honoring Saint Francis Xavier at San Chu'an Tao (Sancian Island). San Chu'an Tao is where Francis Xavier died.

I looked into the face of the early church in Jiangmen (Kongmoon) while visiting the priests, sisters and parishioners of the Cathedral of the Immaculate Conception.

I looked into the face of the early church wherever I went in China, including Beijing and Xi'an, the historic capital.

In San Chu'an Tao, Peter Barry, a Maryknoll priest based in Hong Kong, and I visited a community of Catholics who had been without priests or religious for a long time. Physically isolated from the rest of the church, they had passed on the faith and supported one another through difficult times, meeting in their homes, sharing meals together and joining in prayer.

When we paused on the way to the shrine to visit a school, the site of an old mission, someone asked us, "Are you Christians?" Peter answered, "Yes, we are."

"Are you Catholics?" he asked.

"Yes, we are."

"So am I." And he showed us a medal he wore on a chain around his neck. "My name is James. I have a brother named John. We are fishermen!"

It took me some time to realize that James was a fisherman in the gospel sense. He and his brother were indeed fishermen by trade. They lived in an old fishing village close by the bay, among rice paddies stretching around and behind the town up into the mountains. But as Christians they also cast their nets for human beings, gathering them into the kingdom of God.

We met at James' house in an upper room filled with members of the community, young and old. We had tea and rice cakes together as they told their story, a gospel story as people surely told when they assembled in Jerusalem or Rome.

Today, the memory of that upper room on San Chu'an Tao is connected for me with a passage in the book of Acts describing the early church in Jerusalem: "They devoted themselves to the teaching of the apostles and to the communal life, to the breaking of the bread and to the prayers" (2:42). It is also connected with the story of how the Twelve, unable to meet all the demands of Christian service *(diakonia),* appointed the Seven to serve in their place (6:1–7).

The memory is also connected with Peter's discourse at the home of Cornelius. As one who had eaten and drunk at the table of Jesus, the Lord of all, Peter had to share the gospel with everyone. He had to invite everyone to the breaking of the bread at the table of the Lord (10:34–43).

In China, I looked into the face of the early church. But we do not have to go far away to discover the face of the early church. It is all around us. It has been with us from the beginning of life. The story of the early church is still unfolding, and we have a part in it.

In offering this book, I wish to thank my family: my mom and my dad, Gladys and Laurier; my sister Claudette, MM; my brother, Brother Gary, SSS, manager and art director of *Emmanuel* magazine; my brother Peter, his wife, Cheryl, and my nephews, Jason, Charles and Kevin.

Like Jerusalem and Rome, our home is a moveable feast. In a special way, I thank my religious family, the Congregation of the Blessed Sacrament, my local community serving St. Jean Baptiste Church in New York, and my Provincial Superior, Anthony Schueller, SSS, for their constant support.

I also thank Bishop William McCormack, national director of the Society for the Propagation of the Faith, and the entire staff at the National Office for their friendship and support. Breaking bread with them is very nourishing.

I am also indebted to my colleagues at Catholic Theological Union in Chicago, the University of St. Mary of the Lake in Mundelein, Illinois, and the Saint Paul Seminary School of Divinity of the University of St. Thomas. During the writing of this book, I spent many happy hours in their respective libraries.

I also wish to thank the editors at Liturgy Training Publications for their encouragement, helpful advice, and not least for their patience; my former secretary, Mary Maloney, who is now retired; and my new secretary, Maryanne Macaluso, for reading the manuscript and assisting in its preparation for publication.

I dedicate this book to my sister Claudette, a Maryknoll sister, with whom I have broken bread again and again. Over the years she has shown me the face of the early church in Kenya and Tanzania, where she spent more than twenty years on mission. After her term as president of the Maryknoll Sisters, she is now studying scripture (what else?), preparing for a future mission. Jerusalem and Rome are moveable feasts. It is a blessing and a grace to share them with her.

June 21, 1997
St. Jean Baptiste Church
New York, New York

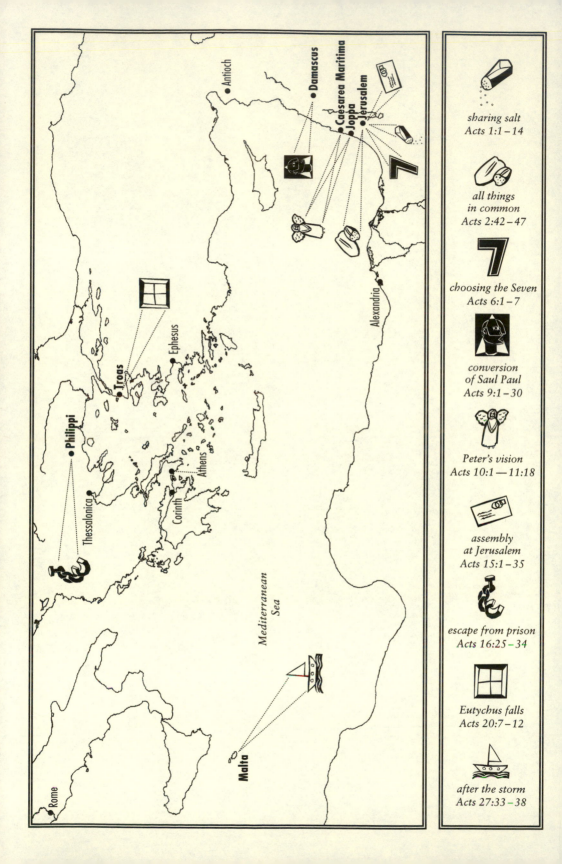

Antioch

Damascus

Caesarea Maritima

Joppa

Jerusalem

Alexandria

Ephesus

Troas

Philippi

Thessalonica

Athens

Corinth

Mediterranean
Sea

Malta

Rome

sharing salt
Acts 1:1 – 14

all things
in common
Acts 2:42 – 47

choosing the Seven
Acts 6:1 – 7

conversion
of Saul Paul
Acts 9:1 – 30

Peter's vision
Acts 10:1 — 11:18

assembly
at Jerusalem
Acts 15:1 – 35

escape from prison
Acts 16:25 – 34

Eutychus falls
Acts 20:7 – 12

after the storm
Acts 27:33 – 38

Chapter I

The Eucharist in the Acts of the Apostles

> *In the first book, Theophilus,*
> *I dealt with all that Jesus did and taught*
> *until the day he was taken up,*
> *after giving instructions through the holy Spirit*
> *to the apostles whom he had chosen.*
>
> > Acts 1:1 – 2

The Gospel of Luke and its story of the origins of the eucharist[1] end with three closely related stories, the visit to the tomb (24:1 – 12), the story of Emmaus (24:13 – 35) and Jesus' appearance to the community assembled in Jerusalem (24:36 – 53). Together, these stories provide a dramatic conclusion for Luke's first book and its story of the origins of the eucharist (Acts 1:1).

After Jesus' ascension, the Gospel leaves us with Jesus' followers "continually in the temple praising (*eulogountes*, blessing) God" (Luke 24:53). Blessed by Jesus as he ascended (*eulogesen, en to eulogein*, 24:50 – 51), Jesus' followers blessed God in return.

As they conclude the story of Jesus, the three stories also announce the story of the church and its mission "to all nations, beginning from Jerusalem" (Luke 24:47; see Acts 1:8). Before ascending, Jesus addressed those who would soon be the church: "And [behold] I am sending the promise of my Father upon you; but stay in the city until you are clothed with power from on high" (Luke 24:49; see Acts 1:1 – 4). The conclusion of the Gospel thus provides a transition to the Book of Acts and its story of the development of the eucharist.

The story of the visit to the tomb tells that two men greeted Mary Magdalene, Joanna, Mary the mother of James, and the other women with them when they came to the tomb (Luke 24:4 – 7). The story of Emmaus tells that two disciples, Cleopas and a companion,

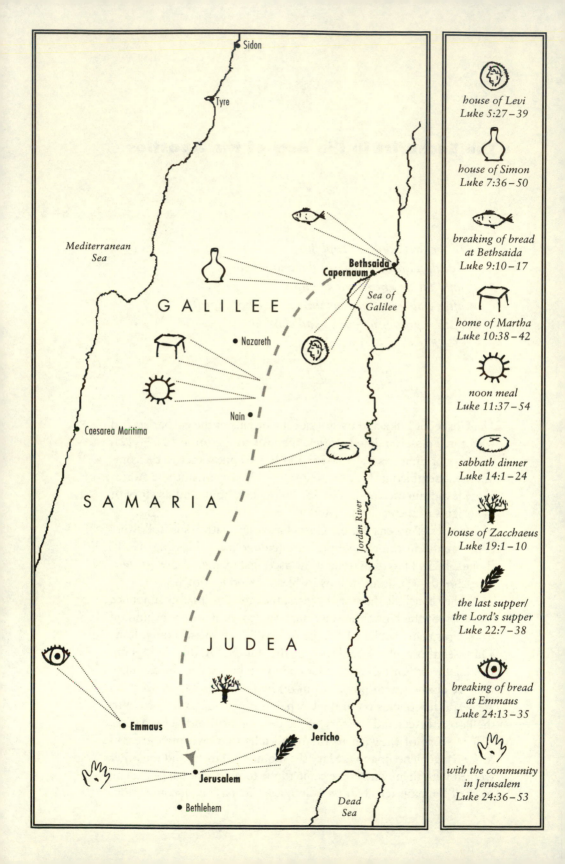

Sidon

Tyre

*Mediterranean
Sea*

G A L I L E E

Bethsaida
Capernaum

*Sea of
Galilee*

• Nazareth

• Nain

• Caesarea Maritima

S A M A R I A

Jordan River

J U D E A

• Emmaus

• Jericho

Jerusalem

• Bethlehem

*Dead
Sea*

*house of Levi
Luke 5:27–39*

*house of Simon
Luke 7:36–50*

*breaking of bread
at Bethsaida
Luke 9:10–17*

*home of Martha
Luke 10:38–42*

*noon meal
Luke 11:37–54*

*sabbath dinner
Luke 14:1–24*

*house of Zacchaeus
Luke 19:1–10*

*the last supper/
the Lord's supper
Luke 22:7–38*

*breaking of bread
at Emmaus
Luke 24:13–35*

*with the community
in Jerusalem
Luke 24:36–53*

recognized Jesus "in the breaking of the bread" (24:31, 35). The story of the community in Jerusalem tells that Jesus reassured "the eleven and those with them" (24:33) by eating fish "in front of them" (24:41 – 43).

Entering the tomb, the women had not found "the body of the Lord Jesus" *(to soma tou kyriou Jesou)* and they were amazed (24:3 – 4a). Seeing their amazement, the two men asked: "Why do you seek the living one *(ton zonta)* among the dead?" (24:5) Jesus was not there. He had been raised (24:6). Where then should they seek him? The answer comes in the story of Emmaus and of Jesus' appearance to the community in Jerusalem.[2]

The story of Emmaus shows that the disciples should seek the Living One among the living, "in the breaking of the bread" (24:35). The story tells that Jesus "took bread, said the blessing, broke it, and gave it to them" (24:30). At that, the eyes of the disciples were opened and they recognized him, even as he vanished from their sight (24:31).

The story of the community in Jerusalem shows that the apostolic community should seek the Living One in the midst of the community (Luke 24:42). The story tells that Jesus ate a final meal with the community (24:41 – 42), opened their minds to understand the scriptures (24:45 – 47) and declared them his witnesses (*martyres,* Luke 24:48; see Acts 1:8) before "he parted from them and was taken up to heaven" (Luke 24:51).[3]

Together, the events of the stories of the visit to the tomb,[4] Emmaus and the community in Jerusalem marked the end of an era. Until then, Jesus had been present with the disciples historically, speaking with them and sharing meals. With the passion-resurrection, Jesus of Nazareth, "a prophet mighty in deed and word before God and all the people" (24:19), disappeared from their sight (24:31) and was taken up to heaven (24:51). They no longer saw him as they had in the Galilean ministry (5:1 – 9:50) and on the great journey to Jerusalem (9:51 – 24:53).

The same stories mark the beginning of a new era in which Jesus would be present to the disciples in a new and unprecedented way, which a later age would call "sacramental." In and through them, he would also be present to countless others, eating and drinking in the kingdom of God (see 22:15 – 18). For that, Jesus would send them the promise of his Father and they would be "clothed with power from on high" (24:49).

In the new era, foreshadowed by Jesus' appearances at Emmaus and in Jerusalem, they would remember Jesus of Nazareth (24:19) taking meals with them and speaking to them (24:6–8, 44). They would take bread, say a blessing or give thanks and break the bread, saying: "This is my body, which will be given for you" (24:30; 22:19), both fulfilling and handing on his command: "Do this in memory of me" (22:19; see also 1 Corinthians 11:24, 25). Doing what he did in his memory, they would recognize the Lord Jesus, the Living One, in the breaking of the bread (24:31–35).

At the beginning of Acts,[5] a brief preface (1:1–2) recalls the events told at the end of the Gospel, in particular the final appearance to the community assembled in Jerusalem (Luke 24:36–53), when Jesus gave "instructions through the holy Spirit to the apostles whom he had chosen" (Acts 1:2). Doing so, the preface presents the story of the church as the continuation of the story of Jesus.

In the Gospel, Luke told what Jesus began *(erxato)* to do and teach "until the day he was taken up" (1:2). In the Acts of the Apostles, Luke tells what Jesus continued to do and teach after the passion (1:3–14), "in Jerusalem, throughout Judea and Samaria and to the ends of the earth" (1:8). For Luke, the Book of Acts, with its story of the church, is the gospel of the risen Lord.[6]

The Breaking of the Bread

The Gospel told the story of the origins of the church in the life of Jesus. Within that story, the Gospel also told the story of the origins of the eucharist. Acts continues the story with the development of the church "in Jerusalem, throughout Judea and Samaria, and to the ends of the earth" (Acts 1:8). Acts also tells the story of the development of the eucharist as part of the life of the church.

At the end of the story of Emmaus, Luke referred to the eucharist as "the breaking of the bread": "Then the two recounted what had taken place on the way and how he was made known to them in the breaking of the bread" *(en te klasei tou artou,* Luke 24:35). At the end of the story of Pentecost, Luke again refers to the breaking of the bread in a little summary describing the life of the church: "They devoted themselves to the teaching of the apostles and to the communal life, to the breaking of the bread *(te klasei tou artou)* and to the prayers" (Acts 2:42). In Luke-Acts, the eucharist has a new name.

Table 1

The Ten Meals with Jesus in the Context of Luke's Gospel[1]

1:1 – 4 Preface: Narrative of events fulfilled in our midst
1:5 — 2:52 Prologue: Ultimate origins and ultimate destiny
3:1 — 4:13 Historical background and preparation
4:14 — 24:53 The story of Jesus

> Beginnings in Galilee (4:14 – 44)
>
> Origins of the church in Jesus' Galilean ministry (5:1 — 9:50)
>> 5:1 — 6:11 The call to discipleship
>>> Banquet at the house of Levi (5:27 – 39)
>> 6:12 — 8:56 Establishing the community of the Twelve
>>> Dinner at the house of Simon the Pharisee (7:36 – 50)
>> 9:1 – 50 The mission of the Twelve
>>> The breaking of the bread at Bethsaida (9:10 – 17)
>
> Life of the church in Jesus' journey to Jerusalem (9:51 — 24:53)
>> 9:51 — 13:21 Setting out on the journey
>>> Hospitality at the home of Martha (10:38 – 42)
>>> Noon meal at the home of a Pharisee (11:37 – 54)
>> 13:22 — 19:48 Proceeding to Jerusalem
>>> Sabbath dinner at the home of a Pharisee (14:1 – 24)
>>> Hospitality at the house of Zacchaeus (19:1 – 10)
>> 20:1 — 21:38 In the temple at Jerusalem
>> 22:1 — 24:53 Passion, resurrection and ascension
>>> The Last Supper (27:7 — 38)
>>> The breaking of the bread at Emmaus (24:13 – 35)
>>> With the community in Jerusalem (24:36 – 53)

1. See Eugene LaVerdiere, *Dining in the Kingdom of God* (Chicago: Liturgy Training Publications, 1994), 12.

The descriptive summary (2:42) tells what the church was like in those very early days after Pentecost, when the original core of disciples (1:13 – 14; 1:15) swelled to more than three thousand (2:41). It also tells what the church would like to be two thousand years later. In our own time, the little summary describes the vision of

Vatican II, a very special and evangelical event in the life of the church. As we approach the new millennium, this summary continues to inspire all those devoted to the renewal of the church.[7]

"The breaking of the bread," one of the four elements in Luke's summary, is Luke's name for the eucharist (see Luke 24:35; Acts 2:42).[8] An earlier name, "the Lord's Supper" *(ho kyriakon deipnon),* spoke of the relationship between the eucharist and Jesus the Lord (see 1 Corinthians 11:17). Another name, "the eucharist" *(he eucharistia),* first attested in the *Didache,* emphasized that the eucharist is a thanksgiving event *(Didache* 8:1).

"The breaking of the bread" *(he klasis tou artou),* Luke's name for the eucharist, highlights the sharing aspect of the eucharist. It speaks of the eucharist as a community event. Bread that is broken is bread to be shared, strengthening and building up the community as an *ekklesia,* an ecclesial community. As a community event, the breaking of the bread is thus an ecclesial event, expressing both "the communal life" *(he koinonia)* and the mission of the church. The breaking of the bread is both a *koinonia* event and a mission event.

This book is about the development of the eucharist according to Acts. In a previous book, *Dining in the Kingdom of God,* I explored "the origins of the eucharist according to Luke," emphasizing how the eucharist is a gospel event.[9] In this companion volume, I emphasize how the eucharist is a community event, that is, an ecclesial event, a *koinonia* event in the life of a missionary church.[10]

After introducing the eucharist as a community event, an ecclesial event and a *koinonia* event, this first chapter will focus on the Book of Acts as Luke's second volume. It will then introduce Acts' story of the development of the eucharist.

A Community Event

When Luke wrote in the mid-eighties, the name "the breaking of the bread" may have been new, but the reality behind it already had a long history, reaching back to the very birth of the church and the life of Jesus. The breaking of the bread also had a rich background in ancient life, early Judaism and the Old Testament.

As the staple food in the ancient Mediterranean world, bread was taken at every meal, so much so that the word "bread" often referred to the entire meal. Sharing bread, sharing a meal, joined people in solidarity. In that context, however, people spoke of "eating bread" or "taking bread together," not of "breaking bread." In the Old Testament, the expression "breaking bread" referred to a particular symbolic act. Later, in early Judaism, it referred to a ritual gesture. Among the Christians, it eventually referred to the eucharist, celebrated in the context of a meal.

The exception in the Old Testament is in the Book of Lamentations, describing the misery of Zion and the hunger of her children (4:4):

> The tongue of the suckling cleaves
> to the roof of its mouth in thirst;
> The babes cry for food (LXX, *arton*),
> but there is no one to give it (LXX, *diaklon*) to them.

Unlike adults, small children cannot eat by themselves. Their bread has to be broken by someone else. With children, breaking bread is not a matter of sharing but of helping them to eat.[11]

A Symbolic Act   The oldest reference to "breaking bread" is in the Old Testament, where it refers to a symbolic act expressing solidarity with people in mourning. After describing Judah's infidelity, the Book of Jeremiah uses the expression "breaking bread" in a severe warning for the people of Judah (16:7):

> They will not break bread (LXX, *klasthe artos*) with the bereaved to console them in their bereavement; they will not give them the cup of consolation to drink over the death of father or mother.

By the same token, the people are not to celebrate with people who have turned away from the Lord and gone astray (16:8):

> Enter not a house where people are celebrating, to sit with them (LXX, *sygkathisai*) eating and drinking (LXX, *phagein kai piein*).

In regard to celebrating, Jeremiah refers simply to eating and drinking. But in regard to consoling the bereaved, he refers to "breaking bread," a symbolic act associated with offering the bereaved "the cup of consolation." In a similar context, Ezekiel refers to the same act as eating "the customary bread" (24:17; see also 24:22–23):

Groan in silence, make no lament for the dead, bind on your turban, put your sandals on your feet, do not cover your beard, and do not eat the customary bread.

A Ritual Gesture

In early Judaism, "breaking bread" represented a simple ritual gesture, accompanied by a Jewish blessing,[12] at the beginning of a meal. The ritual gesture was also a symbolic act uniting all those who took part in the meal. At a family meal, it was the father, the head of the family, who took a loaf of bread, spoke a blessing, broke the bread with his hands and gave a piece to each member of the family and to any guests, to everyone present at the family table.[13] At a community meal, it was the head of the community, for example, a noted teacher or prophetic figure, who took bread, spoke the blessing, broke the bread and gave a piece to each member of the community and to any guests present at the community table.

Like other teachers and prophetic figures in early Judaism, Jesus broke bread at meals with his disciples. In that, Jesus expressed personal solidarity with the disciples, and they with him. He also invited others to join in that solidarity. Performing the ritual gesture, Jesus also blessed *(eulogein)* God. After the passion, resurrection and ascension, the first disciples continued to break bread, in keeping with their Jewish background and the practice of Jesus. As Christians, however, they also gave thanks *(eucharistein)* to God.

Later, however, as more and more of the Christians came from Gentile backgrounds, Christians continued to break bread, but no longer thought of it as a Jewish ritual. Separated from its Jewish origins, breaking bread was practiced as something Jesus had done and his disciples maintained.

Eventually, as communities moved completely away from Judaism, Christians viewed the practice of breaking bread as a Christian tradition with roots in the life of Jesus and the apostolic community. Seen as a distinctively Christian practice, the phrase "breaking bread" gradually came to connote the entire meal.

At this point, it was a small step from the expression "breaking bread" to the name "the breaking of the bread." Unlike the old expression "breaking bread," the name "the breaking of the bread" had no precedent in the Old Testament and early Judaism. Nor was the name used in the Hellenistic and Roman world. "The breaking of the bread" is a distinctively Christian name for a distinctively Christian event, another name for "the Lord's Supper" or "the eucharist."

So it is that Luke-Acts relates "the breaking of the bread" to its origins in the life of Jesus, and presents the ritual gesture of "breaking bread" in relation to its fulfillment in "the breaking of the bread." As teacher and prophet, Jesus broke bread at meals with his disciples, and the first Christians continued the practice as "the breaking of the bread."[14] There was something quite distinctive about "the breaking of the bread," just as there was about Jesus breaking bread. To the dismay of many, Jesus and his followers broke bread with outcasts and those deemed to be sinners (see Luke 5:27–39; 15:1–2; 19:1–10).

By the mid-eighties, when Luke-Acts was written, "breaking bread" and "the breaking of the bread" no longer referred merely to a symbolic act or a ritual gesture performed at the beginning of a meal. Among Christians, the expression "the breaking of the bread" had become the name for the entire eucharistic meal. That development took place in the Lukan communities which were of predominantly Gentile background.

Jesus and the Symbolic Act   As a name for the eucharist, "the breaking of the bread" recalls the simple symbolic act and ritual gesture that Jesus performed at the beginning of a meal. Luke's Gospel refers to Jesus breaking bread on three occasions.

- Feeding a crowd of some five thousand at the city *(polis)* of Bethsaida, Jesus took five loaves and two fish, "and looking up to heaven, he said the blessing over them, broke them, and gave them to the disciples to set before the crowd" (9:16).

- At the Last Supper, Jesus again "took bread, gave thanks *(eucharistesas),* broke it and gave it to them, saying, 'This is my body, which will be given for you; do this in memory of me'" (22:19).

- Later, at Emmaus, Jesus "took bread, said the blessing, broke it, and gave it to them" (24:30).

After the ascension, Jesus' disciples continued to do the same, breaking bread as Jesus did (Acts 2:42). Acts tells about the community at Troas gathering before Paul's departure to break bread (20:7). On that occasion, Paul was the one who broke the bread (20:11).

Breaking bread was in view of sharing. Done at the beginning of a meal, it gave meaning to the entire meal. At Bethsaida, at the Last Supper and at Emmaus, Jesus shared bread with some five thousand, with the apostles and with two disciples, inviting them to share as he did. "The breaking of the bread" was a prophetic event. Breaking and sharing bread, Jesus shared his very person. So did all those who welcomed him personally. In sharing themselves, they shared the person of Jesus, present and acting in and through them.

Jesus and the Ritual Gesture   Jesus' act of breaking and sharing bread was part of a religious, ritual gesture. We see that most clearly in the story of Emmaus, where "the breaking of the bread" (Luke 24:35) refers to what Jesus had done earlier in the story at the home of Cleopas and his companion, when "he took bread, said the blessing, broke it, and gave it to them" (24:30).[15]

In that context, "the breaking of the bread" refers to the whole of Jesus' gesture, which included four steps. In the breaking of the bread, Jesus

- deliberately took bread, calling attention to what he was about to do,
- spoke a blessing, blessing God for blessings received,
- broke the bread that all might partake of the same bread,
- and gave a piece to each, uniting them with one another.

"The breaking of the bread," a sharing event, was a religious event in which Christians blessed God in return for the blessings they received. Those blessings included the companions gathered together at table as well as the bread they would share. At the beginning of the meal, the blessing gave meaning to the whole meal. Blessed by God in the breaking of the bread, the participants blessed God in return.[16]

Jesus and the Lord's Supper   The Christians for whom Luke wrote were mainly of Gentile background. For them, living in Christianity's third generation, the Jewish ritual gesture would have been at most a faint memory. They associated the gesture with something that Jesus and that his disciples continued to do after the ascension. For Luke's early Christian readers, "the breaking of the bread" referred to a Christian gesture described in a liturgical formula used at the Lord's Supper.

This is best seen in the Last Supper, where Jesus "took bread, gave thanks *(eucharistesas),* broke it, and gave it to them, saying, 'This is my body, which will be given for you; do this in memory of me.' And likewise the cup after they had eaten, saying, 'This cup is the new covenant in my blood, which will be shed for you'" (Luke 22:19–20).

In the account of the Last Supper, "breaking bread" is part of a liturgical formula referring to the ritual gesture Jesus performed. The same liturgical formula referred to the words Jesus spoke, proclaiming what he did and commanding the participants to do the same in memory of him.

The setting for the liturgical formula was the Lord's Supper. Celebrated as a symposium,[17] the Lord's Supper was divided into two parts. First there was the meal proper, introduced by the bread gesture. Then there were homiletic reflections in the form of discourse and dialogue, introduced by the cup gesture.

For the Lukan Christians, therefore, "the breaking of the bread" was a name for the eucharist itself, presenting the Lord's Supper as a Christian sharing event. When they gathered for "the breaking of the bread," they fulfilled the command of Jesus to do this in memory of him. They joined him in offering his body, including their own person, as Jesus himself did, saying with Jesus, "This is my body, which will be given for you."

From the very beginning, then, breaking bread was a community event. There is no separating the gesture, "breaking bread," from the family or community meal that followed it. "Breaking bread," which included a blessing prayer, gave the communal meal its religious significance.

And there is no separating "the breaking of the bread" from "the teaching of the apostles," "the communal life" and "the prayers" (Acts 2:42). All four expressions describe the community life of the apostolic church in Jerusalem. A later age might have called them the marks of the apostolic church. None of the four, including "the breaking of the bread," could subsist apart from the others.

An Ecclesial Event

From the very beginning, the breaking of the bread was a community event, but a special kind of community event. The New Testament presents it as an ecclesial event. The New Testament does not speak of the church as a community, but as an *ekklesia,* a people called together by the Lord (see Luke 5:1 – 11; 5:27– 39).

Community is a modern concern connected with a wide range of social needs, especially in the Western world. Human beings need community. In large parts of the world people have community to such an extent that many languages have no word for community.[18] Simply being human is living as part of a community. When people have community, it is not a concern.

Having community means having stable, personal relationships in various levels and spheres of human living. People, for example, need stable family relationships and social environments such as neighborhoods, small towns, workplaces and churches. When these are threatened or disappear, or when populations are very mobile, community is felt as a need.

Today community is often a major preoccupation, especially in societies marked by individualism or collectivism. It was not so in ancient biblical times, when living as part of a community was taken for granted. Nor was it so in New Testament, patristic or medieval times.

Community is very important for the church, but there is a difference between church *(ekklesia)* and what we generally call community. *Ekklesia* describes the church as a faith reality. Community describes the church as a social reality. *Ekklesia* is a theological term. Community is a sociological term.

There is no escaping our modern need for community, but community is no substitute for *ekklesia.* Nor is there setting aside the faith reality of *ekklesia. Ekklesia* must not be reduced to a secular community.

Not that *ekklesia* and community are opposed. They complement one another. That is why we speak of the church as an ecclesial community, a community called together by the Lord Jesus. And that is why the breaking of the bread is not merely a community event but an ecclesial event. The breaking of the bread is celebrated by people called and gathered together by the Lord.[19]

When a community is ecclesial, community represents the concrete outward expression of *ekklesia.* That is why ecclesial communities come in many shapes and forms. The community life of a small rural parish is very different from that of a large urban or suburban parish. The inner reality of *ekklesia,* however, remains the same. In the same way, the outward forms of the breaking of the bread may differ, but the inner reality remains the same.[20]

The New Testament term for church, *ekklesia,*[21] has deep roots in the Old Testament. The word occurs some one hundred times in the Septuagint,[22] where it has the basic sense of "assembly" or "congregation." At times, *ekklesia* is used in a secular sense, as in Sirach 26:5, for the gathering of a crowd *(ekklesia ochlou).* Most often, however, it is used in a religious sense for the assembly of the Lord *(ekklesia kyriou).*

In the greater Hellenistic world, *ekklesia* referred to the assembly *(ekklesia)* of the people *(demou)* of a city *(polis).* Those who formed the *ekklesia,* the *ekkletoi,* were summoned to the assembly *(ekklesia)* by a herald *(keryx).*

Like the Septuagint, the Book of Acts uses the word *ekklesia* for the assembly of the Lord. Before being martyred, Stephen gave a great discourse where he referred to Moses being with the angel in the assembly in the desert *(en te ekklesia en te eremo,* 7:38; see 7:33–34). The secular use of *ekklesia* is also found in the Book of Acts, in relation to a chaotic assembly *(ekklesia)* when the people of Ephesus gathered in the theater (19:32). It appears again in the same story when the town clerk appealed to the crowd that "the matter be settled in a lawful assembly" *(en te ennomo ekklesia,* 19:39), and right after that, when he "dismissed the assembly" *(ten ekklesian,* 19:40).

Most of the time, however, the Book of Acts uses *ekklesia* in a specifically Christian sense. Sometimes it uses the term in referring to a local church, such as the *ekklesia* in Jerusalem (5:11, 8:1; 11:22; 15:4, 22) Antioch (11:26; 13:1; 14:27; 15:3) Caesarea (18:22) or Ephesus (20:17). Sometimes, Acts uses the term to refer to several local churches, as when Barnabas and Paul appointed presbyters at Lystra, Iconium and Antioch of Pisidia "in each church" *(kat' ekklesian,* 14:23), or when Paul traveled through Syria and Cilicia and brought strength to the churches *(tas ekklesias,* 15:41). Later, a summary tells that "day after day the churches *(hai ekklesiai)* grew stronger in faith and increased in number" (16:5). There were obviously many distinct local churches.

When Luke actually names the city, as in the case of Jerusalem and Antioch, he speaks of the church in *(en)* Jerusalem (Acts 8:1;

11:22) and the church in *(en)* Antioch (13:1), not the church *of* Jerusalem or Antioch. This usage invites a broader understanding of the church as a reality transcending the various local churches. That greater notion seems to be present when Luke tells about Saul trying to destroy the church *(ten ekklesian,* 8:3). Saul's efforts were not limited to the church in Jerusalem (see 9:1–2). The notion is surely present when Luke speaks of "the church *(he ekklesia,* singular) throughout *(kath' holes)* Judea, Galilee, and Samaria" (9:31). That may also be the case when King Herod laid hands upon some members of the church to harm them (12:1) and when the church prayed on Peter's behalf (12:5).

Acts approaches the notion of a universal, or catholic, church in Paul's farewell discourse to the the elders of Miletus, gathered at Ephesus: "Keep watch over yourselves and over the whole flock of which the holy Spirit has appointed you overseers, in which you tend the church of God *(ten ekklesian tou theou)* that he acquired by his own blood" (20:28).

A *Koinonia* Event

Community fills a basic human need. So does the breaking of the bread as a community event. But community is not the same as *ekklesia,* only its outward expression. *Ekklesia* fills a basic Christian need. So does the breaking of the bread as an ecclesial event. As Christians, we have been called by God, we have been baptized in Jesus' name and we form a church *(ekklesia).* But what does it mean to be a church, and what keeps us together as a church? The answer is called *koinonia.*[23]

The Book of Acts uses the term *koinonia* only once, describing the primitive community in Jerusalem, in conjunction with "the teaching of the apostles," and "the breaking of the bread and the prayers" (2:42). As in Paul's letters, Hebrews and 1 John,[24] *koinonia* refers to a dynamic set of relationships at the very heart of the *ekklesia.* Baptized in Christ and united to the Lord Jesus, the members of the church are united to one another. *Koinonia* describes their communion. There is no separating the breaking of the bread from *koinonia.* The breaking of the bread is a community event and an ecclesial event. It is also a *koinonia* event.

The Latin word for *koinonia* is *communio,* a term used frequently in the documents of the Second Vatican Council. The *Dogmatic Constitution on the Church,* for example, speaks of the Spirit unifying the church in communion *(communio)* and in the works of ministry (4). Communion *(communio),* is what makes the church one. Quoting Saint Cyprian, the Constitution sees the universal church as "a people brought into unity from the unity of the Father, the Son, and the Holy Spirit" (4).[25]

In relation to the church, communion *(koinonia, communio)* is more basic than community. Community is a social, outward expression of the church. Communion is a constitutive element, integral to the church's very being. Communion may be compared to someone's soul or spirit, a deep inner reality. As an outward expression of communion, community is like someone's body. Just as the body needs the soul to be alive, an ecclesial community needs communion. Without communion, a community is without a soul. Without community, the *ekklesia* and its *koinonia* would be invisible. Community is necessary for the church to be a visible sign, a sacrament of the body of Christ.

Christian communities vary greatly. A family, for example, constitutes a community. So does an extended family. In the New Testament, a household may constitute an ecclesial community, and so does the body of a local church. Today, there is great interest in basic Christian communities. Communities are influenced by cultural, demographic, sociological factors. Some communities are small, some are large.

Communion *(koinonia, communio),* however, is the same for ecclesial communities of every size, shape or form. That is why today we can speak of a parish, a diocese and the entire church as an ecclesial community. Communion *(koinonia)* is what gives life to every Christian community. Without communion, an ecclesial community is reduced to an outward shell. Its members may form a community and join in fellowship but they are not joined in *koinonia* or communion.

Koinonia is often translated as "fellowship," but there is a great difference between fellowship and *koinonia.* Fellowship refers to the set of relationships among those who form the community. The tenth edition of the *Merriam Webster Collegiate Dictionary* defines "fellowship" as "a community of interest, activity, feeling, or experience." For those who enjoy it, fellowship is a source of happiness.

Koinonia refers to two sets of relationships. The first describes the interpersonal union among those who form the ecclesial community. The second describes their common union with Christ. That is why *koinonia, communio,* communion refers to the common-union of an ecclesial community. In relation to Merriam Webster's definition of "fellowship," we may define *koinonia* as an ecclesial community, not merely of interest, activity, feeling or experience, but of being in Christ. Those who enjoy *koinonia* are filled "with great joy" (*meta chara megale,* Luke 24:52).[26]

Koinonia is to *ekklesia* what fellowship is to community. *Koinonia,* the soul or spirit of *ekklesia,* is what makes a community an ecclesial community. As community is the outward expression of *ekklesia,* fellowship can be the outward expression of *koinonia.* Without *koinonia,* however, fellowship is an empty shell.

The New Testament often uses metaphors to describe the ecclesial community as an expression of *koinonia.* Many of these appear in the documents of Vatican II. The *Dogmatic Constitution on the Church,* for example, describes the church as "a sheepfold," "a flock" (6, see John 10:1–10), "a cultivated field, the tillage of God" (6, see 1 Corinthians 3:9), "the building of God" (6, see 1 Corinthians 3:9), "the house of God in which his family dwells, the household of God in the Spirit," (6, see Ephesians 2:19, 22) and "the holy temple" for which we here on earth are "living stones" (6, see 1 Peter 2:5).

The church is also "the body" of Christ: "For by communicating his Spirit, Christ mystically constitutes as his body" all those brothers and sisters of his "who are called together from every nation" (7).[27] "As all the members of the human body, though they are many, form one body, so also are the faithful in Christ" (7, see 1 Corinthians 12:12).[28]

Vatican II also put great emphasis on the role of the eucharist regarding the *communio* of the church. With reference to the church as the body of Christ, the *Dogmatic Constitution on the Church* states: "Really sharing in the body of the Lord in the breaking of the eucharistic bread, we are taken up into communion *(communio)* with him and with one another. 'Because the bread is one, we, though many, are one body, all of us who partake of the one bread' (1 Corinthians 10:17). In this way all of us are made members of his body (see 12:27), 'but severally members one of another' (Romans 12:4)" (7).[29]

Every aspect of the eucharist shows it as a community event flowing from a deep inner communion among the participants. Consider the opening greeting, taken from 2 Corinthians 13:13, where *koinonia* is associated with grace and love: "The grace *(he charis)* of the Lord Jesus Christ and the love *(he agape)* of God and the fellowship *(he koinonia)* of the holy Spirit be with all of you."[30]

Every prayer, every gesture, every hymn that follows the greeting expresses the same communal aspect. That is why the eucharistic prayers *(anaphoras)* speak with the first person plural pronouns, "we," "us," "our," and not with the first person singular pronouns, "I," "me," "my." It was like that from the beginning.

The oldest anaphora we have is that of Hippolytus, composed around 215–220. The Second Eucharistic Prayer in the Missal of Paul VI is basically identical to that of Hippolytus. Here is the beginning of the preface (the thanksgiving) from the anaphora of Hippolytus: "We give you thanks, O God, through your beloved Child, Jesus Christ, whom you have sent us in the last days as savior, redeemer and messenger of your will." And here is the beginning of the epiclesis, the prayer for the sending of the Holy Spirit: "And we ask that you send your Holy Spirit on the offering of your holy Church."[31]

Community, *Ekklesia* and *Koinonia*

The New Testament, including the Book of Acts, presents the eucharist as a community event, but it does not speak explicitly of community. Community is only inferred. What it talks about is communion, in Greek *koinonia*, that is, "common-union" or "shared-union."[32]

In the Gospel, Luke laid the basis for ecclesial and eucharistic *koinonia* in the story of the origins of the eucharist unfolding in a series of ten meals with Jesus.[33] In the Acts of the Apostles, he shows its various ramifications and implications for the church in the story of the development of the eucharist as the church reaches toward "the ends of the earth" (1:8).

For centuries, we were able to take the community aspect of the church and of the eucharist for granted. We can no longer do that today. Paul VI, addressing a general audience on June 2, 1970, stressed the importance of community. He was also careful to relate community to the church as a *communio:*

One of the salient ideas emerging from the Council for Christian spiritual formation is the sense of community.

Those intent on welcoming the conciliar spirit and criteria for renewal realize that they have a new pedagogy as model. This requires such persons to conceive and express their religious, moral, and social life in terms of the ecclesial community to which they belong. Throughout its documents the Council speaks of the Church: the Church now is the people of God; the Church is the Mystical Body of Christ; the Church is *communio*.

Later in the same address, Paul VI focused on the nature of a community, in particular of an ecclesial community:

All this being said, it remains true that the Church, revitalized and explained by the Council, stands out today more than in the past as a community. The more the Church is spread in the world, the more it defines itself, in virtue of an inherent and constitutive need, as *communio*. Note the social aspect of this definition. Humanity can be seen as a mass, a numerical quantity, or as a mere category of human beings, an amorphous crowd, lacking any deep or tested or chosen bonds within. Or it can be seen as a pluralistic and corporate society or community, brought together for particular ends or interests: as a people, a nation, a society of nations. . . . And in the last analysis as a *communio;* this is the humanity Christ wills.

A community is not just a group. Nor is it just an association, as when people come together in a common project or for a common cause. Nor is it a society, made up of people from the same class who have similar needs and like interests. Nor is a community just a club, where one meets congenial people with the same sporting interests. Normally, a group, association, society or club is just a gathering of individuals. And what holds them together is some expression of fellowship.

An ecclesial community is not just a gathering of individuals, but an assembly of Christian persons. Those who form a Christian community may enjoy fellowship, but it takes much more than fellowship to have an ecclesial community. In special situations, as in times of persecution, the church has to do without open community and fellowship. Community and fellowship, however important, are not of the essence. *Koinonia* or *communio,* that is, common-union, is of the essence.

The same applies to the eucharist. Describing the eucharist and "the breaking of the bread" in terms of community and table fellowship is too little. Translating *koinonia,* for example, in Acts 2:42, as "fellowship" and interpreting "the breaking of the bread" as "table fellowship" misses the essential. In the church, community and the eucharist are expressions of ecclesial *koinonia.*

In a community, people share their lives, not only their goods. In an ecclesial and a eucharistic community, they share their life in Christ. It is possible to facilitate a community's emergence, like a midwife at a delivery, removing obstacles stemming from church architecture or the configuration of the assembly, whatever impedes the community from being and acting as a community.

The greater danger is to presuppose that an ecclesial community really exists. Removing obstacles will not bring it about. For that we need something much more basic. That something is *koinonia,* the lifeblood of community and of the breaking of the bread.

Exploring the development of the eucharist according to Acts, I shall focus on the community aspect of the eucharist, as an expression of the ecclesial community and its *koinonia* in and with Christ, a *koinonia* that is the gift of the Holy Spirit.

The Acts of the Apostles

In the Gospel, Luke told the story of Jesus and his followers. In the Acts of the Apostles, he tells the story of the church and the early Christians (see 11:26). Writing Luke-Acts as one work in two volumes, Luke conceived and presented Acts as the continuation of the Gospel. To appreciate Luke's achievement in the Book of Acts, it is helpful to compare it with Mark.

At the end of Mark's Gospel, a young man gives the women who came to the tomb a message for the disciples and Peter, and through them for all who would share their faith. Jesus is preceding them to (or in) Galilee. There they will see him (Mark 16:7). With that, Mark invites us to return to the beginning of the Gospel and read it once again. The first time, we read it as the story of Jesus of Nazareth and his disciples. Having followed Jesus to the passion, burial and resurrection, we now read the Gospel anew as the story of Jesus Christ, the Son of God, and the early church with its mission to the Gentiles. Mark wrote his one-volume Gospel on two levels, that of Jesus and the disciples, and that of the risen Christ and the church.

Mark's Gospel was Luke's principal source in the writing of the Gospel, along with a hypothetical source called "Q," for *Quelle,* a German word meaning "source." Luke also used sources and traditions of his own. By scholarly convention, these are labeled "L," Luke's initial. While following Mark, however, Luke simply took the story of Jesus and his disciples and told it as the story of the origins of the church, leaving out the actual story of the early church. Unlike Mark, Luke in his Gospel announces but does not tell the story of the church and its mission.

It is as though Luke peeled off Mark's second layer, the story of the risen Christ and the church, and set it aside for his second volume, the Acts of the Apostles. What Mark did in one volume, Luke did in two, separating the story of the church (the Acts) from the story of Jesus (the Gospel).

In the Gospel, for example, Luke omitted Mark's story of Jesus and his disciples crossing the Sea of Galilee from the Jewish to the Gentile side (Mark 6:45–52; see Matthew 14:22–33; John 6:15–21). The mission to the Gentiles would be told in the Book of Acts, beginning with the story of Peter and Cornelius, the Roman centurion (10:1–11:18)

Luke also omitted Jesus' teaching about unclean and clean foods (Mark 7:1–23). That issue, involving how the Gentiles would be integrated in the church, is treated in Acts' story of the apostolic council in Jerusalem (15:1–35). He also omitted related stories about Jesus healing a Syrophoenician's daughter (Mark 7:24–30) and a man who was deaf and could not speak (7:31–37). If Jesus could heal a Gentile man, he could also heal a Gentile woman. For Luke, that was not an issue.

After that, Luke left out Mark's story of Jesus breaking bread for a crowd of four thousand people in Bethsaida, one of the Gentile cities of the Decapolis. Unlike the earlier crowd of five thousand (6:34–44), this crowd of four thousand included women and Gentiles (8:1–10). A major issue in Mark's Gospel was the universality and unity of the church. Luke would treat this issue in the stories of Peter and Cornelius (Acts 10:1–11, 18) and of the apostolic council (15:1–35).

While writing the Gospel, "the first book" (1:1), Luke anticipated and announced many of the themes developed in Acts. The Gospel was written with Acts in view. Likewise, in writing Acts, his second book, Luke kept the Gospel in the background, beginning with its story of the word coming to John the Baptist (Luke 3:1–22; see Acts 1:1–5). Like the Gospel, Acts is a story of the word, the word that came to John, that Jesus spoke (see Luke 5:1, 5; 10:39) and that spread through the growth of the church (see Acts 6:7; 12:24). Luke must have worked on the two volumes, Luke and Acts, at the same time or in close succession.

Writing very likely in Antioch or its surrounding region in the mid-eighties of the first century, Luke had in mind a wide range of communities, the heirs to the Pauline mission and the communities founded by them. Those communities would be in present-day Greece, Turkey, Cyprus and Syria. In Acts, Luke tells the founding story of many of those communities, for example, the community at Philippi (16:11–40), Thessalonica (17:1–9), Corinth (18:1–18), Ephesus (18:19–21, 24–28; 19:1–20), Damascus (9:1–22), and not least Antioch on the Orontes (11:19–30), linking all the communities to one another in one great foundation story. Luke did that through their relationship to Paul and his missionary journeys, and Paul's relationship to the church in Antioch, Jerusalem and Rome.

Structure of Acts   The close relationship between the two books is evident in their structure, which is quite parallel. Like the Gospel of Luke, Acts begins with a preface, where the writer addresses the reader in the person of Theophilus (Luke 1:1–4; Acts 1:1–2). The preface of the Gospel introduces both volumes. The preface of Acts connects Acts with the Gospel.

Following the preface, Acts includes a prologue, outlining the major themes and the basic structure of the book. The Gospel of Luke also includes a prologue, perhaps two, giving the impression of the Gospel starting over and over again. At the time Luke wrote the preface of Acts, which summarizes the Gospel as what Jesus began to do and teach (Acts 1:1), the infancy narrative of the Gospel may not yet have been written.

The original prologue giving the major themes of the Gospel, may have consisted of the story of the word coming to John the Baptist

(Luke 3:1–20), of Jesus' baptism by him (3:21–22), the genealogy of Jesus (3:23–38) and the forty-day period of testing (4:1–13). Aside from the genealogy (see Matthew 1:1–17), this original prologue followed the development of the prologue in Mark (1:2–13).

The present prologue, which tells the entire Gospel story in miniature, seems to have been written after the rest of Luke-Acts. If so, Luke intended the infancy narrative, as the prologue is often called, as a prologue for the whole of Luke and Acts.

After the preface (1:1–2) and the prologue (1:3–14), Acts tells the story of the development of the church in three stages, including:

- the early church in Jerusalem (1:15 — 5:42),
- the spread of the church from Jerusalem to Antioch (6:1 — 12:25),
- and the missions from Antioch (13:1 — 19:20).

Each stage is introduced by a story about a major development in the basic ministerial structure of the church. The first stage is introduced by the choice of Matthias to replace Judas as one of the Twelve (1:15–26). The second stage is introduced by the selection and appointment of the Seven (6:1–7). The third is introduced by the selection and appointment of Barnabas and Saul for the work of the mission (13:1–3).

It was almost the same in the Gospel, except for the addition of a narrative synthesis of the mission of Jesus (Luke 4:14–44). Paralleling Acts, the Gospel tells the story of the origins of the church in three stages, including:

- the church as a people called (5:1 — 6:11),
- the church as the community of the Twelve (6:12 — 8:56),
- and the community of the Twelve sent on mission (9:1 – 50).

As in Acts, each stage is introduced by a passage representing a major development in the establishment of the church. The first stage is introduced by the call of Simon Peter and his partners, James and John (Luke 5:1–11). The second stage is introduced by the selection and appointment of the Twelve (6:12–16). The third is introduced by the story of Jesus sending the Twelve on mission (9:1–6).

The last section of Acts presents Paul's great journey to Rome, a journey that would take him first to Jerusalem (19:21 — 28:31). The journey narrative is introduced with Paul making up his mind about the journey and sending two of his assistants ahead of him (19:21 –

22). The journey ends with Paul in Rome welcoming all who come to him, proclaiming the kingdom of God and teaching about the Lord Jesus Christ (28:30 – 31).

The last section of the Gospel presents Jesus' great journey to Jerusalem, presented thematically as a journey to the ascension (Luke 9:51 — 24:53). The journey to Jerusalem is introduced with Jesus resolutely deciding to journey to Jerusalem and sending messengers ahead of him to prepare the way (9:51 – 56). The journey ends with Jesus' disciples "continually in the temple praising God" (24:53).

Acts and the Development of the Eucharist

To appreciate better the story of the development of the eucharist in Acts, we begin by reviewing the story of its origins in the Gospel. We shall then see how Acts presents the development of the eucharist as part of the development of the church.

The Origins of the Eucharist　In the Gospel, Luke told the story of the origins of the eucharist in a series of ten meals, each developing a basic theme connected with the eucharist.[34] Three of the meals are part of Jesus' ministry in Galilee (5:28 – 39; 7:36 – 50; 9:10 – 17). Seven of the meals are on Jesus' way to the ascension (9:51 — 24:53); four of these are on the way to Jerusalem (10:38 – 42; 11:37– 54; 14:1 – 24; 19:1 – 10), and three are in or near Jerusalem (22:14 – 38; 24:13 – 35; 24:36 – 53).

In the Galilean ministry, the first meal is at the home of Levi, the tax collector who left everything and followed Jesus (5:27– 39). As a follower, Levi gave a great banquet for Jesus, which many tax collectors attended. When the Pharisees and their scribes objected, Jesus defended the presence of the tax collectors. He had not come to call the righteous to *metanoia,* but sinners (5:27– 32). The meal is part of the story of the church as a people called (5:1 – 6, 11). The story of Levi shows that the eucharist is an evangelizing event, where Jesus calls participants to repentance, conversion and a total transformation of their lives.

The second meal in the Galilean ministry is at the home of Simon the Pharisee (7:36–50). Learning that Jesus was at table in the home of a Pharisee, a woman known as a sinner came and placed herself at the feet of Jesus, bathing them with her tears. Seeing this, Simon wondered: "If this man were a prophet, he would know who and what sort of woman this is who is touching him, that she is a sinner" (7:39). In response, Jesus challenged Simon, pointing out that the woman's love for Jesus was greater than Simon's. That showed that she had repented and been forgiven. The meal is part of the story of the church as the community of the Twelve (Luke 6:12—8:56). The story of Simon shows that the eucharist is a reconciling event.

For the third and climactic meal in the Galilean ministry, Jesus himself is the host and for a crowd of five thousand in the city of Bethsaida (9:10–17). Since Jesus, the Son of Man, has no home of his own, no place to rest his head (9:58), the meal does not take place at a home. When the Twelve feel overwhelmed by the crowd and want to send them away, Jesus orders them to give the crowd something to eat. The meal at Bethsaida has Jesus breaking bread for the first time. The story is part of the story of the church as a people sent on mission (9:1–50). The story of the breaking of the bread at Bethsaida shows that the eucharist is a missioning event.

Of the four meals on the way to Jerusalem, the first is at the home of a woman named Martha (10:38–42). The story deals with the issue of *diakonia* in the life of the church as it follows Jesus on his journey to Jerusalem. In the eucharistic ministry *(diakonia),* the one necessary thing is attention to the person of the Lord and listening to his word. Without that one thing necessary, nothing else matters.

At the second meal on the way to Jerusalem, a lunch at the home of a Pharisee, Jesus emphasizes the priority of inner purification over external ritual (11:37–54). The story shows that genuine participation in the eucharist flows from love of God and neighbor.

The third meal on the way to Jerusalem is a Sabbath meal at the home of a leading Pharisee. After addressing the basic purpose of the Sabbath, Jesus shows how people should relate to one another at a dinner (Luke 14:1–24). Speaking first to the guests, he tells a parable about not seeking the first place. Then, speaking to the host, he tells him to invite not only those who would bring him prestige but to invite the poor, the crippled, the lame and the blind. At that, one of the guests announces, "Blessed is the one who will dine in the kingdom of God" (14:15). The story shows that the eucharist must reflect the values of the kingdom.

The third meal on the way to Jerusalem is at the home of Zacchaeus, the chief tax collector in Jericho (19:1 – 10). It is necessary — a matter of salvation — that Jesus come to Zacchaeus' home. When Jesus is our guest at the eucharist, salvation is our guest. The story shows that welcoming Jesus in the eucharist is welcoming our own salvation.

The final three meals are in or near Jerusalem and part of Luke's account of the passion-resurrection. The first is the Last Supper, described in the symbolic language and the liturgical formulas used at the Lord's Supper. Here, in the Last Supper, Luke treats directly of the eucharist. Relating the Last Supper of Jesus' life to the Lord's Supper of the early church, Luke develops the implications of Jesus' passion, Judas' betrayal and Peter's denial for the early church (22:14 – 38).

In the second meal, Jesus speaks to two disciples who have left the community in Jerusalem and are on their way to Emmaus. On the way, Jesus interprets the scriptures that have to do with himself. All the while, the disciples do not recognize him. But, moved by Jesus' words, they invite him to their home. Finally, they recognize Jesus as he takes bread, breaks it and gives it to them, even as he vanishes from their sight (Luke 24:13 – 35). The story shows that the eucharist is related to Jesus' word and that the community of disciples can recognize him in the breaking of the bread.

The third and final meal is with the whole community assembled in Jerusalem. Jesus, the Living One, presents himself to the disciples, eats fish before them and speaks to them of his passion and resurrection. They would be his witnesses once they received the holy Spirit (24:36 – 53). The story shows that the eucharist is related to the mission of church.

Besides these ten stories of meals that Jesus took with his disciples and others, the Gospel includes many other references to the eucharist or references that have implications for the eucharist. One of these is a petition in the Lord's prayer: "Give us each day our daily bread" (11:3), the bread that is truly distinctive of us. Another is in the prologue, the story of Jesus' birth: "She wrapped him (her firstborn son) in swaddling clothes and laid him in a manger, because there was no room for them in the inn" (2:7). She "laid him in a manger." She offered him as nourishment for the flock.

Table II

The Development of the Eucharist in the Context of the Acts of the Apostles

1:1 – 2 Preface: Transitional summary of Luke's Gospel

1:3 – 14 Prologue: "Until the day he was taken up"
    A Covenant of Salt (1:4)

1:15 — 28:31 The story of the church

    Origins and development (1:15 — 19:20)
        1:15 — 5:42 The primitive community in Jerusalem
        The breaking of the bread (2:42 – 47)
        6:1 — 12:25 From Jerusalem to Antioch
        The choice of the Seven (6:1 – 7)
        The conversion of Saul (9:1 – 30)
        The conversion of Cornelius (10:1 — 11:18)
        13:1 — 19:20 The Missions from Antioch
        The council of Jerusalem (15:1 – 35)
        At table with Gentiles in Philippi (16:25 – 34)

    The journey to Jerusalem and Rome (19:21 — 28:31)
        19:21 — 20:38 Through Macedonia and Achaia
        Breaking bread with the community
            at Troas (20:7 – 12)
        21:1 — 23:11 On to Jerusalem
        23:12 — 28:31 On the way to Rome
        Breaking bread in a great storm at sea (27:33 – 38)

The Development of the Eucharist   The story of the development of the
eucharist in Acts is quite different from the story of its origins in the
Gospel. Instead of a series of meal stories showing various aspects
of the eucharist, Acts has only two meal stories (20:7– 12; 27:33 –
38), both of which are part of the story of Paul's great journey to
Rome (19:21 — 28:31).

Acts includes three passages which treat directly of the eucharist.
Of those, the first is a summary describing the life of the early church
in Jerusalem (2:42 – 47). The summary includes Luke's name for the
eucharist, "the breaking of the bread" (2:42). The summary also refers

to the believers who "broke bread in their homes" (2:46). The second passage is the story of the meal at Troas, where Paul broke bread on the first day of the week before leaving the community the following morning (20:7–12). Then there is the story of Paul in the midst of a great storm at sea, who "took bread, gave thanks to God . . . broke it, and began to eat" (27:33–38).

Acts also includes two passages that have indirect bearing on the eucharist. One of those deals with ministry *(diakonia)*, telling how the Seven were chosen and appointed to the ministry at tables *(diakonein trapezais)*. The other tells how Paul and Silas converted a jailer, who "brought them up into his house *(eis ton oikon)* and provided a meal *(paretheken trapezan)* and with his household rejoiced at having come to faith in God" (16:25–34).

Besides these, there are four passages that may not be eucharistic, whether directly or indirectly, but have important implications for the nature of the eucharist and its assembly. That Jesus "shared salt with" the apostles after the passion (Acts 1:4; see 1:1–5) and that they "ate and drank with him after he rose from the dead" (10:41; see 10:34–43) assured that Jesus would be present in and through them in the breaking of the bread. The story of Saul's conversion shows how, through baptism, a convert is integrated in the eucharistic assembly (9:1–31). The apostolic council in Jerusalem shows how Gentiles are integrated at the one table of the Lord (15:1–35).

Like the story of the origins of the eucharist (see Luke 2:6–7), the story of its development begins with the prologue (Acts 1:3–14). After the preface, which recalls all that Jesus did and taught (1:1–2), the prologue relates that Jesus made himself present to the apostles, appearing to them during forty days, speaking to them of the kingdom of God and sharing salt with them (1:3–4). The story of the development of the eucharist begins with those forty days when Jesus shared salt with the apostles, assuring them of his presence after the ascension. The story of the development of the eucharist is thus connected with the story of its origins.

The story of the development of the eucharist continues in the first section of Acts (1:15—5:42), where a summary describes the early church in Jerusalem from the day of its birth on Pentecost (2:42–47). In the summary, the eucharist, "the breaking of the bread," is presented as a constitutive and integral element in the life of the church, together with the teaching of the apostles, the *koinonia* and the prayers. The summary is related to several stories in the Gospel where Jesus broke bread (Luke 9:10–17; 22:14–38; 24:13–35).

The development of the eucharist then continues in the second section of Acts (6:1 — 12:25), with three stories that are indirectly related to the eucharist or have important implications for it.

As the church in Jerusalem grew and became ethnically diverse, problems arose in the exercise of *diakonia*. That story is told in the choice and appointment of the Seven (6:1–7). The *diakonia* of charity to the needy and the *diakonia* at the eucharistic table must flow from the *diakonia* of the word. The story is related to the Gospel's story of Martha and Mary, where *diakonia* first becomes an issue (Luke 10:38–42), as well as to the Last Supper, where Jesus referred to himself as the model of *diakonia* (22:24–27; see also 17:7–10).

Developing from within Judaism, the church soon drew attention to itself, and that attention brought persecution. The second story in this section of Acts that has implications for the eucharist tells how Saul (Paul) the persecutor was converted on the way to Damascus and was integrated into the eucharistic community (9:1–31). When Paul was struck with blindness, he did not eat or drink until after his baptism when his sight was restored. The story of Paul's conversion recalls aspects of the story of Levi the tax collector (Luke 5:27–39).

Paul would be the missionary to the Gentiles, but Peter was the first to preach to the Gentiles and have them baptized (Acts 10:1 — 11:18). The third story in this second section of Acts that has implications for the eucharist takes place at the home of the centurion Cornelius at the Roman capital of Caesarea. Reflecting on the event, Peter spoke to the household of Cornelius. He outlined why Gentiles must be welcomed into the church (10:34–43). This story has important implications for universality and inclusiveness of the church and its eucharistic assembly. Like the story of Paul's conversion, it recalls aspects of the story of Levi (Luke 5:27–39).

With the precedent set by Peter, Paul and Barnabas dedicated themselves to the mission to the Gentiles. The story is told in the third part of Acts as the missions from Antioch (13:1 — 19:20).

Two stories in this third section of Acts have bearing on the eucharist. The success of the church brought to the fore a number of questions affecting the whole church. How could the Gentiles be integrated into the one church? What should be expected of them in regard to the Jewish practices surrounding food and meals? These issues were decided at an apostolic council in Jerusalem (15:1–35). The results have important implications for the unity of the church and its eucharistic assembly. The story recalls a story in the Gospel about a dinner at a Pharisee's house (Luke 11:37–54).

The second story in the missions from Antioch shows that baptism has implications for Christians of Gentile background. Once baptized, the Gentiles were not simply integrated into the one eucharistic community. Like those of Jewish background, they shared responsibility for setting out the eucharistic table. The story is about the conversion of Paul's jailer at Philippi. Once baptized, he brought Paul and Silas to his home and provided a meal of thanksgiving "for having come to faith in God" (Acts 16:25–34).

The final two stories concerning the eucharist are part of Paul's great journey to Jerusalem (19:21 — 28:31). Both are directly eucharistic.

The first story is set at Troas, where Paul broke bread with the community on the first day of the week (20:7–12). This recalls the stories at the end of the Gospel where Jesus, the Living One (Luke 24:5), was recognized in the breaking of the bread (24:13–35), and spoke to the disciples about their mission (24:36–49) before blessing them and ascending to the Father (24:1–53). The story shows the relationship between the eucharist and life in Christ.

The second story on Paul's great journey is also the last in the Book of Acts with implications for the eucharist. It tells that Paul broke bread on a ship at the height of a storm so that all might be saved (27:33–38). The story shows that the eucharist is theologically related to salvation. It recalls the Gospel's story of Zacchaeus (Luke 19:1–10). In welcoming Jesus to his home, Zacchaeus welcomed his own salvation.

In this first chapter, we introduced the breaking of the bread as a community event, an ecclesial event and a *koinonia* event. We also introduced the Acts of the Apostles as Luke's second book. Then, after reviewing the origins of the eucharist according to Luke, we situated Acts' story of the development of the eucharist as part of the development of the church.

In the second chapter, we shall examine the beginnings of the eucharist in relation to the preface (1:1–2) and the prologue (1:3–14) of Acts, where during forty days (1:3) Jesus shared salt with the apostles (1:4) before ascending to heaven.

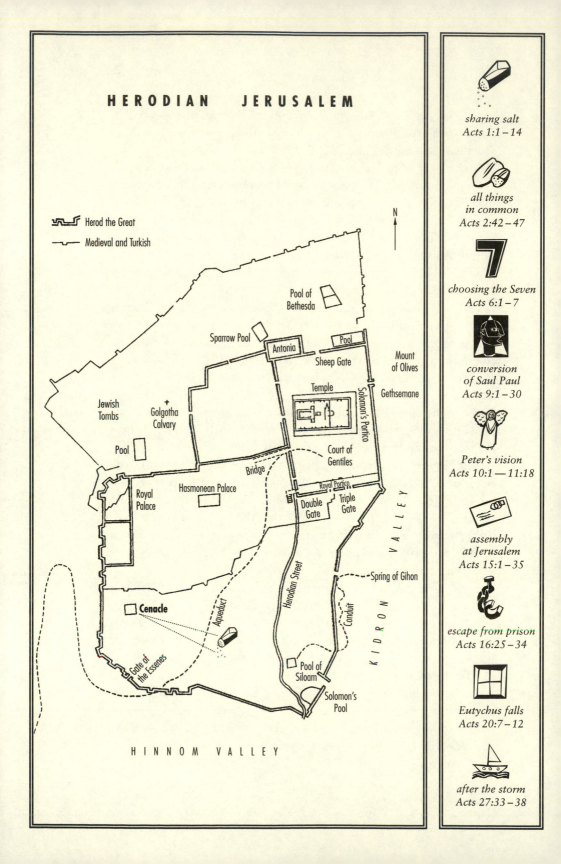

HERODIAN JERUSALEM

N

Herod the Great

Medieval and Turkish

Pool of Bethesda

Sparrow Pool

Antonia

Pool

Sheep Gate

Mount of Olives

Temple

Solomon's Portico

Gethsemane

Jewish Tombs

Golgotha Calvary

Court of Gentiles

Pool

Bridge

Royal Portico

Royal Palace

Hasmonean Palace

Double Gate

Triple Gate

Cenacle

Aqueduct

Herodian Street

Spring of Gihon

Conduit

KIDRON VALLEY

Gate of the Essenes

Pool of Siloam

Solomon's Pool

HINNOM VALLEY

sharing salt
Acts 1:1–14

all things
in common
Acts 2:42–47

choosing the Seven
Acts 6:1–7

conversion
of Saul Paul
Acts 9:1–30

Peter's vision
Acts 10:1—11:18

assembly
at Jerusalem
Acts 15:1–35

escape from prison
Acts 16:25–34

Eutychus falls
Acts 20:7–12

after the storm
Acts 27:33–38

Chapter II

A Covenant of Salt
(1:1–14)

Salt is good,
but if salt loses its taste,
with what can its flavor be restored?
                    Luke 14:34

Acts' story of the eucharist begins right after the passion, when Jesus appeared to the apostles during forty days, preparing them for Pentecost. During those days, Jesus spoke to them of the kingdom of God and shared salt with them (1:3–4).

Luke announces those days in the preface, showing that the Acts of the Apostles are related to the Gospel (1:1–2). He speaks of them, succinctly but tellingly, in the prologue (1:3–14).

In the preface, Luke looks back to the Gospel, his first book:

In the first book, Theophilus, I dealt with all that Jesus did and taught until the day he was taken up, after giving instructions through the holy Spirit to the apostles whom he had chosen.

Looking back, Luke relates the life of the church to the life of Jesus, and with it the development of the eucharist as told in Acts to its origins in the story of Jesus.

In the Gospel, the story of the eucharist began in Jesus' Galilean ministry. It ended in Jerusalem with Jesus' passion-resurrection. In Acts, the story of eucharist coincides with the story of the church "in Jerusalem, throughout Judea and Samaria, and to the ends of the earth" (1:8).

The Preface (1:1–2)

The preface[1] provides a brief summary of "the first book," the Gospel, where Luke "dealt with all that Jesus did and taught" *(erxato . . . poiein te kai didaskein)* "until the day he was taken up" (1:1–2a). To be more precise, Luke "dealt with all that Jesus began *(erxato)* to do and teach."

Focusing on "the day he was taken up" (1:2b), the preface speaks of Jesus' final appearance to the community, when he ate in their presence and instructed them before being taken up (see Luke 24:36–53). The first book, however, was only the beginning. What Jesus began to do and teach in the first book, he would continue in the second book.[2]

What Jesus began "in the first book" included a series of ten meals, starting with a banquet at the home of a tax collector named Levi (Luke 5:27–39) and ending with a meal where he instructed the community on "the day he was taken up" (Acts 1:2; Luke 24:36–53). Of those ten meals, five, including the last, were in the form of a symposium,[3] providing Jesus a good occasion to teach.

It is at Jesus' final meal in Jerusalem, when he ate (Luke 24:36–43) with "the eleven and those with them" (24:33), that Jesus gave "instructions through the holy Spirit to the apostles whom he had chosen (Acts 1:2b; see Luke 24:44–49). It is then, also, after instructing them, that Jesus led the community out as far as Bethany and "was taken up" (Acts 1:2a; see Luke 24:50–53).[4]

Earlier that morning, "the first day of the week," some women had discovered Jesus' tomb empty (Luke 24:1–11). On hearing the news, Peter ran to the tomb and saw the burial cloths alone (24:12). That same day, two disciples met Jesus on the way to Emmaus, "but their eyes were prevented from recognizing him" (24:16). It was only later, at home in Emmaus, that they recognized him in the breaking of the bread, whereupon they returned with the good news to the community in Jerusalem (24:13–35). Jesus' final appearance and meal with the community followed immediately (24:36–53).

In Luke's Gospel, all the events connected with the resurrection, including the ascension (24:50–53), take place on that same first day of the week. In Acts, the events are spread over a period of forty days (1:3). But then, the role the ascension plays in Luke is not the same as in Acts. In Luke, the ascension acts as a climactic conclusion of Jesus' mission. In Acts, it introduces the mission of the church.

The Prologue (1:3 – 14)

After the brief preface (1:1 – 2), Luke continues with a short prologue (1:3 – 14), setting out the point of departure for the story of Acts together with some of its major themes. Short as it is, the prologue can be divided into three small units. The first tells how Jesus presented himself alive to the apostles over a period of forty days, showing them in many ways that he was really alive (1:3 – 5). The second tells of their last gathering with Jesus, when he ascended to heaven from the Mount of Olivet (1:6 – 12). The third describes the nucleus of the community after the ascension gathering in the upper room where they were staying (1:13 – 14).

Acts' story of the development of the eucharist begins in the first part of the prologue (1:3 – 5), which describes Jesus making himself present to the apostles over a period of forty days:

> He presented himself alive to them by many proofs after he had suffered, appearing to them during forty days and speaking of the kingdom of God.
>
> While meeting with them *(synalizomenos),* he enjoined them not to depart from Jerusalem, but to wait for "the promise of the Father about which you have heard me speak; for John baptized with water, but in a few days you will be baptized with the holy Spirit."

Luke's story of the origins of the eucharist ended with an appearance of Jesus "on the first day of the week" when Jesus "presented himself alive to them by many proofs after he suffered" (1:3a; see Luke 24:36, 39 – 40, 44 – 47). In the prologue of Acts, Luke extends that final appearance into a series of appearances lasting forty days, when Jesus met with the apostles and ate with them. The Greek expression for eating with them (Acts 1:4) is *synalizomenos,* literally "while sharing (or eating) salt with them." In the ancient world, sharing salt was a popular expression for having a meal together.

At the end of the Gospel, the meal Jesus took with the community (Luke 24:36 – 53) concluded all that Jesus began to do and teach. In reference to the eucharist, that final meal emphasized the relationship between the eucharist and the passion (see 24:44 – 46; see also 24:19 – 27; 22:7 – 13, 14 – 38), and the community's upcoming mission (24:47 – 48). In the eucharist, the early Christians remembered that the Christ had to suffer and enter into his glory (24:26;

see 24:6 – 8). They also remembered that he prepared them for their Christian mission (Acts 10:40 – 41).

At the beginning of Acts, the meals Jesus took with the apostles, sharing salt with them (1:4), introduce the story of the church and its development. With reference to the eucharist, sharing salt emphasizes the relationship between the eucharist and the risen Lord's presence to the community. In the eucharist, the early Christians looked to the future with hope, knowing that Jesus, who shared salt with them, would remain with them, uniting them in his presence. As his witnesses, they would act and speak in his name.

The reference to Jesus "sharing salt with" the apostles is the point of departure for the development of the eucharist in the story of Acts. Every other reference to the eucharist in Acts presupposes it. It also associates the community meals in Acts to those Jesus took with his followers and disciples in the Gospel. Without Jesus sharing salt with the apostles, we might not see that Jesus, the risen Lord, is present when Christians gather for "the breaking of the bread" (2:42).

For people today, Acts' expression "taking" or "sharing salt with them" (*synalizomenos,* 1:4) can be very puzzling. Few would suspect that Jesus' act of sharing salt with the apostles had something to do with the eucharist. Taking bread, saying a blessing, breaking the bread and giving it to the apostles would have been clearer.

That is what Jesus did with the apostles at the Last Supper (Luke 22:19), with the two disciples at Emmaus (24:30) and at Bethsaida with a crowd of five thousand (9:10 – 17). As here in Acts 1:3 – 5, what Jesus did at the Last Supper and at Bethsaida was related to the kingdom of God (Luke 9:11; 22:16; see also 14:15).

In New Testament times, however, conditions were very different, and sharing salt was an eloquent and powerful gesture. Sharing salt with the apostles, Jesus made himself intimately present to them. Sharing salt over forty days, he made them more and more one with him, preparing them for Pentecost and "the promise of the Father" (Acts 1:4), forming them to be his "witnesses in Jerusalem, throughout Judea and Samaria, and to the ends of the earth" (1:8).

That is what Jesus did in the first part of the prologue (1:3 – 5), preparing the apostles to be baptized with the holy Spirit (1:5). John had baptized with water, but in a few days they would be baptized with the holy Spirit (1:5). We recall Jesus' saying, "the law and the prophets lasted until John; from then on the kingdom of God is proclaimed" (Luke 16:16). Proclaimed by Jesus, the kingdom of God was among them (17:21). Proclaiming it, they would extend it to the ends of the earth (Acts 1:8).

Acts' story of the eucharist starts with Jesus, the risen Lord, "sharing salt with" the apostles, offering them a new covenant and sealing the new covenant by taking salt with them. The new covenant, like the ancient covenant with Aaron and his descendants (see Numbers 18:19) and the Davidic covenant (2 Chronicles 13:5), is a covenant of salt.

To appreciate what it meant for Jesus "to share salt with" the apostles and what it could mean today, we shall begin by examining the expression itself. We shall then explore its background in ancient life and literature, in the Bible as well as in the Greek and Roman world. Finally, we shall analyze its literary role and theological implications in the prologue of Acts (1:3–14).

Sharing Salt with Them (1:4)

The Greek expression *synalizomenos* (1:4), literally, "while sharing salt with them," is a New Testament *hapax legomenon,* appearing only here in the entire New Testament, and many have found its sense unclear.[5] We begin, therefore, by examining it closely, reviewing various efforts at translation in English, analyzing it philologically and exploring the sense it could have.

The Translations   The difficulty so many have with the expression *synalizomenos* is obvious from the various translations. No contemporary English translation renders it literally: "while sharing (taking, having, eating) salt with them." Each one tries to make sense of the expression. Here is how *synalizomenos* is rendered in some widely-used translations:

- The Revised New American Bible (RNAB): "while meeting with them";
- The New King James Version (NKJV): "being assembled together with them";
- The New Revised Standard Version (NRSV): "while staying with them";

- The New American Standard Bible (NASB): "and gathering them together";
- The Revised New English Bible (RNEB): "while in their company";
- The Good News Bible (GNB): "When they came together";
- The New Jerusalem Bible (NJB): "while at table with them"; and
- The New International Version (NIV): "while he was eating with them."

No two translations are the same, showing both the difficulty and the richness of the expression. Each translation brings out a different nuance, not all of them compatible. "Meeting with" the apostles (RNAB) suggests an active presence, "being assembled together with them" (NKJV), a passive presence, "staying with them" (NRSV), an extended stay, and "gathering them together," a particular occasion. Being "in their company" (RNEB) emphasizes Jesus' relationship to the community, and "when they came together" (GNB), their mutual relationship.

The NJB and NIV are more specific in their translation. Focusing on Jesus' presence at table with the apostles (NJB), and on Jesus' eating with them (NIV), these two come closest to saying that Jesus was sharing salt with them. So doing, both relate Jesus' active and extended presence to the community to Jesus' eating with the community in Jerusalem at the end of the gospel (Luke 24:36 – 53). Both also come closest to the understanding of the early Christians, whose translations into Syriac, Coptic, Latin and Ethiopic all referred to Jesus' having meals with the apostolic community after he rose from the dead.[6]

The Greek Expression   The Greek term *synalizomenos* is the present passive participle of the verb *synalizo (synalizomai)*. In Acts 1:4, the participle modifies the grammatical subject, Jesus (*Iesous*, 1:1), who made himself present *(parestesen)* to the apostles for forty days (1:3) and enjoined *(pareggeilen)* them not to leave Jerusalem (1:4). Introducing Jesus' instructions to the apostles, the participle relates Jesus' instructions to his appearances. Appearing to them during forty days, Jesus shared salt with them.

The verb *synalizo* is a compound verb, derived from *syn,* a preposition meaning "with," and the verb *halizo,* meaning "to salt," "to give, restore or intensify flavor." The verb *halizo* itself is derived from the noun *hals,* meaning "salt."[7]

In the New Testament, *halas,* a Hellenistic form of the noun *hals,* and the verb *halizo* appear as metaphors in some of Jesus' most striking sayings: "Everyone will be salted *(halisthesetai)* with fire. Salt *(halas)* is good, but if salt *(halas)* becomes insipid *(analon),* with what will you restore its flavor? Keep salt *(halas)* in yourselves and you will have peace with one another" (Mark 9:49 – 50).[8]

A closely related saying appears in Luke: "Salt *(halas)* is good, but if salt *(halas)* itself loses its taste *(moranthe),* with what can its flavor be restored *(artythesetai)*? It is fit neither for the soil nor for the manure pile; it is thrown out" (Luke 14:34 – 35).[9]

A variant of Luke can be found in Matthew: "You are the salt *(halas)* of the earth. But if salt *(halas)* loses its taste *(moranthe),* with what can it be seasoned *(halisthesetai)*? It is no longer good for anything but to be thrown out and trampled underfoot" (Matthew 5:13).[10]

Outside the synoptic gospels, the only other figurative reference to salt in the New Testament is in Paul's letter to the Colossians: "Let your speech *(logos)* always be gracious *(en chariti),* seasoned *(ertymenos)* with salt *(halati),* so that you know how you should respond to each one" (Colossians 4:6).[11]

In every case, the salt metaphor refers to the personal quality of those addressed (Mark 9:49 – 50; Matthew 5:13; Luke 14:34 – 35) or the quality of their speech (Colossians 4:6). In light of this early Christian context, *synalizomenos* could be understood as Jesus having or taking salt with the apostles, thereby strengthening or intensifying their quality as apostles, forming them as his witnesses in deed and word. Already that would be something. But there is more.

The verb *halizo,* "to salt," is used in the passive with the meaning "to be salted," for example "by fire" (Mark 9:49; see also Matthew 5:13). The verb *synalizo* is also used in the passive, meaning "to share, take, have or eat salt with" one or more people. In Acts 1:4, Jesus did not simply do something to the apostles, nor were they merely passive, albeit open to his action. Jesus did something with the apostles, and they participated in the action. Jesus ate, or dined, with the apostles during a period of forty days, and they joined him at dinner.

Making Sense of the Expression   It is one thing to give a word's literal meaning. In the case of *synalizomai,* the literal meaning is "to share, take, have or eat salt with someone." It is another to show how the literal meaning makes sense, especially when the literal meaning is metaphorical or symbolic.[12]

For many, that Jesus' shared salt with the apostles makes little sense.[13] Some have even suggested that *synalizomenos* may be a defective spelling for *synaulizomenos,* meaning "to be with" or "stay with" (NRSV). But, as many have pointed out, the word *synalizomenos* is firmly attested in the ancient manuscripts. Besides, the ancient translations in various languages all understood the term as a reference to eating together.

Others have suggested that *synalizomenos* is actually not a compound of *syn* and *halizo.* They propose that, in Acts 1:4, *synalizomenos* has a long *a,* whereas a compound with *halizo* would have a short *a.* With a long *a, synalizomenos* would have nothing to do with salt.

In the active voice, *synalizo,* with a long *a,* appears frequently in the writings of Flavius Josephus, with the meaning "to bring together," "to assemble" or "to collect" (NASB).[14] In the passive voice, also frequent in Flavius Josephus, it means "to come together" or "to congregate."[15] In Acts 1:4, *synalizomenos,* which is in the passive voice, would have this same meaning, "to come together" or "to congregate" (GNB). The difficulty with this solution is grammatical. *Synalizomenos* is singular, while the meaning "coming together" requires the plural.[16]

In Acts 1:4, both the context and the sense require the singular. It is a matter of Jesus (singular) sharing salt with the apostles, not of Jesus and the apostles coming together or sharing salt with one another (plural). In sharing salt Jesus both takes and maintains the initiative. From the theological point of view, the difference is extremely significant.

In Acts 1:4, sharing salt is not a mutual act among equals. Jesus has a special role in sharing salt with the apostles, as God has in the Mosaic covenant and Jesus in the new covenant. Jesus' place and role in sharing salt with the apostles is similar to his role at the Last Supper, at the Lord's Supper and in community assemblies for the breaking of the bread.

Salt in the Ancient World[17]

Ultimately, the expression "while sharing salt with them" *(synalizomenos)* is based on common everyday experiences. Salt was a necessary ingredient of any meal, even the simplest, consisting of bread and salt. In the ancient world, to break bread was to share salt.

At the same time, sharing salt, like breaking bread, was rich in symbolism. Sharing salt made for a deep, personal, and enduring relationship. In the Old Testament, people even spoke of a "covenant of salt" (Numbers 8:19; 2 Chronicles 13:5). In the world of Acts, Jesus' sharing salt with the apostles was the basis for their *koinonia* (common-union, 2:42).

Salt, a Basic Necessity   Throughout the ancient world, salt was considered a basic necessity, both as a dietary ingredient and for preserving food. In preparing a meal, salt was used as a seasoning. At the meal itself, it was added as a condiment or taken in the form of a sauce. Taken with bread as an appetizer, it could even constitute a separate course. As a preservative, salt was used to cure fish and meats for future consumption, and to keep food from spoiling until it was eaten. There was no refrigeration in those days.

Salt was an essential element at meals and a preservative for perishable foods. Such were its two most basic functions. There were other uses for salt, for example, in medicine and in cosmetics, but all of them flowed from these two. So did its metaphorical use to designate wit, clever and witty speech, a lively spirit and conviviality. So did its symbolic use in the various sacrifices and in relation to the covenant.

We turn to four authors, two of them in the Bible, as witnesses to the role of salt in filling a basic need in the ancient world. The two biblical authors are Sirach (2nd c. BC) and Job (circa 6th c. BC), both of whom made a great contribution to wisdom literature. The two other authors are Pliny the Elder (AD 23 or 24 – 79), a keen observer of nature, and Plutarch (b. before AD 50, d. after 120), a keen observer of human life. Both Pliny and Plutarch were contemporaries of Luke.

The Book of Sirach   Sirach, praising God the creator for providing everything that is essential for life, included salt among our chief human needs (39:26):

> Chief of all needs for human life
> are water and fire, iron and salt,
> The heart of the wheat, milk and honey,
> the blood of the grape, and oil, and cloth.

Earlier, Sirach had listed "life's prime needs," that is, the indispensable things people should provide for their sustenance, as "water, bread, and clothing, a house, too, for decent privacy" (29:21). The earlier list did not include salt, but it did include bread, and bread was never taken without salt, as we see from the wisdom of Job.

The Book of Job   Perhaps the most dramatic witness to the importance of salt as a food and of its relationship to bread comes from Job. To appreciate his statement, we must attend to its context.

Job had just voiced his first plaint (3:3, 24, 26):

> Perish the day on which I was born,
> the night when they said, "The child is a boy!"
> For sighing comes more readily to me than food,
> and my groans well forth like water.
> I have no peace nor ease;
> I have no rest, for trouble comes!

Responding, Job's friend, Eliphaz, had tried to make sense of Job's plight (4:7 – 8; 5:6 – 7):

> Reflect now, what innocent person perishes?
> Since when are the upright destroyed?
> As I see it, those who plow for mischief
> and sow trouble, reap the same.

> For mischief comes not out of the earth,
> nor does trouble spring out of the ground;
> But man himself begets mischief,
> as sparks fly upward.

Eliphaz' response was of no help, and his attempt at consolation tasteless. Job replied with a renewed cry of anguish (6:2 – 3):

> Ah, could my anguish but be measured
> and my calamity laid with it in the scales,

They would now outweigh the sands of the sea!
Because of this I speak without restraint.

Continuing, Job attributed his misfortunes, not to his personal conduct, but directly to God (6:4):

For the arrows of the Almighty pierce me,
and my spirit drinks in their poison;
the terrors of God are arrayed against me.

With two rhetorical questions, Job then showed the impossible situation he was in and that Eliphaz' explanation made no sense. Eliphaz' response was no consolation (6:5 – 6):

Does the wild ass bray when he has grass?
Does the ox low over his fodder?
Can a thing insipid be eaten without salt?
Is there flavor in the white of an egg?

For both questions, the implied response is, "Of course not." The wild ass does not bray when he has grass, and the ox does not low over his fodder. Nor can something insipid be eaten without salt. Eliphaz' efforts to console him were like insipid food without salt. Such food is unpalatable and should never be served. Nor should Eliphaz try to console Job with empty, insipid words. Job concludes with a cry of disgust over the food of his friend's consolation (6:7):

I refuse to touch them;
they are loathsome food to me.[18]

Job's comparison, as given in the Hebrew Bible, shows how important salt was at a meal in ancient times. The Greek translation in the Septuagint is more concrete than the Hebrew and more striking in relation to Acts' story of the eucharist: "Is bread eaten without salt *(ei brothesetai artos aneu halos)*?" Bread, the staff of life, is always taken with salt.

For those who eat mostly processed food, live in humid climates and enjoy the convenience of automobiles, elevators and escalators, taking salt can be a problem. In the modern world, people are warned to avoid salt. Salt retains water in our system, in some cases, raising a person's blood pressure. For someone suffering from hypertension, salt can be dangerous.

In the ancient Mediterranean world, however, and throughout the biblical world, these conditions did not obtain. The climate was dry and the rains seasonal. People traveled on foot or on muleback, or in the desert sometimes on camelback. In first-century Roman cities, people lived in buildings of up to six stories.[19] In those conditions, people needed salt precisely to retain water in the body. Even the most modest meal included salt. The prevalent danger to health was not hypertension, but dehydration. And people knew that salt was necessary to prevent dehydration.

Pliny the Elder   Pliny the Elder included a long section on salt in his monumental *Natural History,* as part of his treatise on water in Book 31 (xxxix–xlv). In the section, Pliny distinguished among various kinds of salt and how each could be used to greatest advantage. He spoke of the use of salt as a seasoning or a preservative, as a medicine, and even as a cosmetic, smoothing the skin and providing a gloss. In relation to its use in medicine, Pliny referred to an old saying: "Herein is especially applicable the saying that for the whole body nothing is more beneficial than salt and sun."[20]

What Pliny wrote about the use of salt in medicine shows that the situation in the first century was very different from the situation today, when we generally view salt as a health hazard.[21] In New Testament times, salt was considered beneficial for a person's health and was appreciated for its healing properties.

Pliny also wrote discriminatingly about the use of salt to season meats and foods and for preserving meats: "to season meats and foods the most useful one [salt] melts easily and is rather moist, or it is less bitter, such as that of Attica and Euboea. For preserving meat the more suitable salt is sharp and dry, like that of Megara."[22]

Salt could also be eaten as a conserve. With various "fragrant additions," salt was "used as a relish creating and sharpening an appetite for every kind of food, so that in innumerable seasonings it is the taste of salt that predominates" (Book 31, xli, 87).[23]

Pliny concluded that "a civilized life is impossible without salt, and so necessary is this basic substance that its name is applied metaphorically even to intense mental pleasures. We call them *sales* (wit); all the humour of life, its supreme joyousness, and relaxation after toil, are expressed by this word more than by any other" (Book 31, xli, 88).[24]

Pliny ended his treatment of the use of salt in the preparation of foods and at meals by appealing to the authority of Varro, as well as to a popular proverb and to the use of salt in sacrifices: "Varro too is our authority that the men of old used salt as a relish, and that they ate salt with their bread is clear from a proverb.[25] But the clearest proof of its importance lies in the fact that no sacrifice is carried out without the *mola salsa* (salted meal)" (Book 31, xli, 89).[26]

Pliny showed that salt was necessary for human life and that it became a metaphor for wit and humor in conversation. He also referred to a proverb about eating salt with bread. A similar connection between bread and salt was made by the Septuagint for Job 6:6. Unfortunately, Pliny did not actually cite the proverb.

Plutarch   For Plutarch, a meal without salt is like life without hope. Plutarch wrote of the importance of salt in his *Quaestiones Convivales* ("Table-Talk") in response to the question, "Whether the sea is richer in delicacies than the land."[27]

In Plutarch's opinion, no food was comparable to salt, a product of the sea, for stimulating and sustaining appetite. Without salt, all food is tasteless and unpalatable. Without salt, "practically nothing is eatable. Salt is added even to bread and enriches its flavour . . . Salt is also the best relish *(opson)* to season other relishes."

Judging by the heroes of old, salt was part of the most modest and simple diet. Acting as if they were in training, they excluded "all superfluous elaborations and condiments." They "even did without fish, though they were camping by the Hellespont; yet they could not endure to eat meat without salt. They testify that salt is the only relish that cannot be dispensed with. Just as colour requires light, so flavour requires salt to stimulate the sense; otherwise flavours are disagreeable and nauseous to the taste."

Indirectly, salt is even a good seasoning for drinks. "Moderately salty foods, on account of their pleasant taste, bring out the sweetness and smoothness of any kind of wine, and also make any water agreeable and tonic."

Summing up the qualities of salt, Plutarch adds: "Beyond that, salty food aids digestion of any other; it makes any food tender and more susceptible to concoction; the salt contributes at once the savour of a relish and the good effect of a medicine."

From Sirach and Job, and from Pliny and Plutarch, we see that salt was necessary for human life in the ancient Mediterranean climate and culture. Salt even assured, or contributed to, a person's health. From this very basic point of view, then, it made sense for Jesus to share salt with the apostles (Acts 1:4). Symbolically, salt assured the health and vitality of those who would be Jesus' witnesses to the ends of the earth.

Salt and Friendship   With Sirach, Job, Pliny the Elder and Plutarch, we saw that the ancients viewed salt as a necessity from several points of view, sustaining life and contributing to its quality. Anything as essential as salt, like bread, connected with eating and survival, would normally contribute to the culture and the way people relate to one another. In the ancient world, eating was a social event, and meals, especially those taken in the evening, were a significant event. In this context, we can appreciate Pliny's remarks about salt as a metaphor for wit, humor, joyousness and relaxation.

For a family and friends, meals were quality time together, strengthening family ties. When guests were invited or simply dropped by, meals were an expression of hospitality, establishing ties second only to those of blood.[28] For friends, meals were a source of deeper unity, as meal after meal bonded them closer and closer.

To see how eating salt was related to friendship, we turn to two philosophers, one Greek and one Roman — Aristotle (384–322 BC), the teacher of Alexander the Great, and Cicero (106–43 BC), famous as the dean of Roman orators.

Aristotle   In the *Nicomachean Ethics,* Aristotle wrote of the various kinds of friendship. Describing the highest form as that between good people, who resemble each other in virtue: "Such friendships are of course rare, because such men are few. Moreover they require time and intimacy: as the saying goes *(kata ten paroimian gar),* you cannot get to know a man *(ouk estin eidesai allelous)* till you have consumed the proverbial amount of salt in his company *(prin tous legomenous halas sunanalosai).*"[29]

In other words, people have to share many a meal together before they really get to know one another and become fast friends. Friendship has to mature, and the maturing takes place at the meals they share with one another. Since salt is a necessary ingredient at every meal, the depth of a friendship can be measured by the amount of salt they take in one another's company.

In the *Eudemian Ethics,* Aristotle was a bit more explicit, stating that it takes a long time for a friendship to develop. Hence the proverbial reference to "the bushel of salt *(ho medimnos ton halon).*"[30] To take or eat salt together is to have a meal together. To have eaten a bushel of salt together is to have eaten many meals together, to have enjoyed a long history of meals together. Those who have eaten a bushel of salt together are therefore old and very close friends.

Cicero   In his philosophical treatise, "On Friendship" *(De Amicitia),* Cicero wrote eloquently about the value of old friends. First he raised a question, in his estimation not a very difficult question *(quaestio subdifficilis):* "Are new friends who are worthy of friendship, at any time to be preferred to old friends, as we are wont to prefer young horses to old ones?"

Any doubt, in Cicero's opinion, would be unworthy of a human being *(indigna homine dubitatio),* "for there should be no surfeit of friendships as there is of other things." There is no such thing as having too many friends. Friends are in a class by themselves.

"As in the case of wines that improve with age, the oldest friendships ought to be the most delightful; moreover, the well-known adage is true: 'Men must eat many a peck of salt together before the claims of friendship are fulfilled' *(verumque illud est, quod dicitur, multos modios salis simul edendos esse, ut amicitiae munus expletum sit).*"[31]

Both Aristotle and Cicero provide a foundation in ordinary human experience for what Jesus did, sharing salt *(synalizomenos)* with the apostles. Sharing salt with them, Jesus was building up the bond of friendship between the apostles and him and among the apostles themselves. Since salt was an extremely important element in a meal, indeed, a life-giving element, taking salt with the apostles meant sharing his life with them. Taking salt with the apostles over a period of forty days meant Jesus was deepening and strengthening the bond of unity between himself, the risen Lord and the apostles.

Salt and Sacrificial Offerings   For Pliny, the clearest proof for the importance of salt lay "in the fact that no sacrifice is carried out without the *mola salsa* (salted meal)."[32] Roman literature is full of references to the use of salt in Roman sacrifices. There is even reference to it in Virgil's *Aeneid:* "Already the fatal day had come; already everything was prepared for the sacrifice: the salt, the sacred cakes *(salsae fruges)* and the narrow bands with which my forehead was to be encircled."[33]

In the Old Testament, we find the same. Salt was an important, even indispensable, element in the sacrifices offered at the temple.[34] For this, we turn first to Ezra, a great scribe (circa 400 BC), a priestly passage from Exodus (6th century BC) and a passage from Ezekiel (6th century BC).[35] We shall then turn to the Book of Leviticus, a priestly work (6th century BC), and to Philo, the Jewish Alexandrian philosopher (circa 15 BC – AD 50), commenting on Leviticus.

Book of Ezra   Ezra was a major figure in the restoration of Jerusalem, the temple and its worship after the deportation to Babylon. For Ezra and the world he represented, salt was one of the things required for the sacrifices offered in the temple. King Darius of Persia, following up on a decree of King Cyrus, ordered that the house of God "be rebuilt as a place for offering sacrifices and bringing burnt offerings" (Ezra 6:3). In his own decree (6:6 – 10), Darius ordained that the expenses for the rebuilding be provided from royal revenues (6:8), and that (9) whatever else is required — "young bulls, rams, and lambs for holocaust to the God of heaven, wheat, salt, wine, and oil, according to the requirements of the priests who are in Jerusalem — is to be delivered to them day by day without fail, (10) that they may continue to offer sacrifices of pleasing odor to the God of heaven and pray for the life of the king and his sons."

Darius' successor, Artaxerxes, also issued a decree to the royal treasurers of West-of-Euphrates (7:21 – 24) that they continue providing for the worship in the temple of Jerusalem. For everything, however, he set precise limits, except for salt.

Whatever Ezra the priest, scribe of the law of the God of heaven, requests of you, dispense to him accurately, within these limits: silver, one hundred talents; wheat, one hundred kors; wine, one hundred baths; oil, one hundred baths; salt, without limit.

Book of Exodus   Salt was provided without limit, because it was required for every sacrificial offering. Salt was even required in the preparation of incense (30:34 – 35):

> The Lord told Moses, "Take these aromatic substances: storax and onycha and galbanum, these and pure frankincense in equal parts; and blend them into incense. This fragrant powder, expertly prepared, is to be salted and so kept pure and sacred."

In the preparation of incense, salt was considered a preservative to keep the incense pure.[36] In the case of human beings, salt was used as a healing agent. In the case of incense, it was a purifying agent.

Book of Ezekiel   Salt was required both for holocausts and cereal offerings. For the restoration of the temple, Ezekiel paid close attention to the altar and its sacrifices (43:13 – 27). After describing the purification of the altar (43:18 – 22), he attended to the purification of the offerings (43:23 – 24):

> When you have finished the purification, bring an unblemished young bull and an unblemished ram from the flock, and present them before the Lord; the priests shall strew salt on them and offer them to the Lord as holocausts.

After purifying the altar and the offerings, they were to offer sacrifices daily for seven days. When these days were over, beginning with the eighth day, the priests would offer holocausts and peace offerings that would be acceptable to the Lord (43:25 – 27).

Book of Leviticus   For the use of salt in cereal offerings, we turn to Leviticus 2:11 – 13.

> Every cereal offering that you present to the Lord shall be unleavened, for you shall not burn any leaven or honey as an oblation to the Lord. Such you may indeed present to the Lord in the offering of first fruits, but they are not to be placed on the altar for a pleasing odor.

In the offering of first fruits, leaven and honey should be offered. But, since they contribute to the deterioration of the offerings, making them impure, they could have no part in sacrifices. Not so, however, with salt.

> However, every cereal offering that you present to the Lord shall be seasoned with salt (LXX, *hali halisthesetai,* be salted with salt). Do not let the salt of the covenant of your God (LXX, *hala diathekes kyriou,* the salt of the covenant of the Lord) be lacking from your cereal offering. On every offering you shall offer salt.

> As a preservative, salt guaranteed that the offerings would be pure, making them an enduring offering acceptable to God. Salt also assured the offerings would have a pleasing odor (see 2:12), agreeable to God. In a communion sacrifice, salt preserved the offering for later consumption. Symbolically, it assured that the union between the Lord and the people would endure.
> It was only fitting that their offering should be seasoned with salt. God's covenant with them was a "covenant of salt." By seasoning their offerings with salt, they remembered and renewed their covenant commitment.
> The expression "the salt of the covenant" is especially striking. It refers to the profound relationship between God, the Lord of the covenant, and the people, God's friends eating at the Lord's table. Using salt in the sacrifices was a reminder of the people's covenant relationship with the Lord.

Philo of Alexandria   Commenting on Leviticus 2:13, "On every offering you shall offer salt," Philo emphasized the qualities of salt as a preservative, as did Exodus 30:34 – 35 and Leviticus 2:11 – 13.

> Salt acts as a preservative to bodies, ranking in this as second in honour to the life-principle. For just as the life-principle

causes bodies to escape corruption, so does salt, which more than anything else keeps them together and makes them in a sense immortal.[37]

For Philo, salt signified complete permanence. Just before, concerning Leviticus 6:2, 5–6, specifying that the fire on the altar must burn continously, Philo commented:

> That, I think, is natural and fitting, for since the gracious gifts of God *(hai tou theou charites)* granted daily and nightly to men are perennial, unfailing and unceasing, the symbol of thankfulness also *(kai to symbolon tes eucharistias),* the sacred flame, should be kept alight and remain unextinguished for ever.[38]

Continuing in the same vein, he spoke of the sacrifice consisting "not in the victims but in the offerer's intention and his zeal which derives from its constancy and permanence from virtue."[39] The salt, preserving the offering from corruption, was symbolic of the offerer's virtuous intention, which must be constant and permanent.

Several texts on the role of salt in sacrifices of various kinds help us appreciate that, as a preservative, salt can be symbolic of permanence. By sharing salt with the apostles (Acts 1:4), Jesus guaranteed that their relationship with him would endure.

Salt and the Covenant   With Leviticus 2:11–13, we began to see that sacrificial salt was related to the covenant of their God. With Philo, we saw that sacrificial salt was symbolic of the virtuous intention and zeal of the one who offered the sacrifice, as the fire on the altar was symbolic of the offerer's attitude of thanksgiving. Both Leviticus and Philo, emphasizing the preservative qualities of salt, highlighted the people's relationship with God. Seasoning the offerings with salt made the relationship a permanent one.

For this final section on the background for Jesus' sharing salt with the apostles, we turn again to the Book of Ezra, to a passage showing very clearly what it means to eat salt at someone's table. The passage provides a good starting point for understanding the implications of an ancient covenant, and what salt had to do with it. We shall then turn to the Book of Numbers (6th century BC)[40] and 2 Chronicles (circa 400 BC), both of which use the expression "the covenant of salt."[41]

The Book of Ezra   In the biblical world, as in the Hellenistic and Roman world, partaking of someone's salt meant enjoying someone's hospitality and being on friendly terms. It also entailed a sense of obligation and responsibility toward the person.

In the book of Ezra, we find the following in a letter to King Artaxerxes from officials living in Samaria (see 4:17): "Now since we partake of the salt of the palace, we ought not simply to look on while the king is being dishonoured" (4:14). Partaking of "the salt of the palace" meant they depended on the king for their position as his representatives. As such, they may even have received hospitality at the palace and partaken of the king's table.

In a sense, the Samaritans were related to the king, at least by salt if not by blood. Already that implied solidarity with the king and called for loyalty to him. Referring to the grounds of that relationship as "the salt of the palace," emphasized their enduring, even permanent, relationship to the king, as in a covenant.

Book of Numbers   From Leviticus, we are already familiar with the expression "the salt of the covenant of your God," in Greek, *hala diathekes kyriou,* "the salt of the covenant of the Lord" (Leviticus 2:13). In Numbers 18:19, we have a slightly different expression, "an inviolable covenant," or more literally, "a covenant of salt forever" (NRSV).[42]

The covenant in question is the one with Aaron and his descendants, granting them a share in the offerings:

> By perpetual ordinance I have assigned to you and to your sons and daughters all the contributions from the sacred gifts which the Israelites make to the Lord; this is an inviolable covenant to last forever before the Lord for you and for your descendants.

The difference between the expression in Leviticus, "the salt of the covenant," and the one in Numbers, "a covenant of salt," is significant. Leviticus was talking directly about salt. The Israelites must not allow salt to be lacking in their cereal offerings. Sacrificial salt was not ordinary salt. It was the salt of the covenant. As such, it was a symbol of their covenant relationship with God.

The Book of Numbers, however, was talking directly not about salt but about the covenant. To show the value of the covenant, the author emphasized that it was a covenant of salt. The Greek translation of the Septuagint described the salt as everlasting: *diatheke halos aioniou,* "a covenant of everlasting salt." As a covenant of salt, the covenant would be enduring, since salt was a preservative. Everlasting salt, however, would make the covenant not only enduring but everlasting.

Second Book of Chronicles   Like the priestly author of the Book of Numbers, the chronicler also refers to "a covenant of salt" (2 Chronicles 13:5). In this case, the covenant is the one the Lord made with David, to whom God gave the kingdom of Israel, that is, the rule over Israel, forever:

> Do you know that the Lord, the God of Israel, has given the kingdom of Israel to David forever, to him and to his sons, by a covenant made in salt (literally, a covenant of salt)?

Once again, the preservative power of salt makes the covenant everlasting. A covenant of salt is a permanent covenant. The Lord gave David rule over Israel by a covenant. The quality of the covenant came from the salt, making it a lasting covenant. David's rule would last forever. Since the rule had been already described as everlasting, there was no need to stress that the salt itself was everlasting.

With these references to "a covenant of salt" in the background, it becomes clear that Jesus' sharing of salt with the apostles was meant to make his presence to them an abiding presence. By the same token, their relationship to him would be everlasting.

In light of the expression "the salt of the covenant," Jesus "taking salt with" the apostles evokes Jesus' words at the Last Supper: "This cup is the new covenant in my blood, which will be shed for you." By eating salt with the apostles, Jesus was forming them as witnesses for the new covenant.

Summary and Conclusions

Summing up, in Acts 1:4, the term *synalizomenos* refers to Jesus' sharing salt with the apostles. As the subject, Jesus shared salt with them and, thanks to his initiative, they participated in the event. There is no reason to substitute another word *(synaulizomenos)* or propose a different etymology *(synalizomenos* with a long *a)*. On various grounds, the substituted or proposed alternatives are even more problematic than *synalizomenos* with a short *a,* meaning "sharing salt with them."

In the ancient world, salt was a basic necessity, as a preservative and as a food, even as a medicine. Indispensable for human life, salt was part of every meal, as a condiment, as a special sauce, sometimes as a separate dish, taken with bread. If Jesus shared meals with the apostles after the passion, before he was taken up, it was quite normal for him to share salt with them.

Salt also contributed to the culture. It was a small step from taking salt as a basic life necessity or for medical purposes to sharing salt as an expression of friendship. The same can be said about bread. We can understand, then, that Jesus, sharing salt with the apostles, made himself intimately present to them, bonding them to him and to one another. Jesus sharing salt with the apostolic community was the basis for their *koinonia,* their common-union (see Acts 2:42).

Salt was an essential element of sacrifices in the ancient Near East, in the Roman world, and in Israelite worship, at least from the sixth century and Israel's deportation to Babylon. Sprinkled on the sacrifical offerings, salt assured that these would remain pure, making them an enduring offering, acceptable to God. In relation to the covenant, it was a symbol of the people's ongoing fidelity to the Lord, preserving their covenant relationship. Jesus' sharing salt with the apostolic community was the basis of their steadfast application to prayer (Acts 1:14), to the teaching of the apostles and to the *koinonia,* to the breaking of the bread and to the prayers (2:42).

As a preservative, salt symbolized the enduring relationship between Jesus, the risen Lord, and the apostolic community. In relation to the new covenant, Jesus' sharing salt with the apostles established a bond between him and the community of the Twelve, making and forming them into an enduring sign of his abiding presence.

We shall conclude by situating Jesus' act of sharing salt with the apostles in the context of the preface and the prologue, showing the great importance of its contribution to the Book of Acts and its story of the development of the eucharist.

In My First Book (1:1 – 2)

In the first book to Theophilus, Luke dealt with all that Jesus began *(erxato)*[43] to do and teach until the day he was taken up after instructing the apostles he had chosen through the holy Spirit (1:1 – 2). What Jesus began to do and teach in the Gospel, he continued in the Acts of the Apostles. For Luke, Acts is the gospel of the risen Lord.

Acts, however, is the story of the development of the church and its mission. The story often refers to Jesus, especially in the teaching of the apostles, but rarely presents Jesus in an active role. But that does not mean that Jesus was not present. How else could Jesus continue to do and teach what he began in the Gospel? A later age would call this form of presence "sacramental." Without using the word, Acts presents the apostolic church as the sacrament of Jesus, expressing, indeed fulfilling, in deed and word, what Jesus began to do and teach in the Gospel. The basis for this is given in the prologue (1:3 – 14).

From the point of view of the church, this is shown in stories of Peter, Paul and others, doing what Jesus did, preaching, teaching, healing, raising people from the dead and announcing the kingdom of God. They also broke bread in their homes and in full assembly as Jesus had done for and with them. In all this, the apostolic church acted in Jesus' name, the only "name under heaven given to the human race by which we are to be saved" (4:12).

The basis for the sacramentality of the church, for doing and teaching what Jesus did and taught, for making him present in the world of Acts, is given in the prologue (1:3 – 14). Such is the prologue's purpose: to show how Jesus would continue in and through the apostolic church what he began to do and teach in the gospel. Each statement, each phrase, each word is important, but only as part of the prologue's total message.

To understand and appreciate why over and over again Jesus took salt with the apostles for forty days, we must see the event as part of the prologue. Doing that, it becomes clear that Jesus' taking salt with the apostles was the basis for the development of the eucharist in the life of the church as told in the Acts of the Apostles.

The prologue can be divided into three sections:

- Jesus and the apostles after his passion (1:3 – 5);
- The final assembly and the ascension (1:6 – 12);
- The community after the ascension (1:13 – 14).

Table III

Setting for Jesus' Sharing Salt with the Apostles

1:1 – 14 Preface and Prologue

    Preface: "In the first book" (1:1 – 2)

    Prologue: Introducing the second book (1:3 – 14)
        Jesus appeared to them (1:3 – 12)
            For forty days (1:3 – 5)
                1:4 While sharing salt with them
            The final appearance (1:6 – 12)
                The mission of the church (1:6 – 8)
                The ascension (1:9 – 12)
            The community in Jerusalem (1:13 – 14)

Together the three sections form the prologue, not only in general for the Acts of the Apostles, but for the development of the eucharist according to Acts.

After the Passion (1:3 – 5)

The first section of the prologue tells what Jesus did and taught between his passion and the day he was taken up. It also focuses on the instructions Jesus had given to the apostles he had chosen through the holy Spirit (see 1:1 – 2). The account begins with a general summary statement and becomes increasingly more specific.

As the prologue opens in verse 3, we hear the narrator's voice. In the middle of verse 4, we begin to hear the voice of Jesus, but very faintly. By the end of verse 5, Jesus' voice becomes loud and clear, and the "you" being addressed is no longer Theophilus (1:1) but the apostles (1:2).

> He presented himself alive to them by many proofs after he
> had suffered, appearing to them during forty days and speak-
> ing about the kingdom of God. While meeting with (eating salt

with) them he enjoined them not to depart from Jerusalem, but to wait for "the promise of the Father about which you have heard me speak; for John baptized with water, but in a few days you will be baptized with the holy Spirit."

He Presented Himself Alive to Them   After his passion, Jesus presented himself alive to the apostles in many convincing ways.[44] Acts describes how he did that: "appearing *(optamenos)* to them during forty days and speaking *(logon)* about the kingdom of God" (1:3).

The basic statement is that Jesus presented himself alive *(parestesen heauton zonton)* to the apostles. Jesus is the Living One. At the end of the gospel, those who appeared to the women in the tomb asked them, "Why do you seek the living one *(ton zonta)* among the dead?" (Luke 24:5). The story of Emmaus would then show where to find the living one (24:13 – 35), namely, in the breaking of the bread (24:31, 35). A dramatic story, told later in Acts, helps us to appreciate what it meant for Jesus to present himself alive, that is, as the Living One.

When a disciple in Joppa,[45] a woman named Tabitha, fell sick and died, the disciples sent for Peter.[46] When Peter arrived, he was taken upstairs to the upper room *(hyperoon,* Acts 9:37, 39), where Tabitha was laid out. After dismissing everyone, Peter knelt down and prayed. Then, turning to her body *(soma),* he commanded her, "Tabitha, arise!" Tabitha opened her eyes, saw Peter, and sat up. Peter gave her a hand and raised her up *(anestesen).* Calling the holy ones *(hoi hagioi)* and the widows, Peter presented her alive *(parestesen auten zosan)* (9:36 – 43).

Peter presented Tabitha alive to the disciples after Peter raised her from the dead. Jesus presented himself alive to the apostles after he suffered and rose from the dead. Jesus, the risen Lord, was not simply the Living One. He was the Living One for them. The story of Tabitha recalls the story of Jesus and Jairus' daughter (Luke 8:40 – 42, 49 – 56). In and through Peter, Jesus, the risen Lord, was continuing to do and teach what he had begun to do and teach in the course of his historical life.

In the story of Jesus and Jairus' daughter, Jesus did not present the little girl alive to her family and those present. Instead, he directed that she be given something to eat (8:55).[47] That is also how Jesus had presented himself to the community of disciples assembled at Jerusalem. When Jesus stood *(este)* in their midst, the disciples thought they were seeing a spirit. To show that that he was really himself, Jesus, the same who died but was now alive, Jesus asked them for something to eat. They offered him a piece of fish, which he took and ate in front of them (24:36 – 42). In the same way, the prologue of Acts would show Jesus eating salt with the apostles (Acts 1:4a).[48]

Appearing to Them during Forty Days How did Jesus present himself alive to the apostles? By appearing to them, not once, but repeatedly, "during forty days." The present participle, "appearing," in Greek, *optanomenos,* comes from the verb *optanomai* (to appear). This is the only time that the verb is used in the entire New Testament. Usually, referring to Jesus, the risen Lord, the verb used is *ophthe,* a passive form of the verb *horao* (to see), also meaning "he appeared," or more literally, "he made himself be seen" (1 Corinthians 15:5 – 8; Luke 24:34; see also Acts 1:11). Both verbs refer to an act of Jesus.

The form *ophthe* emphasizes the transforming and empowering effects of Jesus' appearing to someone. In the Septuagint — the Greek version of the Old Testament used by the early Christians — *ophthe* is used only for God, the Lord, the glory of God and the angel of the Lord appearing. The term thus evokes the story of Moses when the angel of the Lord appeared to him in a bush aflame without being consumed. That is when Moses, called by God, was given a special mission (Exodus 3:1 – 22). It also evokes the story of Abraham and Sarah, when the Lord appeared by the terebinth of Mamre (Genesis 18:1 – 15). The verb *ophthe* associates the appearances of Jesus as risen Lord with the appearances of God, the Lord, the angel of the Lord and the glory of God.

The use of *optanomenos* instead of *ophtheis,* the participle corresponding to *ophthe* (see Luke 9:31) suggests a lesser form of appearance, one that would be represented by the word *optasia,* describing a vision or apparition. Such a vision made one an eyewitness (*autoptes,* Luke 1:2) but of itself did not make one a witness (*martys,* Acts 1:8, 22; 10:41, 43; Luke 24:48). More was required. Before they could be witnesses, Jesus would have to speak to them about the kingdom of God and eat salt with them and pour forth the holy Spirit upon them (see Acts 2:33).

The forty days *(di' hemeron tessarakonta)* Jesus was appearing to the apostles recall the forty days *(hemeras tessarakonta)* Jesus spent in the desert tested *(peirazomenos)* by the devil. Jesus did not eat anything in those days, and when they were fulfilled, he was hungry (Luke 4:1 – 2). A similar story is told in Matthew 4:1 – 2 and at the end of Mark's prologue (1:12 – 13).[49]

Jesus' forty days in the desert were days of testing and preparation for his mission, which was about to begin. They recall the forty days and forty nights Moses spent on the desert heights of Mount Sinai (Exodus 24:18; 34:28; Deuteronomy 10:10). During forty days and forty nights on the mountain, Moses neither ate bread nor drank water (Deuteronomy 9:9, 11). The same was true of the forty days and forty nights he lay prostrate on coming down from the mountain (9:18, 25). For Moses, the forty days and forty nights were a period of purification to enter God's presence and preparation for his exodus mission.

Jesus' forty days also recall the story of Elijah's desert journey of forty days and forty nights to Mount Horeb.[50] On the strength of the food given to him by an angel before his departure, Elijah fasted all the way to Mount Horeb (1 Kings 19:1 – 9).

The forty days Jesus presented himself alive to the apostles, appearing to them and speaking to them of the kingdom of God, were also days of preparation and formation for their mission in view of the kingdom of God. Like Moses, Jesus had fasted, preparing for his mission in desert solitude. Not so the apostles, whom Jesus prepared for their mission by dining with them, eating salt with them, in the upper room *(hyperoon)* where they were staying in Jerusalem (Acts 1:13). The bridegroom was still with them! But the day was approaching when the bridegroom would be taken away from them (see Luke 6:33 – 35).

The Day He Was Taken Up (1:6 – 14)   Acts' story of the eucharist begins with the prologue (1:3 – 14), which recapitulates and amplifies the story of Jesus' appearances and the ascension already told at the end of Luke (Luke 24:13 – 53). In the gospel, Jesus' appearances and the ascension conclude the story of Jesus. They also conclude the story of the origins of the eucharist according to Luke. In Acts, a sequel to the gospel, they introduce the story of the church. They also introduce the story of the development of the eucharist according to Acts.

Before Acts' prologue, a very brief preface summarized what Jesus began *(erxato)* to do and teach *(poiein te kai didaskein)* "until the day he was taken up" (Acts 1:1–2). After the prologue, beginning with the choosing of Matthias as a witness to the resurrection (1:15–26), Acts tells what Jesus continued to do and teach after the day he was taken up, but with a difference. In the gospel, Jesus acted as a historical figure, who was born, grew to adulthood, fulfilled a God-given mission and died. In Acts, Jesus acted through the church, which continued Jesus' mission in his name.

Having shared salt with the apostles during forty days, Jesus prepared the apostles for their mission in history. When they asked Jesus if he was about to restore the kingdom of Israel, he answered that it was not for them to know the times or seasons that the Father had established by his own authority (1:6–7).

Having shared salt with Jesus, the apostles were ready to receive power when the holy Spirit came upon them. They would be his "witnesses in Jerusalem, throughout Judea and Samaria, and to the ends of the earth" (1:8).

As Jesus finished this final instruction, outlining the history of the church as told in the Acts of the Apostles, "he was lifted up and a cloud took him from their sight" (1:9). Jesus had entered into the presence of God. In the Old Testament, the cloud that came over the tent of assembly in the desert (Exodus 40:34–35) and over the temple of Jerusalem at its dedication (1 Kings 8:10) was a sign of God's presence. At the transfiguration, the cloud came over Jesus, Moses and Elijah, and from it came a voice declaring: "This is my chosen Son; listen to him" (Luke 9:34–45).

At the ascension, the cloud indicates that Jesus has now entered into his glory (see 24:26), where he will remain "until the time of universal restoration" (Acts 3:21).

Having shared salt with the apostles, however, Jesus' presence would strengthen them in the upper room as they devoted themselves to prayer together with some women, Mary, the mother of Jesus and his brothers and sisters (1:13–14). After the coming of the holy Spirit, he would then continue to be present to and through them as they pursued their mission to the ends of the earth.

In this second chapter we explored the meaning of *synalizomenos* (sharing salt with) in Acts 1:4. For that, we researched the symbolism of salt in the Old and New Testaments as well as in the Hellenistic and Roman world. Concluding, we then saw how Jesus' act of sharing salt with the apostles during forty days contributed to the preface and the prologue of Acts. Sharing salt with them, Jesus assured the apostles and the whole church they would fulfill their mission in history, making Christ present "in Jerusalem, throughout Judea and Samaria, and to the ends of the earth" (1:8).

In the third chapter, we shall turn to the first section of the body of the Book of Acts (1:15 – 2:42). There we shall explore the meaning of the expression, "the breaking of the bread" (2:42; see 2:46), and its contribution to the life of the church in Jerusalem.

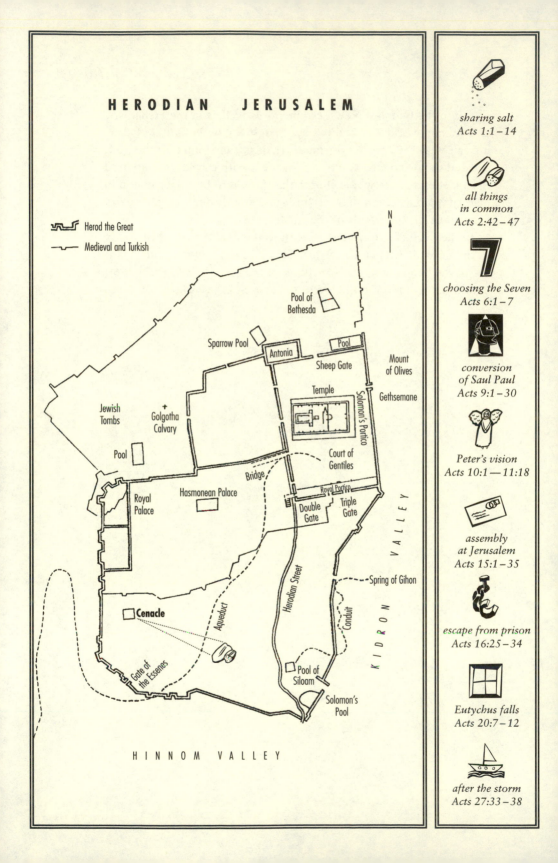

HERODIAN JERUSALEM

Herod the Great
Medieval and Turkish

N

Pool of
Bethesda

Sparrow Pool

Pool

Antonia

Sheep Gate

Mount
of Olives

Temple

Jewish
Tombs

Golgotha
Calvary

Solomon's Portico

Gethsemane

Pool

Court of
Gentiles

Bridge

Royal Portico

Royal
Palace

Hasmonean Palace

Double
Gate

Triple
Gate

K I D R O N   V A L L E Y

Herodian Street

Spring of Gihon

Cenacle

Aqueduct

Conduit

Gate of
the Essenes

Pool of
Siloam

Solomon's
Pool

H I N N O M   V A L L E Y

sharing salt
Acts 1:1–14

all things
in common
Acts 2:42–47

7

choosing the Seven
Acts 6:1–7

conversion
of Saul Paul
Acts 9:1–30

Peter's vision
Acts 10:1—11:18

assembly
at Jerusalem
Acts 15:1–35

escape from prison
Acts 16:25–34

Eutychus falls
Acts 20:7–12

after the storm
Acts 27:33–38

Chapter III

The Primitive Community in Jerusalem (1:15 — 5:42)

Those who accepted his message were baptized,
and about three thousand persons were added that day.
They devoted themselves
to the teaching of the apostles and to the communal life,
to the breaking of the bread and to the prayers.

Acts 2:41 – 42

Acts' story of the eucharist began immediately after the passion and resurrection of Jesus. Before being taken up to heaven (1:9–11), Jesus presented himself alive to the apostles. Appearing to them for forty days, he spoke to them about the kingdom of God (1:3). Joining them at table, he shared salt with them (1:4a).

Sharing salt with the apostles, Jesus prepared them to receive "the promise of the Father" (1:4; see Luke 24:49). A few days after the ascension, they would "be baptized with the holy Spirit" (1:5) that they might be his witnesses "in Jerusalem, throughout Judea and Samaria, and even to the ends of the earth" (1:8).

Jesus' appearances to the apostles (1:3–9) connect the birth and development of the church with "all that Jesus did and taught until the day he was taken up" (1:1). In doing that, the appearances also connect the development of the eucharist to the many meals Jesus took with his followers and disciples in the course of his life. In Luke-Acts, the story of the origins (Luke) and the development (Acts) of the eucharist is one continuous story.

Some of those meals were in Galilee (Luke 5:32–39; 7:36–50; 9:10–17), some on the great journey to Jerusalem (10:38–42; 11:37–54; 14:1–24; 19:1–10) and some in Jerusalem, on Passover, when

Jesus shared the Last Supper with the disciples (22:14 – 38), "on the first day of the week," when Jesus broke bread with the disciples of Emmaus (24:13 – 35) and with the whole community (24:36 – 49) the day he was taken up to heaven (24:50 – 53).

Later, in Acts, Peter would recall that God granted that Jesus be visible to the apostles, to "the witnesses *(martysin)* chosen by God in advance, who ate *(synephagomen)* and drank *(synepiomen)* with him after he rose from the dead" (10:40 – 41). Those appearances include Jesus' appearance at the end of the Gospel, when he ate and drank with "the eleven and those with them" (Luke 24:36 – 42; see 24:33), as well as the appearances at the beginning of Acts, when he shared salt with the apostles during forty days (Acts 1:3 – 4).

On those occasions, Jesus "opened their minds to understand the scriptures" (Luke 24:45) and spoke to them "about the kingdom of God" (Acts 1:3). He also declared them his witnesses *(martyres,* Luke 24:48; Acts 1:8; see 10:39 – 41). Their mission would begin on Pentecost, when Jesus sent the promise of the Father upon them (Luke 24:44 – 49).

At the beginning of Acts, Luke did not describe the meals Jesus took with the apostles, from the day he appeared to them "on the first day of the week" (see Luke 24:1, 13, 36) until the day he was taken up to heaven. The expression he used, however, tells a great deal about those meals. "Sharing salt with" *(synalizomenos)* the apostles, Jesus made himself intimately present to them.[1] Sharing salt with them during forty days, Jesus was laying the basis for their "common-union" (in Greek *koinonia,* in Latin *communio,* Acts 2:42), their union with him and their union with one another.[2]

Jesus was also laying the basis for his presence to them, with them, in them and through them when they assembled for the breaking of the bread and fulfilled his command to do this in memory of him (Luke 22:19). In the breaking of the bread, Jesus would continue what he began to do and teach until the day he was taken up (Acts 1:1 – 2). For their part, they would act and speak in his name, that is, in his very person.

In the breaking of the bread, Jesus would continue to nourish them with his very person, as he announced at the Last Supper, when "he took the bread, gave thanks, broke it, and gave it to them, saying, 'This is my body, which will be given for you'" (Luke 22:19). At the breaking of the bread, Jesus would be present to them as a participant and as nourishment. In the eucharist, Jesus, sacramentally present, would act in and through them. And they would be living, personal "sacraments" of his presence, acting in his name, as they fulfilled his command, "Do this in memory of me" (Luke 22:19b; see 1 Corinthians 11:24, 25).

In the Beginning (1:15 — 5:42)

The preface (Acts 1:1 – 2) and the prologue (1:3 – 14) showed how Jesus prepared the apostles for the coming of the holy Spirit and the birth of the church in Jerusalem. The first section of Acts (1:15 — 5:42) tells about the birth of the church on Pentecost and its early development.

In the beginning, the life of the church was a continual series of wonders and signs (see 2:19, 43; 4:22, 30; 5:12): the stuff of prophesy, visions and dreams (see 2:17). Told in story form, the wonders and signs are inseparable from the preaching and teaching of Peter. They are also linked by three great summaries describing the life of the church. Together, the stories, the preaching and teaching and the summaries show the joyful vitality, the irrepressible spirit and the extraordinary growth of the primitive church in Jerusalem.

In all this, Luke painted an idealized portrait of Christianity's founding community, offering it as an ideal for every community. For Luke, the beginnings of the church in Jerusalem represented a golden age[3] that should inspire the whole church as it spread from Jerusalem "to the ends of the earth" (1:8). The apostolic church in Jerusalem was the mother church of all the churches, including the church in Antioch, in Ephesus and in Rome. In Acts, Luke carefully relates every development of the church to its origins in Jerusalem.

All was not perfect, of course. The community experienced internal problems, as we see in the story of Ananias and Sapphira (5:1 – 11). Like Joseph Barnabas (4:36 – 37), Ananias and Sapphira sold a piece of property. However, they deceived the church about the amount for which they sold it (5:1 – 2). Lying to the church, whose very life sprang from the holy Spirit, they lied to the holy Spirit (5:4).

The community also suffered persecution from the outside. Soon after Pentecost, Peter healed a crippled beggar at the entrance of the temple (3:1 – 10). Then, while teaching and preaching in the temple (see 3:11 – 26), Peter and John were taken into custody (4:1 – 3) and brought before the Sanhedrin (4:5 – 22). Later, the apostles were arrested by the chief priest and the party of the Sadducees, put in the public jail and again brought before the Sanhedrin (5:17 – 33).

Every problem, however, internal or external, turned to the good. After the judgment of Ananias and Sapphira, "great fear *(phobos megas)* came upon the whole church *(holen ten ekklesian)*[4] and upon all who heard of these things" (5:5, 11; see also 2:43). No ordinary fear, the great fear that came upon them evokes the religious awe *(phobos)* that came upon Zechariah on seeing the angel of the Lord (Luke 1:11 – 12) and upon the shepherds when "the angel of the Lord appeared to them and the glory of the Lord shone around them" (2:9).

In spite of persecution, the number of Christians kept growing (Acts 4:4). On being arrested, the apostles had an opportunity to preach the Christian message before the Sanhedrin (4:8 – 12; 5:29 – 32). Strengthened by persecution, the whole community raised its voice in prayer (4:23 – 31). Nothing could stop the apostles from teaching and proclaiming the Messiah, Jesus, both at the temple and in their homes (5:42).

From the beginning, the eucharist played an integral part in the life of the primitive community in Jerusalem. Luke gave the eucharist a prominent place in his idealized portrait of the church, holding up its assembly and "the breaking of the bread" as an ideal and an inspiration for all the churches.

The first major summary describing the life of the community (2:42 – 47) shows that the members devoted themselves "to the teaching of the apostles and to the communal life, to the breaking of the bread and to the prayers" (2:42). The same summary shows that "every day they devoted themselves to meeting together in the temple and to breaking bread in their homes," and that "they ate their meals with exultation and sincerity of heart, praising God and enjoying favor with all the people" (2:46 – 47a).

"The breaking of the bread" *(he klasis tou artou)*, as we have already seen, is Luke's name for the eucharist. In Luke-Acts, the name itself appears in two places. Besides in the description of the church in Acts 2:42, we find it at the end of the story of Emmaus, when the disciples reported that Jesus "was made known to them in the breaking of the bread" (Luke 24:35). Note the wording in 24:35. Jesus was not made known to the disciples *by* the breaking of the bread, that is, by the way Jesus physically broke the bread, but *in* "the breaking of the bread," that is, in and through the whole eucharistic event.[5]

In Luke-Acts, "the breaking of the bread" refers to two different events, both of which are related to the eucharist. In one, the early Christians celebrate the breaking of the bread weekly when the whole community assembled as a church *(epi to auto)*. In the other, Christians break bread daily in their own homes *(kat' oikon)*.

As a weekly event, "the breaking of the bread" corresponds to what Paul called "the Lord's Supper" (see 1 Corinthians 11:20). From the story of Emmaus (see Luke 24:13) and the story of Troas (Acts 20:7–12), we learn that the weekly celebration of the breaking of the bread was on "the first day of the week."

As a daily event (see 2:46–47a), "the breaking of the bread" corresponds to what we might call a Christian or religious meal. Besides gathering as a church, Christians gathered as a family or household, as friends or neighbors, even perhaps as former members of the same synagogue. Paul may have referred indirectly to such meals in 1 Corinthians, when he dealt with the divisions in the assembly (1 Corinthians 11:17–22). When the community assembled as a church *(en ekklesia, epi to auto)*, it was not to eat the Lord's Supper. Would it not then be better for them to eat and drink in their own homes?

Before examining the summary (Acts 2:42–47) and its references to the breaking of the bread, we must first situate the summary in the context of this first part of Acts and its story of the beginning of the church in Jerusalem (1:15 — 5:42).

The Church in Jerusalem (1:15 — 5:42)

After the ascension (1:9–11), the apostles returned to Jerusalem (1:12) and the upper room *(hyperoon)*[6] where they were staying (1:13a). In this first section of Acts, the story of the church unfolds entirely in Jerusalem, which was home for "devout Jews from every nation under heaven" (2:5). With Jews from all over the world dwelling there *(katoikountes)*,[7] Jerusalem was an appropriate symbol for the church's mission to the ends of the earth.

With the defection of Judas, the twelve apostles had been reduced to eleven. At the end of the prologue, Luke lists their names (1:13; see Luke 6:12–16).[8] A summary adds that "all these devoted themselves with one accord to prayer, together with some women, and Mary the mother of Jesus, and his brothers" (1:14).

Table IV

Setting for the Breaking of the Bread in the Jerusalem Community

1:15 — 5:42 The primitive community in Jerusalem

The choice of Matthias as one of Twelve (1:15 – 26)

The story of Pentecost (2:1 – 47)
      The coming of the holy Spirit (2:1 – 13)
      Peter's inaugural discourse (2:14 – 41)
      Transitional summary of life
        in the Jerusalem community (2:42 – 47)
          2:42 Introduction: the marks of the apostolic church
          2:43 – 47a Body: a more detailed description
            2:43 Awe, wonders and signs
            2:44 – 45 Communal life, sharing with the needy
            2:46 – 47a Meeting in the temple,
              breaking bread in their homes
          2:47b Growth of the church

The ministry of Peter and John (3:1 — 4:31)
      Cure of a beggar at the gate of the temple (3:1 – 10)
      Peter's second discourse (3:11 – 26)
      The arrest of Peter and John
        with Peter's third discourse (4:1 – 22)
      Prayer of the community (4:23 – 31)
      Transitional summary of life
        in the Jerusalem community (4:32 – 35)

The community and the sharing of goods (4:36 — 5:16)
      A positive example: Joseph Barnabas (4:36 – 37)
      A negative example: Ananias and Sapphira (5:1 – 11)
      Transitional summary of life
        in the Jerusalem community (5:12 – 16)

The wonders and signs performed by the apostles (5:17 – 42)
      Trial before the Sanhedrin
        with Peter's fourth discourse (5:17 – 41)
      Concluding summary (5:42)

The first section of Acts (1:15 — 5:42) begins with the story of how Matthias was chosen to replace Judas as one of the Twelve (1:15 – 26). Once the Twelve had been restored to their full complement, Acts continues with the birth and early development of the church. For Luke, the story of the apostolic church in Jerusalem, the church of the Twelve, is the story of the church everywhere.

The rest of this first section can be divided into four parts:

- Pentecost and the breaking of the bread (2:1 – 47),
- the ministry of Peter and John (3:1 — 4:35),
- the community and the sharing of goods (4:36 — 5:16) and
- the wonders and signs performed by the apostles (5:17 – 42).

The first part (2:1 – 47) begins with the story of Pentecost, telling how the apostles were filled with the holy Spirit (2:1 – 4) and how the people in Jerusalem reacted to them and their message (2:5 – 13). It continues with Peter's inaugural discourse, proclaiming the gospel that underlies the whole Book of Acts (2:14 – 41).[9]

The first part ends with a summary that describes the Jerusalem community in the weeks and months after Pentecost (2:42 – 47). It is in this major summary, the first of three (see 4:32 – 35; 5:12 – 16), that Luke refers to "the breaking of the bread" as an integral element in the life of the church.

The whole summary, and each element in it, including "the breaking of the bread," must be read in the light of Pentecost, the coming of the holy Spirit and Peter's discourse. The summary describes the first fervor, the honeymoon, of those who had just been baptized on Pentecost. The summary also introduces the second part (3:1 — 4:35).

The second part (3:1 — 4:31) begins with the story of Peter and John going to the temple for the three o'clock hour of prayer. At the gate of the temple, the one called "the Beautiful Gate," Peter cured a beggar who had been crippled from birth (3:1 – 8). As in the story of Pentecost, Luke then tells how people reacted (3:9 – 10), and how Peter responded with a kerygmatic discourse, emphasizing and developing some key aspects of the gospel (3:11 – 26).[10]

The second part continues with the arrest of Peter and John, their trial before the Sanhedrin and their release (4:1 – 22). It includes Peter's third discourse, presenting the basic elements of the gospel before the Sanhedrin very succinctly (4:8 – 12). It also tells that when

Peter and John returned to the community their own people raised their voices in prayer (4:23 – 31).

Like the first, the second part ends with a summary (4:32 – 35), continuing the description of the early church in Jerusalem, newly filled with the holy Spirit (4:31). This second major summary further develops the sharing of goods, an element introduced in the first summary (2:44 – 45). It also introduces the third part (4:36 — 5:16).

Introducing the third part, the summary (4:32 – 35) tells that "the community of believers was of one heart and mind," and that "they had everything in common" (4:32). This idealized description is followed by two examples, one positive, encouraging the community to be generous, the other negative, warning the community against lying. The positive example tells that Joseph Barnabas sold a field and gave the proceeds to the apostles (4:36 – 37). The negative example tells that Ananias and Sapphira lied, saying they gave the apostles the entire proceeds from a property they sold (5:1 – 11).

Like the first and second parts, the third also ends with a summary (5:12 – 16). This third major summary further develops the wonders and signs performed by the apostles, an element introduced in the first summary (2:43). The summary also introduces the fourth part (5:17 – 42).

The fourth part tells that the wonders and signs performed by the apostles provoked an angry response from the high priest and the Sadducees, who brought the apostles before the Sanhedrin. This gave Peter a second occasion to present the basic elements of the gospel before the Sanhedrin. Like the third discourse, the fourth is very succinct (5:29 – 32). At the trial, the wisdom of a Pharisee, a member of the Sanhedrin named Gamaliel, prevailed, and the apostles were set free (5:17 – 41). The fourth and final part ends with a concluding summary: "And all day long, both at the temple and in their homes, they did not stop teaching and proclaiming the Messiah, Jesus" (5:42).

Besides the stories, the first section of Acts thus includes four discourses of Peter (2:14 – 41; 3:12 – 26; 4:8 – 12; 5:29 – 32),[11] three major summaries describing the life of the community (2:42 – 47; 4:32 – 35; 5:12 – 16)[12] and a great prayer of the community (4:23 – 30), all artistically woven into a tapestry of the church in Jerusalem. Along with the major summaries, this first section of Acts (1:15 — 5:42), includes a few brief concluding summaries,[13] one of which concludes the whole first section of Acts (5:42).[14]

In its use of stories, discourses, summaries and prayers, the story of the birth and early development of the church can be compared to the story of the birth and infancy of Jesus (Luke 1:5 — 2:52). Like the story of the church, that of Jesus includes discourses and summaries. The discourses announce the birth of John the Baptist (1:13 – 20) and the birth of Jesus (1:30 – 38). The summaries describe their early development (1:80; 2:40, 52). In place of prayers, the story of Jesus' birth has four canticles (1:46 – 55, 68 – 79; 2:14, 29 – 32). As in the story of the birth of the church, these literary elements are woven into a wonderful tapestry of the birth of Jesus.

A Descriptive Summary (2:42 – 47)

The three longer summaries (Acts 2:42 – 47; 4:32 – 35; 5:12 – 16) contribute significantly to Luke's portrayal of the church in Jerusalem. Drawing on traditional elements associated with the early years of the church, Luke integrated these in a new composition.[15]

Of the three summaries, the first (2:42 – 47) gives the most comprehensive picture of the church. Throughout, the summary speaks in universals, using the word "all" *(pas, pasa, pan)* repeatedly, as well as the words "many" *(polla)* and "whole" *(holon),* describing "the whole people" *(holon ton laon).* It is also in this first summary that Luke presents the breaking of the bread as a key element in the life of the church. We begin with an overview of the whole summary, which can be divided into three segments, including an introduction (2:42), a body (2:43 – 47a) and a conclusion (2:47b).

Introduction: The Marks of the Apostolic Church (2:42)   The summary opens with a summary of its own, presenting the four distinguishing marks of the apostolic church (2:42). The introductory summary includes the breaking of the bread as a constitutive element of the church, along with the teaching of the apostles, the common-union and the prayers. The breaking of the bread is further developed later in the summary (2:46 – 47a).

Body: A More Detailed Description (2:43 – 47a)   After the introductory summary (2:42), Luke gives a more detailed description of the church

(2:43 – 47a), telling how the early Christians lived as an ecclesial community. The elements described in the body are further developed in the other summaries (4:32 – 35; 5:12 – 16). The body itself can be divided into three segments:

Awe, Wonders and Signs (2:43)   In the first segment, Luke tells that religious awe *(phobos,* see 5:5, 11) came upon everyone *(pase psyche),* and that many *(polla)* wonders and signs were done by the apostles (2:43). The wonders and signs are touched upon in the second major summary (4:33) and are the principal theme of the third (5:12 – 16). Both the universal awe and the wonders and signs flowed from the community's ecclesial life (2:42).

Communal Life, Sharing with the Needy (2:44 – 45)   All *(pantes)* the believers were together as a church *(epi to auto)* and held everything *(apanta)* in common *(koina),* so much so that they sold personal property and possessions to divide with each one *(pasin)* according to need (2:44 – 45). The communal sharing is the principal theme of the second major summary (4:32 – 35), showing why the apostles were able to bear witness to the resurrection with great power, and why great grace *(charis megale)* came upon everyone (4:33). The communal life and their sharing with the needy flowed directly from their common-union *(koinonia).*

Meeting in the Temple, Breaking Bread in Their Homes (2:46 – 47a)   Every day they devoted themselves to meeting in the temple area (see Luke 24:53) and to breaking bread in their homes (Acts 2:46a). At this point, the summary focuses on the spirit of the community and the atmosphere pervading the breaking of the bread: "They ate their meals with exultation and sincerity of heart, praising God and enjoying favor with all the people" *(holon ton laon,* 2:46b – 47a; see Luke 24:19). Gathering daily in the temple and breaking bread in their homes showed that they devoted themselves to the breaking of the bread and to the prayers.

Conclusion: The Growth of the Church (2:47b)   Acts' first portrait of the church began with an introductory summary, describing the marks of the apostolic church (2:42). It ends with a concluding summary, describing its ongoing growth: "And every day the Lord added to their number those who were being saved" (2:47b).[16] With this concluding note, Luke recalls Peter's final plea in the Pentecost discourse: "Save yourselves from this corrupt generation" (2:40) and the response of those present: "Those who accepted his message were baptized, and about three thousand persons were added that day" (2:41).

Introduction: The Marks of the Apostolic Church (2:42)

The introductory summary (2:42)[17] describes the members as devoting themselves to four different aspects of the life of the church:

> They devoted themselves to the teaching of the apostles and to the communal life, to the breaking of the bread and to the prayers.

The summary presents the four elements or aspects in two sets. The first set is extremely basic, describing the very life of the church. It includes "the teaching of the apostles" and "the communal life." These first two elements are very closely related. "The teaching of the apostles" is the foundation for "the communal life." And "the communal life" is a concrete expression of "the teaching of the apostles." Together, the two form the basis for the second set.

Building on the first, the second set describes the basic life activities of the church. These include "the breaking of the bread" and "the prayers." Like the first two elements, the third and fourth are closely related. "The breaking of the bread," including a prayer of blessing or thanksgiving (see Luke 9:16; 22:17, 19; 24:30; Acts 27:35), is the source and the summit of other activities including "the prayers." Persevering in "the prayers," blessing and thanking God daily in the temple (Acts 2:46a; see 3:1) and in their homes, provides a general religious context for the breaking of the bread.

They Devoted Themselves (2:42a)

The opening expression, "they devoted themselves" *(esan de pro-skarterountes),* is very significant, introducing the four distinctive elements in the life of the church. A more literal translation would be "they were devoting (or kept devoting) themselves." The expression refers to the ongoing baptismal life of the believers.

Later in the summary, Luke uses the expression to describe the community's daily activities: "Every day they devoted themselves *(proskarterountes)* to meeting together in the temple area and to breaking bread in their homes" (2:46). The same expression was used at the end of the prologue, describing the community at prayer while awaiting the gift of the holy Spirit: "All these devoted themselves *(esan proskarterountes)* with one accord to prayer" (1:14). Later, the same expression will introduce the two most basic activities in the mission of the Twelve: "We shall devote ourselves *(proskarteresomen)* to prayer and to the ministry of the word" (6:4).

In all four instances (1:14; 2:42, 46; 6:4), the expression "devoting oneself to" refers to a special value or activity. In every case, it implies perseverance, especially in prayer (see also Romans 12:12; and Colossians 4:2). Luke stresses the need for perseverance in Jesus' teaching on prayer.

The theme first appears in a little commentary on the Lord's Prayer. Once when Jesus was praying in a certain place, just as he finished, one of his disciples said to him: "Lord, teach us to pray just as John taught his disciples" (Luke 11:1). In response, Jesus taught them the Lord's Prayer (11:2–4). Then, by way of commentary, Jesus continued with a series of parables and sayings, all of them emphasizing the need for persevering in prayer (11:5–13). Perseverance is also the theme of one of Luke's special parables on prayer: "Then he told them a parable about the necessity *(pros to dein)* for them to pray always *(pantote)* without becoming weary" (18:1, see 18:1–8).[18]

In Acts, "devoting oneself" also refers to devoting oneself to a person. Simon, the Magus,[19] for example, after hearing Philip preach the good news of the kingdom of God and being baptized, became devoted to Philip *(proskarteron to Philippo,* 8:13). Later, Cornelius sent two of his servants and a godly soldier who were devoted to him *(proskarterounton auto)* to summon Peter, who at the time was in Joppa (10:7).

Here, in Acts 2:42, these two different aspects, persevering in an activity and being devoted to someone, complement one another. The believers devoted themselves to the teaching of the apostles, to the breaking of the bread and to the prayers. Devoting themselves

to the common-union, they also devoted themselves to the Lord
Jesus and to one another.

As Believers   Before going any further, we need to focus on those
who so "devoted themselves to the teaching of the apostles and to
the communal life, to the breaking of the bread and to the prayers"
(2:42). In English, the subject is expressed as a personal pronoun,
"they." In Greek, however, the subject is not expressed directly but
implied in the verb. From the immediate context, we learn that
"they" refers to "all who believe" (2:44; see also 4:4, 32; 5:14).

As the Book of Acts tells it, at first the community of believers
was very small, including the eleven apostles, some women, Mary
the mother of Jesus and his brothers, all staying in the upper room
(1:13 – 14). By the time they chose Matthias to replace Judas, the
community had grown to about one hundred and twenty, possibly
still meeting as a community *(epi to auto)* in the same place (1:15).

After hearing Peter's message on Pentecost, about three thousand
persons were baptized and became members of the community
(2:41). In the Greek text, the connective particle *de* in the expression
esan de proskarterountes shows that those who were devoting themselves included not only the apostles and those with them in the upper
room, but all those who were baptized on Pentecost after hearing
Peter's message (2:14 – 40). A little later, at the time Peter and John
were arrested, the number had risen to about five thousand (4:4).

Those devoting themselves "to the teaching of the apostles and to
koinonia, to the breaking of the bread and to the prayers" included
"devout Jews from every nation under heaven staying in Jerusalem"
(2:5; see 2:14). The community of those who devoted themselves
had accepted Peter's teaching and his invitation to repent. They had
also been baptized in the name of Jesus Christ. Their sins were forgiven and they had received the holy Spirit (2:38).

Receiving the gift of the holy Spirit (2:38; see 2:41), they became
part of the new creation manifested on Pentecost when "a noise like
a strong driving wind" (see Genesis 1:2) filled the house where the
apostles stayed (Acts 2:2). Like the apostles, the baptized were
empowered to preach and teach the gospel with tongues of fire (see
2:3). The community in Jerusalem was the first community of the

new creation. Every facet of the community's life was the gift of the
Spirit (see Luke 11:13).

All who were baptized, who believed and "devoted themselves,"
were with the apostles, with whom Jesus had shared salt for a formative period of forty days (Acts 1:4). In the apostolic *koinonia,*
they were party to the new covenant of salt (see Luke 22:30), whose
quality as a preservative assured that they would continue devoting
themselves to the teaching of the apostles and to the common-union,
to the breaking of the bread and to the prayers of the new covenant
(see Luke 22:20).

The Teaching of the Apostles (2:42b)

"They devoted themselves to the teaching of the apostles" *(te didache
ton apostolon).* "The teaching of the apostles" is spelled out in the
discourses Peter gave on Pentecost (Acts 2:14–40), in the temple
area (3:11–26) and before the Sanhedrin (4:8–12; 5:29–32). Later,
there would also be Peter's discourse at the home of Cornelius
(10:34–43) and Paul's discourse at Antioch of Pisidia (13:16–41).[20]

Every reference to "teaching" in the Book of Acts (noun, *he
didache;* verb, *didasko*) is found either in a Lukan summary (1:1;
2:42; 5:42; 11:26; 15:1, 35; 18:11; 28:31) or in a summary report
made by someone in the story (4:2, 18; 5:25, see 5:21; 5:28; 13:12;
17:19; 18:25; 20:20; 21:21, 28). The theme of "teaching," very
basic in both Luke and Acts, shows that the teaching of the apostles
continued the teaching of Jesus after the passion (see 1:1).

In their teaching, the apostles spoke of Jesus' life and mission and
how these were in fulfillment of the scriptures. Special emphasis was
given to the passion and the resurrection. In his own teaching (Luke
4:15), Jesus also spoke of his life and mission as fulfilling the scriptures, beginning with his inaugural discourse in the synagogue at
Nazareth (4:16–19). Like the apostles and the early church, Jesus
also emphasized his passion and resurrection, both before and after
the passion.

Before the passion, in a series of prophetic announcements (9:22,
44–45; 18:31–34), Jesus announced that the passion and resurrection of the Son of Man was necessary *(dei)* as part of the history of
salvation. After the passion, the passion and resurrection would be

Jesus' main theme while interpreting the scriptures for two disciples on the way to Emmaus (24:25 – 27) and while opening the minds of the community in Jerusalem (24:44 – 49).

As an expression, "the teaching of the apostles" refers to a wide range of activities. Acts makes no distinction among teaching, preaching and announcing the good news, so much so that in all of Luke-Acts, the word "preaching" (noun, *to kerygma*) never refers to the preaching of Jesus or of the apostles. The only reference to preaching is to "the preaching of Jonah" (Luke 11:32). The verb "to preach" *(kerysso)* is used quite often, but interchangeably with "to teach" *(didasko)*.[21] Note how Acts situates two of Peter's kerygmatic discourses, those made before the Sanhedrin, in the context of the apostles teaching *(didaskein,* Acts 4:2; 5:28) and proclaiming *(kataggellein,* 4:2).

Like Jesus, the apostles taught the word of God (18:11; see Luke 5:1), and in their teaching they proclaimed the kingdom of God (28:31; see Luke 4:43). But there were some major differences between the teaching of the apostles and the teaching of Jesus. For the apostles, teaching the word of God meant teaching the word of the Lord (Acts 15:35), that is, the word of the Lord Jesus. And proclaiming the kingdom of God meant teaching about the Lord Jesus Christ (28:31). As the Son of God (Luke 1:35), Jesus spoke in his own name. Jesus' word was the word of God. The apostles, however, taught "in Jesus" (Acts 4:2) or "in the name of Jesus" (4:18).

In the context of 2:42, "the teaching of the apostles" refers immediately to Peter's Pentecost discourse. That "they devoted themselves to the teaching of the apostles" says that the newly baptized attended unwaveringly to Peter's teaching. Like Mary at the feet of Jesus (Luke 10:39), the church in Jerusalem was attentive to the word of Jesus, fulfilling the one thing necessary (see Luke 10:42). Hearing the word and acting on it, they were Jesus' true family. All in the community were mother, brothers and sisters to him (Luke 8:19 – 21; see Acts 1:14).

Devoting themselves to the teaching of the apostles meant not only receiving but handing on the teaching of the apostles. As a community of believers, they therefore devoted themselves to the ministry of the word (*te diakonia tou logou,* Acts 6:4). The apostles had assured the continuity between the teaching of Jesus and their community. As a link in the chain of tradition, the believers then assured the continuity between the teaching of the apostles and the

Lukan communities. It was now up to the Lukan communities to pass on what they had received.

The Common-Union (2:42c, 44–45)

Devoting themselves to the teaching of the apostles, the community listened to the word, made it their own and reflected on it. Having heard the word, the community then handed on the word to others, teaching as the apostles taught, devoting themselves to the ministry of the word. The teaching of the apostles gave meaning to every aspect of their life, beginning with the common-union *(koinonia)*.

The summary in Acts 2:42 is the only time that the word *koinonia* appears in all of Luke-Acts. But that does not make it less important. As a mark of the primitive community, together with the teaching of the apostles, *koinonia* was a constitutive element in the life of the church. The teaching of the apostles established the community in continuity with the teaching of Jesus. The *koinonia* established the community in continuity with the life Jesus shared with his disciples. The story of the Jerusalem community is a story of shared faith and shared life.

Ultimately, the *koinonia* was the gift of Jesus, who presented himself alive to the apostles after he suffered, appearing to them, speaking to them about the kingdom of God and sharing salt with them during forty days (1:3–4). Sending the holy Spirit on them (Luke 24:49) on Pentecost (Acts 2:1–4), Jesus transformed them into a missionary community. With Peter as their spokesman, the apostles offered the gift of *koinonia* to everyone who heard them in Jerusalem (2:14–40). That day, about three thousand people accepted the word and became part of the community (2:41).

By devoting themselves to the teaching of the apostles, those who believed joined in the *koinonia* of the apostles and shared their life in Christ. Then, by devoting themselves to the *koinonia*, they joined the apostles in a common ministry of the word and handed on what they themselves received. In their *koinonia* with the apostles, they were from the very beginning a missionary church.

Devoting themselves to the *koinonia* had a direct effect on their life as a community. In sharing their life in Christ with one another, they also shared their property and possessions. As we read later in the summary, "all who believed were together *(epi to auto)* and had all things in common *(hapanta koina);* they would sell their property and possessions and divide them among all according to each one's need" (2:44 – 45).

This general statement (2:44 – 45) is taken up and developed somewhat further in the second major summary: "The community of believers was of one heart and mind, and no one claimed that any of his possessions was his own, but they had everything in common *(panta koina)*" (4:32). It is not that the first Christians renounced the right to own private property (see 5:4). Rather, while retaining private property, they gave priority to the needs of their brothers and sisters in the community. They thought of what they owned as belonging to all.[22]

As a result, "there was no needy person among them, for those who owned property or houses would sell them, bring the proceeds of the sale, and put them at the feet *(para tous podas)* of the apostles, and they were distributed to each according to need" (4:34 – 35). The summary's reference to the needy recalls Deuteronomy 15:4, "there should be no one of you in need" (see also 15:1 – 11).

The attitude of the community toward property and wealth was similar to the attitude found in most Essene communities, which like the early Christians lived alongside other Jewish communities and interacted with them. The way of life in these Essene communities is presented in the *Damascus Document*, which refers to the private property of a member as belonging to the community:

> When anything is lost, and it is not known who has stolen it from *the property of the camp*[23] in which it was stolen, *its owner* shall pronounce a curse, and any man who, on hearing [it] knows but does not tell, shall himself be guilty (IX).[24]

Only those who entered the Essene community at Qumran placed all their property at the disposal of the community. Their way of life is presented in the *Rule of the Community*, whose introduction specifies that

> all who devote themselves to his truth shall bring all their knowledge and their power and *their wealth into the community of God*, to purify their knowledge by the truth of the precepts of God and to order their powers according to the perfection of his ways and *all their wealth* by the counsel of his righteousness (compare Acts 1:11 – 13).[25]

Putting the proceeds "at the feet of the apostles" is an idiomatic expression, like sitting or being at the feet *(para* or *pros tous podas)* of someone (see Luke 7:38; 8:35; 10:39; Acts 22:3) and falling at the feet *(peson para tous podas)* of someone (Luke 8:41; 17:16; Acts 10:25). Sitting or being at someone's feet means being a disciple. Falling at someone's feet is a gesture of submission to authority. Putting things at someone's feet means placing them at someone's disposition.

In all this, the community abided by the teaching of Jesus, whose concern for the poor and needy marked his life from the beginning.[26] In the synagogue at Nazareth, Jesus announced that he was anointed to bring good news to the poor (Luke 4:18). Asked by messengers from John the Baptist whether he was "the one who is to come" (7:20), Jesus answered, "Go and tell John what you have seen and heard: the blind regain their sight, the lame walk, lepers are cleansed, the deaf hear, the dead are raised, the poor have the good news proclaimed to them" (7:22).

At the home of one of the leading Pharisees, Jesus challenged his host to invite the poor, the crippled, the lame, the blind when he held a banquet (14:13). That is when one of his fellow guests exclaimed, "Blessed is the one who will dine in the kingdom of God" (14:15). In reply, Jesus told the parable of the great feast (14:15–24), where "the poor and the crippled, the blind and the lame" were invited (14:21). Later there would be the parable of the rich man "who dined sumptuously each day" while a poor man named Lazarus "would gladly have eaten his fill of the scraps that fell from the rich man's table" (16:19–31). In Jesus' teaching, sharing with the poor is closely related to sharing a meal together.

As a Church (epi to auto)   Before going further, we need to see how the community lived as a community. Did they, for example, live in one place? At the beginning, when the community was quite small, the members very likely lived in the same place, "in the upper room where they were staying" (Acts 1:13).

Later, however, when the community grew to one hundred and twenty, the upper room would have been too small for the whole community to live in. The reference to Peter standing in the midst of the community (1:15) does not require that they lived in one place, only that they gathered in one place.

After Pentecost, when the community grew to more than three thousand (2:41), it was not possible even to assemble in one place; a fortiori, when the number grew to five thousand (4:4). As we read later in this first major summary, "every day they devoted themselves . . . to breaking bread in their homes" (2:46). That presupposes that the community not only lived but assembled to break bread in a number of homes. That, however, did not take away from their *koinonia*. Nor did it prevent them from sharing life with one another and sharing their possessions with those who were needy.

Referring to the community as a whole, Acts uses the Greek expression *epi to auto.*[27] In the Septuagint, the expression appears very frequently, always as the translation for the Hebrew word *yahdau,* meaning "together." In the New Testament, however, the expression *epi to auto*[28] has a quasi-technical meaning, designating the community as such and stressing the *koinonia* (common-union) of its members. In 1 Corinthians 11:20, Paul places the expression *epi to auto* parallel to the expression *en ekklesia,* meaning "as a church" (11:18).

The expression *epi to auto,* therefore, does not mean that they lived or assembled "in one place" or "together," as it meant in the Septuagint.[29] It means that they met "as a body" (Acts 1:15; 2:1), and after Pentecost "as a church," as a community of believers who were one in Christ. That was true whether they assembled in the same place or in various places. A good translation for 2:44, therefore, would be, "And all who believed were united as a church" or in "common-union" *(epi to auto).* A good translation for 2:47 would be, "And every day, the Lord added those being saved to their common-union *(epi to auto).*"

Devoting themselves to the common-union *(koinonia)* included the small ecclesial community or sub-community to which they belonged. So did their sharing with the poor. Devoting themselves to the common-union, however, reached beyond their immediate ecclesial community to the greater ecclesial community in Jerusalem. And so did their sharing with the poor. That is why those who sold their possessions placed the proceeds at the feet of the apostles, for the apostles to distribute throughout the church in Jerusalem. Eventually, devoting themselves to the common-union would include the church in Judea and Samaria, even "to the ends of the earth" (1:8).

The Breaking of the Bread (2:42d, 46–47a)

The teaching of the apostles and the common-union belong to the very life of the church. Receiving and handing on the teaching of the apostles was absolutely vital for the community. As a community of faith, the primitive church was a missionary community. The common personal union with Christ was equally vital. United with Christ, the members of the community were united with one another.

We understand, then, why Luke names the teaching of the apostles and the common-union *(koinonia)* in first place. But that does not make the breaking of the bread and the prayers less important. Together, the teaching of the apostles and the *koinonia* constitute the life of the church. Together, the breaking of the bread and the prayers are primary expressions of the life of the church. They also nourish, sustain, strengthen and bring the life of the church to fulfillment.

The teaching of the apostles was savored at the assembly for the breaking of the bread. It was also shared. The common-union, the very soul of the breaking of the bread, found its highest expression at the Christian table. Conversely, the breaking of the bread was celebrated in a community devoted to the teaching of the apostles and to the common-union, bound to one another and the Lord Jesus with bonds of *koinonia.*

Devoting themselves to the breaking of the bread, the early Christians were faithful to Jesus' command at the Last Supper. After taking the bread and giving thanks, Jesus broke the bread and gave it to them, saying, "This is my body, which will be given for you; do this in memory of me" (Luke 22:19). In the breaking of the bread, they did what Jesus did in memory of him.

In the breaking of the bread, they continued what Jesus did with his followers and disciples during his Galilean ministry, on his journey to Jerusalem and in Jerusalem before the passion and after he rose from the dead. Jesus himself enabled them to do this by taking salt with the apostles during forty days (Acts 1:4) and sending the Spirit upon them (Luke 24:49; Acts 2:1–4, 38). In the breaking of the bread, the members of the community shared salt with one another, blessing God and giving thanks for the salt they had received through the apostles.

The Bread that Jesus Broke   The name for the eucharist in Luke-Acts is not "the breaking of bread" *(he klasis artou)* but "the breaking of *the* bread" *(he klasis* tou *artou)*. The first definite article, "the," indicates that "the breaking of the bread" is not just any breaking of the bread, but a definite and very special event. Paul called that event "the Lord's Supper" *(to kyriakon deipnon)*. Today, we usually call it "the eucharist." The second definite article, "the," indicates that the bread that is broken is not just any bread, but a particular and very special bread. The definite article also assumes that we already know about this bread.

"The bread" in "the breaking of the bread" is the bread that Jesus broke and gave to his apostles to distribute at Bethsaida. In the breaking of the bread, the community continued to break the bread that Jesus had broken, sharing it with one another and thousands of others. They did that first in Jerusalem. Eventually, they would do that "to the ends of the earth" (Acts 1:8).

It was at the climax of Jesus' Galilean ministry. Jesus had already been a guest for dinner at the home of a tax collector named Levi (Luke 5:27 – 39) and at the home of a Pharisee named Simon (7:36 – 50). He would now be the host for a crowd of five thousand in the city of Bethsaida (9:10 – 17).[30]

The apostles had just returned from their first mission, and Jesus "took them and withdrew to a town called Bethsaida" (9:1 – 10). But a crowd of about five thousand followed him. Jesus welcomed them and spoke to them about the kingdom of God. He also healed all who needed to be cured. At day's end, the Twelve suggested he dismiss the crowd that the five thousand might find a place to stay and something to eat. All the apostles had was five loaves and two fish (9:11 – 14a).

In the New Testament stories of the breaking of the bread, the number "five thousand" is very traditional (see Mark 6:44; John 6:10). In Luke's Gospel, the crowd of five thousand is symbolic of the whole church, looking back to a time when the church was still quite small. Even so, there would have been no place in Bethsaida large enough for an assembly of five thousand. In relation to Acts, the number five thousand prefigures the church in Jerusalem, which soon grew to some five thousand (4:4).

Jesus told the Twelve to have the crowd of five thousand sit down in companies of fifty. The number "fifty" corresponds to the size of a typical community assembling as a church *(epi to auto)* for the breaking of the bread.[31] Jesus then broke the five loaves and the apostles offered them to the five thousand. "They all ate and were satisfied" (Luke 9:14b–17a).

The breaking of the bread for the five thousand at Bethsaida represents a general assembly of the entire church, made up of small ecclesial communities, each numbering about fifty. Ordinarily, the small communities assembled on their own for the breaking of the bread. At Bethsaida, however, Jesus hosted a great assembly of all the assemblies.

If the story of Bethsaida had ended there with the feeding of the five thousand, it would already have been a great gospel story, telling one of the most striking wonders and signs Jesus performed. But the story continues. The loaves Jesus broke were more than the five thousand could eat. After the crowd ate and were satisfied, the apostles gathered twelve baskets of the bread left over from the bread that Jesus had broken. The twelve baskets correspond to the twelve apostles, whom Jesus made the foundations of a church that would reach to the ends of the earth.

"The bread" in "the breaking of the bread" is the bread left over when Jesus broke the bread at Bethsaida. The summary in Acts describes the church as nourished by the bread from the twelve baskets the apostles had gathered. In Jesus' name, the apostles continued to break the five loaves. Jesus had nourished five thousand with those five loaves. They would nourish many thousands more. The bread they broke was the bread of the kingdom of God (see Luke 9:11; 14:15).

"The bread" is also the bread that Jesus broke at the Last Supper, when he took bread, gave thanks and gave it to the Twelve, saying, "This is my body, which will be given for you; do this in memory of me" (Luke 22:19). "The bread" in "the breaking of the bread" is the body of Christ.

In the breaking of the bread, the community continued to break the bread Jesus had broken and offered it in his name. One with Christ, they repeated his words, "This is my body, which will be given for you" (22:19). As Christians, they made Christ's eucharistic words their own. They also repeated Christ's command: "Do this in memory of me" (22:19), so becoming a link in the chain of eucharistic tradition. They would do this that the whole human race might do what Jesus had done in memory of him.[32] Like the gospel, the eucharist was intended for all people.

"The bread" in "the breaking of the bread" is also the bread Jesus broke at the home of two disciples at Emmaus, presenting himself to them as a stranger, a sojourner in Jerusalem, accompanying them on their journey and interpreting for them "what referred to him in all the scriptures" (24:27). Arriving at Emmaus, they thought they were inviting a stranger to stay with them at their home (24:28 – 29). But when he took bread, said the blessing, broke it and gave it to them, "their eyes were opened and they recognized him, but he vanished from their sight" (24:30 – 31).[33]

The disciples then returned to the community in Jerusalem (24:33). Intending to share the good news of what happened to them "on the way" and "in the breaking of the bread" (24:35), they were greeted with the good news of the resurrection and that Jesus had appeared to Simon (24:34).

In Acts' summary of the life of the church, "the bread" is also the bread Jesus broke and gave to the disciples at Emmaus. Like the disciples, therefore, the Jerusalem community should be able to recognize the risen Lord. For that they needed to invite to their homes (see 24:29) those visiting in Jerusalem who did not yet know of the events that had taken place there (see 24:18).

In their Homes The summary in Acts says that "every day they devoted themselves to meeting together in the temple area *(en to hiero)* and to breaking bread in their homes *(kat' oikon)*" (2:46). In Jerusalem, the temple area and the home were the two main centers for the community's religious life. Greek-speaking Christians may also have attended the synagogue. That would explain the persistence of Christian Hellenists as a distinct group within the community (see 6:1) as well as the recurring conflict with Jewish Hellenists (6:9; 9:29). Away from Jerusalem, the two settings were the synagogue and the home.

At first, Christians who were of Jewish origin joined the Jews for worship and prayer in the temple as well as in the synagogue, in both places witnessing to the faith. When visiting Jerusalem, Christians who were of Gentile origin could join them in the court of the Gentiles (21:26). The temple and the synagogue also provided a setting for Peter and John (3:1 – 26), and later for Paul (9:29; 21:27 — 22:21) to teach the good news of Jesus Christ.

The Christian community in Jerusalem continued to frequent the temple until it was destroyed in AD 70. In the diaspora, however, Christians either left the synagogue or were expelled from it over the issue of admitting Gentiles to the community. With their separation from the synagogue, the home became the main setting for Christian life and ministry. Hence the prominent place given to the home in Luke-Acts and throughout the New Testament.

At first, the community stayed in the upper room (*hyperoon,* 1:13)[34] in a private home in Jerusalem, the same upper room *(anagaion)* where Jesus had celebrated the Last Supper with his disciples (Luke 22:12). Luke described this upper room as a guest room *(katalyma),* where "the master of the house" (22:11) had provided the hospitality Jesus needed to eat the Passover with his disciples. The word *katalyma* refers to any place or space where hospitality is given to someone on a journey.[35] After the passion, the community continued to receive hospitality in the same upper room (see Luke 24:36 – 49; Acts 1:13 – 14).

Early tradition situates the "upper room" on Jerusalem's western hill, a very affluent part of the city.[36] Jesus, the Son of Man, who had "nowhere to rest his head" (Luke 9:58), could not have afforded such a room. Some of his followers, however, had the means to rent it.

During Jesus' ministry in Galilee, a number of women accompanied him and the Twelve. Among these women were "Mary called Magdalene, . . . Joanna, the wife of Herod's steward Chuza, Susanna, and many others who provided for them out of their resources" (8:2 – 3). These women also followed Jesus from Galilee to Jerusalem (23:49, 55; 24:10). After the passion, at least some of the women stayed in Jerusalem and were part of the first community (Acts 1:14). A woman like Joanna, "the wife of Herod's steward," had the means and the influence to ensure that the community had a good place to stay, especially when Herod himself was staying in Jerusalem (Luke 23:7).

When the community gathered to choose Judas' successor and Peter stood up in the midst of some one hundred twenty (Acts 1:15), and on Pentecost, when he stood up with the Eleven (2:1 – 4), the community was still staying in the same place, but not necessarily in the upper room. The story of Pentecost says that "there came from the sky a noise like a strong driving wind and it filled the entire house *(holon ton oikon)* in which they were" (2:2). The house where the community had first stayed in the upper room was now entirely at their disposal.

The house seems to have been quite large, enough for one hundred twenty people to gather, but not enough for the three thousand who were baptized and added to the community that day (2:41). The house with the upper room became symbolic of the Christian community in Jerusalem. Luke presented it as the center from which the Christian message radiated throughout Jerusalem (2:5 – 13).

The same house probably remained a central house for the Christian community in Jerusalem. There were surely other houses where Christians gathered as a church. When Peter was freed from prison, for example, "he went to the house of Mary, the mother of John who is called Mark, where there were many people gathered in prayer" (12:12). After explaining "how the Lord had led him out of the prison," Peter asked that they "report this to James and the brothers" (12:17). The account presupposes that James, "the brother of the Lord" (Galatians 1:19),[37] and the other "brothers of the Lord" (Acts 1:14) lived at another house.

Later, when Paul visited Jerusalem, he and some of the disciples from Caesarea stayed at the home of Mnason, a Cypriot, "a disciple of long standing," who welcomed them warmly (21:16 – 17). The following day, Paul and the others went to visit James, in a place where all the presbyters were gathered (21:18). Again, the account presupposes that James lived at another house, and that this house was the center of the church in Jerusalem. Very likely, this house was the same where the community had stayed in the upper room after the passion.

Within a short time, James had become the leader of the church in Jerusalem. Very likely, the house where James lived hosted the apostolic council where a decision was taken regarding Gentiles and their observance of the Mosaic Law (15:1 – 35; see also 21:20 – 25). If so, the most important events, critical to the very nature of the church, all took place in the same house. These events included the Last Supper (Luke 22:7 – 13, 14 – 38), the Easter assembly (24:36 – 53), the post-ascension assembly (Acts 1:13 – 14), the choosing of Matthias to replace Judas as one of the Twelve (1:15 – 26), the coming of the holy Spirit on Pentecost (2:1 – 4) and the apostolic council (15:1 – 35). But there were other houses where the Christians gathered, like the home of Mary, the mother of John Mark, and the home of Mnason.

Hospitality and Ministry From the very beginning, the Christian home was a place of hospitality and ministry. For the Last Supper, someone offered hospitality to Jesus in an upper room that he might extend hospitality to the disciples for the Passover. After the passion, the early Christian community stayed in the same house, including the upper room, where they continued to receive hospitality and give it to others. Very soon, there would be other homes, all of them offering hospitality to other Christians, especially those visiting Jerusalem from elsewhere.

Hospitality was a very basic ministry together with ministry of evangelization, not only in Jerusalem but wherever the church spread.[38] The conclusion of the first section of Acts (1:15 — 5:42) sums up the life of the church in terms of hospitality and evangelization: "And all day long, both at the temple and in their homes, they did not stop teaching and proclaiming the Messiah, Jesus" (5:42). At the temple, they proclaimed Jesus at the historic heart of Judaism. In their homes, they proclaimed Jesus to all those who accepted their hospitality.

Hospitality was a key element in the church's missionary efforts. Those engaged in the Christian mission depended on hospitality. They also offered it. Take Peter, for example, who received hospitality in Joppa in the home of Simon the tanner (10:5 – 6) and offered hospitality in the same home to the messengers sent by Cornelius (10:17 – 23). And take Paul, who received hospitality in Damascus after he was baptized (9:18 – 19) and over and over again in his life as a missionary. At the end of Acts, Paul himself offered hospitality for two years in his lodgings in Rome, proclaiming the kingdom of God and teaching about the Lord Jesus Christ to everyone who came to him (28:30 – 31).

As a place of hospitality and evangelization, the home was a place of ministry *(diakonia),* much of which took place at the table. In this, the community in Jerusalem continued in the footsteps of Jesus, whose ministry unfolded in settings of hospitality. Whether as a guest or as the host, Jesus did much of his teaching at the meals he took with his disciples and many others.

If the home was a place of hospitality, the church was a community of hospitality, providing a home for the homeless and a meal for the hungry. The meal included the teaching of the apostles, inviting guests to join in the common-union of faith. It also included the breaking of the bread, inviting the guests to go forth and extend Christian hospitality to others.

The summary in the Book of Acts introduces "the breaking of the bread" as a distinctive mark of the early church in Jerusalem (2:42). In that, it recalls the breaking of the bread at Emmaus, where the disciples offered hospitality to someone on the way and recognized the risen Lord when he broke bread for them on the first day of the week (Luke 24:13–35). Later, the summary adds that "every day they devoted themselves . . . to breaking bread in their homes. They ate their meals with exultation and sincerity of heart, praising God and enjoying favor with all the people" (Acts 2:46–47a).

In the introductory statement (2:42), "the breaking of the bread" refers to two distinct events, one weekly, the other daily. The early Christians assembled to break bread on the first day of the week. They also broke bread every day in their own homes. The second statement (2:46–47a) is more limited, specifying that they broke bread every day. We need to examine the difference and the relationship between the breaking of the bread "on the first day of the week," and the breaking of the bread "every day." How did these differ? How were they related to one another?

On the First Day of the Week   For the breaking of the bread on the first day of the week, the community assembled "as a church" *(epi to auto),* as people who devoted themselves to the teaching of the apostles and to the common-union. When they assembled as a church, they assembled as Christians, pure and simple, irrespective of each one's human background.

We can best appreciate what that meant from an ancient baptismal formula that Paul cited in his letter to the Galatians: "For all of you who were baptized into Christ have clothed yourselves with Christ. There is neither Jew nor Greek, there is neither slave nor free person, there is not male and female; for you are all one in Christ Jesus" (Galatians 3:27–28).[39]

Being a Christian does not come from someone's conception and birth. It has nothing to do with human generation. When Christians assemble as a church, "there is neither Jew nor Greek, there is neither slave nor free person." Being a Jew or a Greek came from a person's birth. Very often, being a slave or a free person also came from birth.

For the Christian community, these distinctions were irrelevant, since being a Christian had nothing to do with someone's conception and birth. Being a Christian depended on baptism, when someone put off his or her former person and put on Christ, and on the gift of the holy Spirit. Natural and social distinctions had no meaning because being a church did not depend on the relationship between "male and female" (*arsen kai thely,* see Genesis 1:27).

Paul could have added that there is neither man *(aner)* nor woman *(gyne),* again precisely because "there is not male and female." As a church, all, Jew and Greek, slave and free person, man and woman, all who are baptized and have put on Christ are one in Christ Jesus. When the Christians assembled for the breaking of the bread on the first day of the week, they assembled as a church. That meant the assembly was open to all, excluding no one by reason of race, sex, nationality, ethnic background, tribe, caste, social or economic status, or language. Ideally, the community preached the gospel to everyone and welcomed everyone who accepted it.

The Christians did not assemble as a church *(epi to auto)* every day but once a week, on the first day of the week. Like the expression "as a church," the reference to "the first day of the week" tells us a great deal about the community's weekly assembly for the breaking of the bread.[40]

In Luke-Acts (Luke 24:35; Acts 20:7), as in the other Gospels (Mark 16:2; Matthew 28:1; John 20:1, 19), the first day of the week is associated with the resurrection of Jesus. It was on the first day of the week that the women visited the tomb and that Peter also visited the tomb, that Jesus broke bread with two disciples at Emmaus, that he appeared to the Eleven and those who were with them in Jerusalem and that he blessed them on the Mount of Olives[41] as he was taken up to heaven (Luke 24:1–53).

The Greek expression for "on the first day of the week," *te de mia ton sabbaton,* literally, "on day one *(mia)* of the week," is at the very least extremely awkward. Instead of the ordinal number, *prote* (first), it uses the cardinal number, *mia* (one). The usage, which first appeared in Mark 16:2, was not corrected but maintained until the second century. We would expect at least Matthew to have corrected the expression, as he did quite often for other expressions in favor of a better Greek idiom.

There must have been something very special about the expression to explain why neither Matthew nor Luke corrected it and why it also appears in the Gospel of John. The first time we find the ordinal number, *prote,* is in the longer ending appended to Mark's Gospel early in the second century (16:9 – 20). In the longer ending, we finally read the expression we would normally expect, *prote sabbatou,* "on the first day of the week" (16:1).

The expression can be traced to the Septuagint, which translated the Hebrew phrase for the first day of creation *(yom echad)* very literally into Greek as *hemera mia,* "day one" (Genesis 1:5). Unlike Greek, Hebrew has no ordinal number corresponding to the cardinal "one" *(echad)*.[42] In Hebrew, the first ordinal is "second" *(sheni),* corresponding to the cardinal "two" *(shenayim).* Beginning with the second day of creation, the Hebrew has the ordinal, *yom sheni,* which the Septuagint rendered as *hemera deutera,* "second day" (1:8).

"The first *(mia)* day of the week," therefore, associates Jesus' resurrection with the first day of creation, presenting it as the beginning of the new creation *(kaine ktisis),* inviting all people to put on Christ and join him in the new creation (see 2 Corinthians 5:17; Galatians 6:15; Colossians 1:15). To maintain the association between the resurrection and creation, the early Christians retained the Septuagintal expression "day one."

The first day of the week was the day the early Christians proclaimed Jesus as the Living One (Luke 24:1 – 12), listened to him on the way and recognized him in the breaking of the bread (24:13 – 35). The first day of the week was the day they reflected on their mission and renewed their commitment to be his witnesses (24:36 – 49). It was also the day they celebrated the fulfillment of the promises made to Abraham that in his progeny all the families of the earth would be blessed (24:50 – 53; see Luke 1:55, 73; Acts 3:21 – 26).

On the first day of the week, when the early Christians assembled for the breaking of the bread, they celebrated and proclaimed the new creation. The sabbath, the last day of the week, was a day of rest, and the early Christians continued to observe it as a day of rest (see Luke 23:56). The first day of the week, however, was a day of work, and the early Christians continued to observe it as a day of work, associating themselves with Christ in the work of the new creation.

On the first day of the week, the community assembled as a church in the home of a member who placed his or her home at the disposition of the community. For that, the house had to be large enough to accommodate the whole community as well as any guests visiting from other communities. The owner of the house was recognized as the community's host *(keklekos)* for the breaking of the bread (see Luke 14:12).

While the house belonged to a particular member of the community, it was considered to be the home of the ecclesial community (see Acts 2:44; 4:32), serving as the home for the church when it assembled there as a church. After the breaking of the bread, when the community dispersed, the house continued to function as an ordinary home. In the beginning, it was the same for the Jewish synagogue, which also met in a private home, as well as for popular Egyptian and eastern cults.

When the Egyptian cult of Serapis and the eastern cult of Mithras spread to various Hellenistic and Roman cities, the cult very often was established in a private home. For this, the house did not need to be modified architecturally, but a room or a designated space had to be set aside as a domestic sanctuary, with a permanent altar, a statue, special symbols and other appointments.[43]

For a Christian assembly and the Jewish synagogue, none of this was required. By their very nature, the cults needed a sanctuary, however modest, to house their "god." The private house in which a cult was set up was regarded as a temple. By contast, what the Christians and the Jews needed was a place to assemble. For the Christians, that meant a space for dining.

Today, many refer to such a home as a "house church." For me, that suggests that a house has been set aside to serve as a church. For that reason, I prefer the term "a home for the church." The term "house church" refers to a physical structure with rooms, doors, walls, windows, floors and ceilings. The term "a home for the church" refers to the community that gathers there and how they relate to one another.

The assembly centered on the dining room, the main reception room in a large house, or any spacious room that could accommodate the community. Depending on the size of the community, the community often spilled out of the dining room into other rooms. This, of course, could become a source of division and conflict, as guests vied for the highest places (see Luke 14:7–11).

Only in the latter half of the second century, after AD 150, did Christians begin to take over a house, modifying and adapting it architecturally to meet the needs of the community and its assembly.[44] Today many refer to such a house as a *domus ecclesiae*, the house of the church.[45]

Every Day Besides breaking bread as a church on the first day of the week, the early Christians also broke bread every day in their own homes. The summary in Acts says that "every day they devoted themselves . . . to breaking bread in their homes" (Acts 2:46). This too was a religious event, very closely related to the breaking of the bread on the first day of the week, so closely that the same name, "the breaking of the bread," referred to both.

That suggests that when the early Christians in Jerusalem broke bread in their own homes, they very likely performed the traditional ritual gesture of taking bread, pronouncing a blessing, breaking the bread and giving a piece to everyone gathered at the table. Every day, then, they remembered what Jesus did when he broke bread with his disciples and others.

There was a difference, however, between the breaking of the bread on the first day of the week and the breaking of the bread on the other days of the week. On the first day of the week, the community assembled and broke bread as a church. On the other days, they broke bread as a family, household or group of friends.

On the first day of the week, the assembly was open to all and the breaking of the bread was a symbol of the universality or catholicity of the church. On the other days, the meals were for members of the community who enjoyed a special relationship, natural or social, over and above being Christians together. Breaking bread daily in their homes, they had something in common that others did not. The breaking of the bread was a celebration of intimacy, strengthening the bonds that united them.

The expression "every day" *(kath' hemeran)* appears several times in Luke-Acts. We find it, for example, when Jesus developed the implications of his passion for the disciples: "If anyone wishes to come after me, he must deny himself and take up his cross daily *(kath' hemeran)* and follow me" (Luke 9:23). Mark had recorded the same basic teaching, but without the indication "daily" (Mark 8:34). We also find it in the Lord's Prayer: "Give us each day *(to kath' hemeran)* our daily *(ton epiousion)* bread" (Luke 11:3). Instead of "each day," Matthew's version of the Lord's Prayer has "today" *(semeron;* see Matthew 6:11). In the parable of the rich man and Lazarus (Luke 16:19–31), it enters into the description of the rich man "who dressed in purple garments and fine linen and dined sumptuously each day" *(kath' hemeran,* 16:19). As we might expect, the expression is especially frequent in summary statements (Luke 19:47; see also 22:53; Acts 2:47; 16:5; 17:11, 17; 19:9).

In Luke's version of the Lord's Prayer, the bread of each day evokes the manna, the bread of each day that God provided for the Israelites in the exodus (see Exodus 16:4–5, LXX). As the *epiousios* bread, the bread characteristic of them, the new manna was the bread they needed to pray for that they might extend hospitality. In the Lord's Prayer, the Lukan communities did not ask for the bread they needed to satisfy their own hunger, whether spiritual or physical. They asked for the bread they needed to welcome others at their table, as the friend does in Jesus' parable (Luke 16:5–9) commenting on the Lord's Prayer (11:2–4).

"The bread" in the expression "the breaking of the bread" is the same bread for which the early Christians prayed in the Lord's Prayer. In relation to their assembling as a church, the petition asks for the bread they needed to extend hospitality to other Christians, thereby witnessing to the universality of the church. In relation to breaking bread in their respective homes, the petition asks for the bread they needed to extend gospel hospitality to everyone, that they might fulfill their mission as evangelizers and devote themselves to the teaching of the apostles (see Luke 5:27–32).

As we read in Acts, "they ate their meals with exultation and sincerity of heart, praising God and enjoying favor with all the people" (2:46b–47a). Every day, the members of the community experienced the good news in the intimacy of their homes, breaking bread with all who accepted their hospitality and teaching them about the Lord Jesus. Then, on the first day of the week, they shared the good news with the whole community when it assembled as a church.

The Prayers (2:42e, 46a)

They devoted themselves also "to the prayers" *(tais proseuchais)*. In the introductory summary (2:42), the prayers are closely related to the breaking of the bread. Together, the two express the very life of the community constituted by the teaching of the apostles and the common-union. Just as the Christians assembled "as a church" *(epi to auto)* for the breaking of the bread, they assembled "with one accord" *(homothumadon),* with one mind and heart, for the prayers (1:14; 2:46; 5:12). Like the breaking of the bread, the prayers flowed from their *koinonia.*

The early Christians in Jerusalem were faithful to the prayers offered in the temple. They also assembled for prayer as a church in conjunction with the breaking of the bread, when they blessed God and gave thanks on the first day of week. Every day, they observed times of prayer, "praising God" (2:46) in their homes as well as away from home. For the Christians, as for the Jews, the prayers were a matter of religious observance.

Faithfully attending to the prayers, the early Christians were in continuity with the life of Jesus, where prayer constituted an extremely important element.[46] They also devoted themselves to praying as Jesus taught his disciples (Luke 11:1 – 13), thereby opening themselves to the gift of the Spirit (11:13).

In Luke-Acts, prayer has an important role at critical junctures of salvation history, with significant developments presented as a response to prayer. Every stage in the life and mission of Jesus and in the life and mission of the church is prepared for by prayer. For the mission of Jesus, witness his baptism (Luke 3:21 – 22), the choosing of the Twelve (6:12 – 16), his passion (22:39 – 46) and his death (23:46). For the mission of the church, witness the community "continually in the temple praising God" (24:53) and in the upper room (Acts 1:13 – 14) awaiting the promise of the Father.

Acts associates the very growth of the church with the way the community attended to the prayers (2:42 – 47) as well as with their teaching and proclaiming Jesus as the Christ (5:42). It was while Peter was at prayer that he received the vision preparing him and the church for the mission to the Gentiles (10:9). It was while the church in Antioch was at prayer that its mission to the Gentiles was disclosed and that they entrusted that mission to Barnabas and Paul (13:1 – 3).

"Devoting themselves to the prayers" does not refer to a set of formulas or a particular body of prayers, but to the saying of prayers at set times during the day. For example, public prayers were offered in the temple at the ninth hour (three o'clock in the afternoon). Once when Peter and John went to the temple for the three o'clock hour of prayer, a beggar at the gate, a man who had been crippled from birth, pleaded for alms. Peter, who had neither silver nor gold, cured him. Walking and jumping, the man followed Peter and John into the temple for the public prayers, praising God to the amazement of all (3:1 – 10).

The prayers punctuated the day as the prayers still do in a monastery, where monks and nuns assemble for the hours, such as terce (the third hour), sext (the sixth hour) and none (the ninth hour). The prayer of the hours, like the prayers for the early Christians, represents a community exercise. Until recently, in traditional Catholic societies the Angelus did the same for the general population. In a growing number of parishes, parishioners gather for the prayer of Christians, especially in the morning, but also in the evening.

From Psalm 55:18 we learn that a devout Jew prayed three times a day: "At dusk, dawn, and noon I will grieve and complain and my prayer will be heard." We have partial confirmation for that in the Book of Daniel. Even when Jews were forbidden to pray, Daniel continued his custom of going home and kneeling in prayer, giving thanks to God in the upper chamber three times a day with the windows open toward Jerusalem (Daniel 6:11, 14). It was while Daniel was at prayer at the time of the evening sacrifice that the angel Gabriel came to him (9:21). Later, Gabriel returned to announce the birth of John the Baptist to Zechariah, who was in the sanctuary burning incense "while the whole assembly of the people was praying outside at the hour of incense offering" (Luke 1:9 – 11).

For the Christians in Jerusalem, the most important hour was the ninth, the hour when Jesus spoke his final prayer, "Father, into your hands I commend my spirit," and breathed his last (24:44, 46). Jesus died as people gathered in the temple at the end of the workday for the afternoon sacrifice. It is not surprising, then, that Peter and John went to the temple at the ninth hour (Acts 3:1), and that the angel of the Lord came to Cornelius as he was praying at the ninth hour (10:3, 30). We note also that Peter was praying at the sixth hour when he received the vision of the large sheet coming down from the sky (10:9).

In describing the heroism of the Jewish priests throughout Pompey's assault on the temple, Josephus refers to two daily hours of sacrifice: "The priests were not hindered from performing any of the sacred ceremonies through fear, but twice a day *(dis tes hemeras)* they performed the sacred ceremonies *(hierourgounton)* at the altar *(epi tou bomou),* and did not omit any of the sacrifices *(tas thysias)* even when some difficulty arose because of the attacks" (*Jewish Antiquities* xiv, 65). Earlier in the same work (iii, 237), Josephus had referred to the sacrifice of a lamb each day *(kath' ekasten hemeran),* both at the beginning and at the close of the day *(archomenes te hemeras kai legouses).*

The law regarding the evening sacrifice stipulated that it was to be offered "between the two evenings," that is, at dusk, between sunset and the darkness of night (Exodus 29:39). That is when Judith prayed to the Lord, "while the incense was being offered in the temple of God in Jerusalem that evening" (Judith 9:1). The Mishna, compiled around AD 200, indicated that "the daily whole-offering was slaughtered at a half after the eighth hour [2:30 PM], and offered up at a half after the ninth hour [3:30 PM]" (*Pesahim* 5.1).

The *Shema'* (see Deuteronomy 6:4 – 5) was recited both in the evening and in the morning (*Berakoth* 1.1 – 4). In the morning, two benedictions *(berakoth)* were said before the *Shema'* and one after. In the evening, two were said before and two after, one long and one short (*Berakoth* 1.4).

Besides the *Shema'*, there was the morning *tefillah* (prayer) of the *Shemoneh Esreh* (the Eighteen Benedictions), which could be said until midday, the evening *tefillah*, which had no set time, and an additional *tefillah* which could be said any time during the day (*Berakoth* 4.1). When away from Jerusalem, Jews turned toward Jerusalem for their prayer and directed their hearts to the Holy of Holies. Even in Jerusalem, when away from the temple area, they directed their hearts to the Holy of Holies (*Berakoth* 4.5 – 6). Together with the *Shema'*, the *Shemoneh Esreh* was to the Jews what the Lord's Prayer was to the Christians.

From the *Didache*, we learn that the early Christians prayed the Lord's Prayer three times a day, probably at the hours referred to in Psalm 55:18 and Daniel 6:11, 14. From the many times the Psalms are quoted in the Book of Acts, as in the rest of the New Testament, the Christians must have also prayed the Psalms not only in the temple (3:1; 5:12), but in the upper room (see Mark 14:26; Matthew 26:30) and later when they gathered as a church on the first day of the week and daily in their homes.

Acts gives a good example of a spontaneous prayer that must have been typical for the early Christian community. When Peter and John were released from custody and returned to their own people, the community raised its voice in prayer, addressing God as "Sovereign Lord, maker of heaven and earth and the sea and all that is in them." Their prayer was according to the scriptures. Praying with Psalm 2:1 – 2, they applied it first to Jesus and then to themselves (Acts 4:24 – 31).

So was it that members of the community in Jerusalem "devoted themselves to the teaching of the apostles and to the communion *(koinonia)*, to the breaking of the bread and to the prayers" (2:42). In this third chapter, we described the beginnings of the church in Jerusalem, situated a major summary of its life in the first section of Acts (1:15 — 5:42) and analyzed the summary as a whole. We then analyzed each of the elements included in its introduction: the teaching of the apostles, the *koinonia*, the breaking of the bread and the prayers.

In the fourth chapter, we shall turn to the second section of Acts (6:1 — 12:25) and explore three particular passages: the appointing of the Seven (6:1 – 7), the conversion of Paul (9:1 – 31) and the conversion of Cornelius (10:1 — 11:18). In a different way, each of these stories contributes to the development of the eucharist according to Acts.

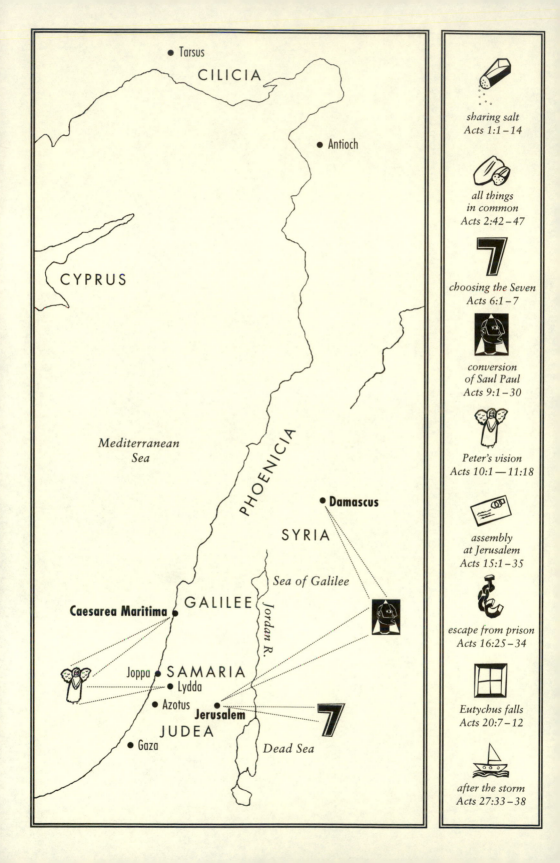

Tarsus

CILICIA

Antioch

CYPRUS

Mediterranean
Sea

PHOENICIA

Damascus

SYRIA

Sea of Galilee

Caesarea Maritima

GALILEE

Jordan R.

Joppa
SAMARIA
Lydda
Azotus
Jerusalem
JUDEA
Gaza

Dead Sea

sharing salt
Acts 1:1–14

all things
in common
Acts 2:42–47

choosing the Seven
Acts 6:1–7

conversion
of Saul Paul
Acts 9:1–30

Peter's vision
Acts 10:1 — 11:18

assembly
at Jerusalem
Acts 15:1–35

escape from prison
Acts 16:25–34

Eutychus falls
Acts 20:7–12

after the storm
Acts 27:33–38

Chapter IV

From Jerusalem to Antioch
(6:1 — 12:25)

It was at Antioch
that the disciples were
first called Christians.
                    Acts 11:26

The first section of the Book of Acts (1:15 — 5:42) told the story of the primitive Christian community in Jerusalem. Beginning with the choice of Matthias (1:15 – 26) and the coming of the holy Spirit at Pentecost (2:1 – 13), the section described the church's early years as a golden age, an idealized portrait of the beginnings, given as the ideal for all Christian communities, present and future.

The section presented the breaking of the bread *(he klasis tou artou)* as one of four constitutive elements in the life of the community, along with the teaching of the apostles *(he didache ton apostolon)*, the common-union *(he koinonia)* and the prayers *(hai proseuchai)*. Integral to the life of the community, the four elements may be viewed as the marks of the apostolic church.

"The breaking of the bread" is Luke's name for the eucharist (Luke 24:35; Acts 2:42). Acts describes the breaking of the bread as a meal celebrated in two distinct but complementary forms: as a community meal "on the first day of the week" *(he mia ton sabbaton)* when the community assembled as a church (Acts 20:7; see 2:42) and as a family meal taken "every day" *(kath' hemeran)* in their respective homes (2:46).

The second section (6:1 — 12:25) shows how the word of God spread from Jerusalem, the Jewish religious capital, to Antioch, the Hellenistic and Roman capital of Syria. The story tells of internal difficulties regarding the ministry *(diakonia)* as the community grew and became more diverse (see 6:1 – 7). It also tells of a great persecution that resulted in an early Christian diaspora, scattering much of the community (see 8:1b, 4; 11:19).[1] Those scattered brought the gospel of Christ with them "through Judea and Samaria" as far as Antioch, on the way "to the ends of the earth" (1:8).

The growth, persecution and scattering of the church brought about several developments in the celebration and the understanding of the eucharist. The section shows that the eucharist is related to ministry, concern for the poor, evangelization, and prayer (6:1 – 7). It also shows that eating and drinking with others implies solidarity with them (9:1 – 31) and that eating and drinking at the table "of the Lord of all" calls the church to be truly universal (10:1 — 11:18).

Overview of 6:1 — 12:25

The section opens in Jerusalem with a serious problem regarding "the daily distribution" *(he diakonia he kathemerine)*. The widows among the Greek-speaking Christians were being neglected. Serious as it was, the problem brought an even greater problem to the surface. Overwhelmed by the demands of the table ministry *(diakonia)*, the apostles had no time for prayer and the ministry *(diakonia)* of the word. Both problems were resolved by the choice of "the Seven" (6:1 – 7; see 21:8).

The section then shows that the Seven were instrumental in bringing the church from Jerusalem to Antioch (6:8 — 11:26) as a result of "a severe persecution of the church in Jerusalem" (8:1) after the martyrdom of Stephen (7:54 – 60). The section ends where it began, in Jerusalem, where Barnabas and Saul returned after fulfilling a relief mission *(diakonia)* from the Christians of Antioch to the Christians in Judea (12:25; see 11:27 – 30).

With the spread of the church from Jerusalem to Antioch, what began as a local ministry *(diakonia)* responding to local needs in Jerusalem became a much wider ministry *(diakonia)* responding to needs in other communities. The missionary church at Antioch recognized its responsibility for the poor in Jerusalem and in Judea. The common-union *(koinonia),* a mark of the apostolic church in Jerusalem (see 2:42), now embraced all the churches in one great common-union *(koinonia).*

Table V

**Setting for the Choice of the Seven, the Conversion of Saul
and the Conversion of Cornelius**

6:1—12:25 From Jerusalem to Antioch

The choice of the Seven (6:1 – 7)
A case of neglect (6:1)
The Twelve present a proposal (6:2 – 4)
Response and implementation (6:5 – 6)
Growth of the word of God (6:7)

The story of Stephen (6:8 — 8:3)

The story of Philip (8:4 – 40)

The conversion of Saul (9:1 – 31)
Saul's journey to Damascus (9:1 – 9)
For three days, Saul neither ate nor drank (9:9)
The baptism of Saul (9:10 – 19)
After eating, he regained his strength (9:19a)
Saul in Damascus (9:19b – 22)
Saul in Jerusalem (9:23 – 30)
Growth of the church (9:31)

Peter in Lydda and Joppa (9:32 – 43)

The conversion of Cornelius (10:1 — 11:18)
The vision of Cornelius (10:1 – 8)
The vision of Peter (10:9 – 16)
The messengers from Cornelius (10:17 – 23a)
At the home of Cornelius the Centurion (10:23b – 49)
Dialogue between Peter and Cornelius (10:23b – 33)
Discourse of Peter (10:34 – 43)
Baptism of Cornelius (10:44 – 49)
Back in Jerusalem (11:1 – 18)

The church established in Antioch (11:19 – 30)

Persecution of the Christians and the death of Herod (12:1 – 25)

Popularly, the story of the Seven (6:1 – 7) is often referred to as the institution of the diaconate in the church. Actually, the term "deacon" is never used in the story, nor for that matter in all of Luke-Acts. As in the Gospel, there are "people serving" *(diakonountes),* but no deacons *(diakonoi).* Acts situates the story of the Seven in the mid-thirties of the first century, when the office of deacon had not yet emerged.

It is legitimate, of course, to ground the office of deacon, once it emerged, in the story of the Seven. But the same is true for all the other ministries. It is one thing to see the story as a historical report on when the diaconate was instituted. It is another, looking back, to see later developments such as the diaconate and other ministries, including the priesthood, flowing from the choice of the Seven. As such, the story of the Seven is singled out as a high point in the origins of the diaconate and becomes symbolic of it.

The story shows that the Seven, recognized as leaders by those called "the Hellenists," were related historically and ecclesiologically to the Twelve. It also shows how the beginning of the church in Antioch was related to the beginnings and the early development of the church in Jerusalem.

After the choice of the Seven (6:1 – 7) come the story of Stephen (6:8 — 8:3) and the story of Philip (8:4 – 40), the first and second named in the list of the Seven (6:5). Acts remains silent concerning the other five, as Luke-Acts does for most of the Twelve.[2]

The story of Stephen (6:8 — 8:3), an eloquent and provocative preacher, ends with his martyrdom, which was the beginning of a great persecution of the church in Jerusalem, scattering the community throughout the whole of Judea and Samaria. It is in the story of Stephen's martyrdom at Jerusalem that Saul is first introduced: "The witnesses laid down their cloaks at the feet of a young man named Saul" (7:58; see also 8:1, 3).[3]

The story of Philip (8:4 – 40), a very effective exorcist, healer and evangelizer, shows that he preached the good news of Christ in Samaria and on the Palestinian coast, beginning on the Gaza road, then in Azotus and in all the cities until he reached Caesarea.[4] It is in the story of Philip that Peter, who played a great part in the previous section (1:15 — 5:42), is reintroduced in the second section of Acts (8:14 – 25).

After the stories of Stephen and Philip, we have the story of Saul's conversion to the Lord Jesus (9:1 – 31) and the stories of Peter's early ministry outside Jerusalem (9:32 – 43) and Peter's conversion to the Gentile mission (10:1 — 11:18). The Lord appeared to Saul, the persecutor, on the way to Damascus, where Saul intended to seek out the Christians and bring them back to Jerusalem in chains (9:1 – 19a). After his conversion, Saul spent time with the disciples in Damascus (9:19b – 25). After visiting the community in Jerusalem (9:26 – 30), he left for Tarsus, passing through the port of Caesarea (9:30).

Peter's mission brought him to Lydda and Joppa (9:32 – 43) and eventually to Caesarea, the Roman capital of Palestine, where he baptized the Gentile household of Cornelius (10:1 — 11:18). Philip had gone as far as Caesarea (8:40) and Saul had passed through Caesarea (9:30), but it was Peter who began the mission among the Gentiles in Caesarea. Luke presents Cornelius as the first Gentile to receive the holy Spirit, accept the Word and become a Christian. Saul, also called Paul (see 13:9), was destined to be the apostle to the Gentiles (see 9:6, 15), but the mission to the Gentiles began in the ministry of Peter.

The section ends with the coming of the Christian message to Antioch and the beginnings of the church in that city (11:19 — 12:25). In the first century, Antioch was a major city, the capital of a strategic Roman province in the eastern Mediterranean, one of only four cities in the Mediterranean world with a population approaching 1,000,000. The other three cities were Alexandria in Egypt, Carthage in North Africa and, of course, Rome, the imperial capital.

Christianity came to Antioch as a result of "the persecution that arose because of Stephen" (11:19; see 8:1b, 3) around AD 35 – 36. As the community in Antioch grew and prospered, Herod Agrippa, who ruled as king of Judea in AD 41 – 44, launched a new persecution of Christians in Jerusalem (12:1 – 24). The persecution took place while the Christians of Antioch were sending a relief mission "to the brothers who lived in Judea" (11:27 – 30; 12:25).

The church in Antioch continued to mature. Recognizing its responsibility to those who had not yet heard the gospel, it sent missionaries to neighboring provinces. The story of the missions from Antioch is told in the third section of Acts (13:1 — 19:20).

In Relation to the Eucharist

Like the first section of Acts (1:15 — 5:42), the second section (6:1 — 12:25) sheds a great deal of light on the development of the eucharist in the early church. Three stories critical to the whole story of Acts are especially significant, each in its own way. A story need not be directly and explicitly eucharistic to have implications for the eucharist.

The first story, introducing the entire section (6:1—12:25), is a story of ministry *diakonia*, set in Jerusalem (6:1–7), where the demands of ministry had become overwhelming for the Twelve. It tells how seven men, of Jewish background but Greek-speaking, were chosen to serve at tables *(diakonein trapezais)* in the rapidly growing community. The story has important implications for the development of eucharistic ministry in relation to the church's ministry to the poor and its ministry of the word, as well as for the *koinonia* of the church.

The second story with implications for the eucharist is that of the conversion of Saul (9:1–31). Struck blind by the Lord's presence on the way to Damascus, Saul had to be led by the hand into the city, where he neither ate nor drank for three days (9:1–9). In Damascus, Saul recovered his sight when Ananias laid his hands on him. After being baptized, he began to eat again and stayed with the disciples in Damascus (9:10–22). In the context of Acts, the story has important implications concerning the eucharist in relation to conversion *(metanoia),* baptism and Christian solidarity.

The third story with implications for the eucharist is the story of Peter and the conversion of Cornelius, which is set in Joppa, Caesarea and Jerusalem (10:1—11:18). It tells that Peter first gave hospitality to Gentiles and then accepted the hospitality of a Gentile, a Roman centurion named Cornelius whose entire household was baptized. Peter's experience at Joppa and Caesarea marked his conversion to the Gentile mission. The story gives the theological rationale for the mission to the Gentiles. It relates the eucharist to the apostolic witness *(martyria),* to the person of Jesus Christ as Lord of all and to the universal mission of the church.

The Choice of the Seven (6:1 – 7)

It is not right for us
to neglect the Word of God
to serve at table.

> Acts 6:2

The first story in the section with important implications for the development of the eucharist is the choice of the Seven (6:1 – 7).[5] The story shows that the eucharist is related to various ministries, in particular the ministry to the poor, the ministry at the eucharistic table and the ministry of the word.

The story of the Seven introduces the whole section on the spread of the church from Jerusalem to Antioch (6:1 — 12:25), just as the choice of Matthias (1:15 – 26) introduced the previous section (1:15 — 5:42), and the choice of Barnabas and Saul (13:1 – 3) will introduce the next section (13:1 — 19:20).

Matthias was selected to replace Judas as a special witness to the resurrection of Jesus, bringing the Twelve, Peter and the Eleven, back to their full complement (1:15 – 26). The story of the early church in Jerusalem (1:15 — 5:42) is told as the story of Peter and the Eleven in the midst of the community, witnessing to the resurrection of Jesus. The section spells out what it was like in the primitive foundational community at Jerusalem, led by the Twelve.

Later, Barnabas and Saul were selected for the work to which the holy Spirit called them, that is, to lead missions from Antioch (13:1 – 3). The story of the missions from Antioch (13:1 — 19:20) is told as the story of Barnabas and Saul, also known as Paul (13:9).[6]

The section tells how the missions of the church at Antioch began under Barnabas and Saul (13:1 — 15:35), until the two separated after a serious disagreement (15:36 – 41). At that point, Barnabas returned to Cyprus with Mark, while Paul continued with Silas (15:40 — 19:20). The section also shows that the missions were related through Antioch to the mother church in Jerusalem and through the Seven of Antioch to the foundational community of the Twelve.

The Seven were selected to assure the service *diakonia* at the community tables in Jerusalem that the Twelve might devote themselves to the word of God through prayer *(proseuche)* and the ministry *diakonia* of the word (6:1 – 7). The story of the spread of the church from Jerusalem to Antioch (6:1 — 12:25) is thus told as the story of the Seven.

Diakonia, Diakonein

The story of the Seven contains two key words, the noun *diakonia* (6:1, 4), whose general meaning is "ministry" or "service," and the verb *diakonein* (6:2), meaning "to minister" or "serve." With this general meaning, however, the words *diakonia* and *diakonein* can refer to various kinds of ministry and many ways of serving.

The story of the Seven (6:1–7) applies the terms *diakonia* and *diakonein* to three different ministries, of which only one refers to ministry at tables *(diakonein trapezais),* when the community assembles as a church for the breaking of the bread (6:2). The other two refer to the daily ministry to the poor *(he diakonia he kathemerine),* "the daily distribution" (6:1) and to the ministry of the word *(he diakonia tou logou,* 6:4).

In the Acts of the Apostles as a whole, *diakonia* refers first to the ministry of the Twelve (1:17), a ministry of apostleship (1:25), witnessing to the Lord Jesus' resurrection (see 1:22). Closely related to the ministry of the Twelve is the ministry *diakonia* which Paul "received from the Lord Jesus, to bear witness to the gospel of God's grace" (20:24). On his final visit to Jerusalem, Paul would tell James and all the presbyters "what God had accomplished through his ministry" *(diakonia,* 21:19). *Diakonia* also refers to the ministry of Timothy and Erastus, who assisted *(diakonein)* Paul (19:22) in his ministry (see 16:1–4; 17:14–15; 18:5; 20:4–5).

Elsewhere in Acts, the term *diakonia* also refers to the relief mission *diakonia* that the disciples at Antioch entrusted to Barnabas and Saul for the brothers and sisters in Judea (11:29–30; 12:25). A similar use can be found in Luke, where the Gospel refers to some women, including Mary Magdalene, Joanna, the wife of Herod's steward Chuza, Susanna and many others "who provided for" *(diakonein)* Jesus and the Twelve out of their resources (Luke 8:1–3). Both of these provide a broader context for the use of *diakonia* in the story of the Seven (Acts 6:1–7), where it refers to the "daily distribution" (6:1).

In Luke's Gospel, with the exception of Luke 8:1–3, *diakonia* and *diakonein* always refer to table ministry or service at meals (4:39; 10:38–42; 12:37; 17:8; 22:26–27). Ministry at tables *(diakonein trapezais)* includes welcoming the guests (10:38), attending to them (10:38–42, 7:36–50), having them recline, if the situation called for that (12:37) and personally serving them (22:26–27). Serving at tables means serving people at tables, not just preparing the food (17:8) and setting it out.[7]

Overview of 6:1 – 7

The story of the Seven is told in three short units. Like most stories in Luke-Acts, it has an introduction (Acts 6:1), a body (6:2 – 6) and a conclusion (6:7). Each of these units plays a significant role in the story as well as in the greater context of Acts.

The first unit, the introduction (6:1), is very short but extremely important, as is so often the case with introductions in Luke-Acts. It provides the story with its setting. A problem had arisen in the Jerusalem community regarding the daily distribution *diakonia* to the poor. A group called "the Hellenists" were complaining to those called "the Hebrews" that their widows were being neglected in the community's ministry *diakonia* to the poor.

In relation to the greater context of Acts, the verse continues to develop the theme of communal sharing in the community which was so prominent in the first section of Acts (1:15 – 5:42; see 2:42 – 47; 4:32 – 35). It also prepares the broader issue of sharing, not only within the same community, but between different communities, such as those of Antioch and Jerusalem (11:27 – 30; 12:25).

The second unit, the body of the story (6:2 – 6), shows that the problem regarding the widows was but a symptom, pointing to a deeper underlying problem. The Twelve were "neglecting the word of God to serve at table" (6:2). The body of the story focuses on that deeper problem and tells how the problem was resolved through the choice of the Seven. The story shows how, with the Seven, the early church expanded the number of those engaged in ministry by appointing people for specific ministries. In that way, the church ensured the fulfillment of all the ministries, including the ministry *diakonia* of the eucharistic table (6:2), and respected the complementary nature of the various ministries.

In relation to the greater context, the body of the story diversifies and extends the leadership of the church, reshaping it by including the Seven. It also shows how the church at Antioch and those that sprang from its missions were related to the mother church in Jerusalem.

The third unit, the conclusion (6:7), tells that the word of God, thanks to the apostolic ministry *diakonia* of the word, continued to spread, now that the basic problem had been resolved (6:2 – 6) and its symptom cured (6:1). It also tells how the community continued to grow.

The spread of the word of God is a unifying motif for the entire Book of Acts. The growth in the number of disciples is a recurrent theme, especially in the first and second parts of Acts, including here in the story of the Seven. As part of the introduction (6:1) and of the conclusion (6:7), it provides the story with a literary frame.[8]

Parallels in Luke's Gospel

The story of the Seven has two close parallels in Luke's Gospel, both concerned with ministry *diakonia* in situations where those ministering found themselves overwhelmed by the demands of their ministry. The first is a story of the breaking of the bread for the five thousand. In it, the Twelve asked Jesus to "dismiss the crowd so that they can go to the surrounding villages and farms and find lodging and provisions" (Luke 9:12). In response, Jesus asked them to give them food themselves. The food they gave consisted of two fish and five loaves, which he broke, and after a blessing, gave to them to set before the crowd (9:10 – 17).[9]

The second, the story of Martha and Mary (10:38 – 42), parallels even more closely the story of the Seven. Martha, who was burdened with much serving *diakonia*, complained that her sister left her to serve *(diakonein)* all by herself (10:40). Mary, however, a true disciple attending to the word of the Lord (Luke 10:39; see Acts 6:2, 4), would not be deprived of the better part.[10]

A Case of Neglect (6:1)

The story begins with a serious problem that arose in the community. The widows of the Hellenists were being neglected in the daily distribution (*diakonia,* Acts 6:1). To address the problem, the Twelve called the community together and proposed that seven be chosen and appointed to serve at table. The proposal was accepted (6:2–6). The measure would assure the continued growth of the community (6:7):

> At that time, as the number of disciples continued to grow, the Hellenists complained against the Hebrews because their widows were being neglected in the daily distribution.[11]

The expression "at that time" is a common introductory device, announcing a new section or story and connecting it with the preceding story. In this case, the expression links the story of the Seven (6:1–7) with the previous verse, a summary concluding the section on the life of the community in Jerusalem: "And all day long, both at the temple and in their homes, they did not stop teaching and proclaiming the Messiah, Jesus" (5:42).

The expression "at that time" thus connects the story of the Seven (6:1–7) and the section on the movement of the church from Jerusalem to Antioch (6:1—12:25) with the story of the church in Jerusalem (1:15—5:42). In those early days, the life and ministry of the Jerusalem community had two principal foci, one at the temple and one in their homes.[12] In both places, everything the community did could be considered teaching *(didaskein)* and preaching *(euaggelizein)*, announcing the good news of Jesus Christ.

The concluding summary of the life of the community in Jerusalem (5:42) is related to the section's other summaries, especially the great transitional summaries that present the life and growth of the community in detail (2:42–47; 3:32–35; 5:12–16). The reference to teaching and evangelizing every day *(pasan te hemeran)* at the temple *(en te hiero)* and at home *(kat' oikon,* 5:42) parallels a statement in the first of those summaries: "Every day *(kath' hemeran)* they devoted themselves to meeting together in the temple area *(en te hiero)* and to breaking bread in their homes *(kat' oikon)*" (2:46).

Taken together, the three transitional summaries with their emphasis on the growth of the community (see 2:47; 5:14), on the common-union *(koinonia)* and on the sharing of goods provide the background to understand the problem that arose concerning the widows (6:1). The neglect of the widows who belonged to "the Hellenists" reflected a serious breakdown in Christian *koinonia* and the sharing of goods. As a community, the Christians were committed to share according to each one's ability and in relation to each one's need (see 2:42, 44–45; 4:32, 34–35), an ideal that did not allow for discrimination or neglect.

This was the first time the community had problems regarding *koinonia* and sharing. Previous problems in Acts had to do with specific individuals. A Christian couple, for example, Ananias and Sapphira, pretended to contribute the entire amount they received from the sale of a piece of property. In reality, they had retained part of the proceeds for themselves (5:1 – 11).

The problem that now arose concerning the widows was much more serious. Neglecting the widows belonging to "the Hellenists" involved the leaders of the community and affected the whole community. Directly or indirectly, discrimination in a community destroys *koinonia* and affects everyone.

Hellenists and Hebrews   The distinction between "the Hellenists" and "the Hebrews" in the Jerusalem community had nothing to do with ethnic identity. Both were of Jewish background. The distinction had to do with language, culture and personal history.[13] Acts' designation for "the Jews," *hoi Ioudaioi,* includes both "the Hellenists" and "the Hebrews."[14]

The Hebrews *(Hebraioi)* were converts to Christianity who came from Jewish families and synagogues where the scriptures were read in Hebrew and worship was conducted in Hebrew and Aramaic.[15] As Jews, and later as Christians, their roots were mainly in Jerusalem and Judea. The Hebrews were the very first Christians to join the first disciples and others who had followed Jesus from Galilee to Jerusalem.

The Hellenists *(Hellenistai)* were converts to Christianity who came from Jewish families and synagogues where the scriptures were read in Greek and worship was conducted in Greek. As Jews, their roots were in the Greek-speaking diaspora, but they had migrated back to Jerusalem, the religious center of Judaism.[16] They came to Christianity somewhat later than the Hebrews, as a second wave, as it were.[17]

"As the number of the disciples continued to grow," the number of those ministering to the community did not keep pace. By itself, the growth of the community would have been a problem. But the problem was compounded by cultural diversification. With the Hellenists representing a good part of the community's growth, the community could be divided into the Hebrews and the Hellenists.

We can understand the intent to keep ministering to those who had come earlier, namely, the Hebrews. We also can understand the complaint of the Hellenists who came later, that their widows were being neglected in the daily distribution *diakonia*. Similar situations have been replicated countless times over the years and continue to be a challenge today for the church in many parts of the world.

Widows   Many might wonder why the story singles out widows *(cherai)*. There must have been others who were being neglected. As women, however, widows were in a particularly vulnerable position. In Old and New Testament times, a woman depended on her father, her husband or a son for support. If a woman lost her husband and became a widow, she depended on her son or her father for support. If a widow had neither, she was often left helpless.

In the Old Testament, widows are mentioned along with orphans and strangers among those chronically in need, making them an apt symbol for all the needy (see Deuteronomy 10:18; 16:11, 14; 24:17; 26:12 – 13; 27:19). Those who act justly toward widows, orphans and strangers are singled out for a special blessing (see 14:28 – 29; 24:19 – 21). Those who oppress them are singled out for special condemnation (Malachi 3:5; Isaiah 1:17, 23; 10:2; Jeremiah 7:6; Ezekiel 22:7; Deuteronomy 27:19).

In the New Testament, the Letter of James speaks of a religious person as one who cares for orphans and widows in their affliction: "Religion that is pure and undefiled before God and the Father is this: to care for orphans and widows in their affliction and to keep oneself unstained by the world" (1:27).

The First Letter to Timothy gives special pastoral instructions regarding widows, exhorting everyone to honor them. The letter also encourages younger widows to remarry and asks that older widows be enrolled to be cared for by the community (5:3 – 16).[18]

Not that all widows were poor. Some were quite wealthy. In the Old Testament, there is Judith, for example, whose "husband, Manasseh, had left her gold and silver, servants and maids, livestock and fields, which she was maintaining" (Judith 8:7). In the New Testament, there is Tabitha, who "was completely occupied with good deeds and almsgiving, especially on behalf of other widows" (Acts 9:36 – 42).

Wealthy widows, however, were the exception. Most widows were poor and depended on the community for their needs. In providing for them, Jewish communities acted in the name of God, the "Father of the fatherless, defender of widows" (Psalm 68:5; see also Psalm 146:9; Proverbs 15:25; Jeremiah 49:11). The Christian community also acted in the name of Christ while following the example of Jesus on behalf of widows and observing his teaching with regard to them.[19]

The Daily Distribution   Reference to a "daily distribution" *(he diakonia he kathemerine)*,[20] literally, "daily ministry" or "service," suggests that the community described by Luke had become quite well organized. To have a "daily distribution," the community had to have a common fund to which members of the community contributed voluntarily, as we saw in the previous section of Acts (see 2:44–45; 4:32–35, 36–7; 5:3–4). It also presupposes a central place, such as a large home, at which or from which the distribution *diakonia* was made.

There also had to be someone in charge of the collection and of its distribution. At the beginning and for some time, the apostles were in charge (4:34–35), in particular, Peter (see 5:1–11). The story of the Seven implies that the Seven eventually were given this responsibility, but this is not explicitly stated.

A Special Assembly (6:2–6)

The complaint of the Hellenists that their widows were being neglected in the daily *diakonia* brought up an even greater concern, also regarding *diakonia* but of a different sort. This time the problem did not have to do with the beneficiaries of the *diakonia,* those being served or ministered to, but with those who were engaged in the *diakonia,* those serving others, ministering to them in various ways.

The body of the story unfolds in two parts. The first tells that the Twelve assembled the community of disciples and addressed the assembly (6:2–4). The second tells how their proposal was accepted and implemented (6:5–6).

The Twelve Present a Proposal (6:2–4)   To address the problem, the Twelve assembled the community, described the situation affecting their ministry, and proposed a solution. Their speech contains three distinct elements.

> So the Twelve called together the community of the disciples and said, "It is not right for us to neglect the word of God to serve at table. Brothers, select from among you seven reputable men, filled with the Spirit and wisdom, whom we shall appoint to this task, whereas we shall devote ourselves to prayer and the ministry of the word."

With the Twelve assembling the community, the story moves into a new setting. In the introduction, the setting was the daily life of the community, with the Hellenists complaining against the Hebrews that "as the number of disciples continued to grow *(plethunein)* . . . their widows were being neglected in the daily distribution" (6:1). In the body, the setting consists of a general assembly of the community for which the Twelve have called "the number" *(plethos),* that is, the whole community "of the disciples" together (6:2a).

The change in setting is comparable to that in the story of Levi, where the setting moved from the customs post where Levi had been called (Luke 5:27 – 28) to his home, where he invited Jesus to a great dinner and exercised his mission as a follower (5:20 – 31).[21] Consider also the story of Zacchaeus, which began with Jesus making his way through Jericho (19:1 – 6a) and moved to Zacchaeus' home (19:6b – 10).

Unlike these stories, however, the story of the Seven gives no specific sense of place, no indication of where the community assembled. Since the disciples broke bread (Acts 2:46), taught and proclaimed the Christ, Jesus (5:42), in their homes, we assume they assembled in a large home. But since the disciples now numbered more than 5,000 (4:4; 5:14), they could not possibly have assembled in one home.

Literarily, those who actually assembled are symbolic or representative of the whole. The problems experienced by some affected the whole community, and they had to be presented as such. Hence the story's setting in a general assembly.

This is the second of four times in Acts that the greater community is assembled to decide on a critical issue. The first was when the whole community was assembled to choose a successor for Judas (1:15 – 26). That first assembly, when the community was still relatively small, introduced the first section of Acts (1:15 — 5:42).

The third, also in this second section (6:1 — 12:25), is when Peter met with the circumcised believers in Jerusalem to account for entering the home of Gentiles and eating with them (11:1 – 18). The fourth, in the section on the missions from Antioch (13:1 — 19:20), is when Paul, Barnabas and some of the presbyters from the various churches met with the apostles and the presbyters in Jerusalem and decided what should be expected of Gentile converts (15:1 – 35).

The second assembly was occasioned by the complaint of the Hellenists regarding the daily *diakonia*. The Twelve, however, did not deal with that problem, at least not directly. The neglect of the widows among the Hellenists (6:1) was symptomatic of a deeper and more fundamental problem in other areas of *diakonia*. The Twelve, therefore, passed over what could be regarded as a symptom to deal with the more basic problem.

In the gospel, Jesus had done something very similar. When a lawyer asked, "Who is my neighbor?" Jesus did not answer the lawyer's question, at least not directly. Instead, he answered the question the lawyer should have asked: "To whom am I a neighbor?" With the parable of the Good Samaritan, Jesus showed the lawyer not so much who was his neighbor but that he himself should be a neighbor to others (Luke 10:29 – 37).

Again, when Martha complained that her sister left her to do all the serving *diakonia* by herself, Jesus did not address Martha's complaint but addressed her real problem. Martha was forgetting what gave her *diakonia* meaning and value: being a disciple and attending to the word of the Lord (10:38 – 42).

For the lawyer and for Martha, the issue or the complaint was but a symptom. In both cases, Jesus responded to the symptom indirectly by dealing with the deeper issue. And that is what the Twelve do in the story of the Seven.

The whole first part of the assembly is taken up with the Twelve addressing the disciples. The speech of the Twelve presents them as speaking collectively. The intention, therefore, is to give a stylized account representing the mind of the Twelve, rather than their actual words.

Neglecting the Word of God   The speech begins with a principle: "It is not right for us to neglect the word of God to serve at table" (Acts

6:2b). In Luke-Acts, as elsewhere, the wording of a principle can be very general, as when Jesus says, "Those who are healthy do not need a physician, but the sick do" (Luke 5:31). Only from the context (5:27 – 32) can we see the principle's application.

How the principle applied may also be seen from its own wording. In this case, the principle could imply that the Twelve in fact were neglecting the word of God because of being taken up with serving at table. It could also imply that this is what would happen if they tried to address the problem affecting the daily distribution by themselves.

Neglecting the word of God is not the same as neglecting the ministry of the word. "The word of God" may refer to "the ministry of the word," but its scope is much broader. In this context, "the word of God" refers to other ministries as well, including table ministry, indeed, the whole life of the church.[22] The opposite of neglecting *(kataleipo)* the word of God is attending or being devoted to *(proskartereo)* the word of God.

In Acts, the word of God is something that spreads and grows like a living being and is practically identified with the church *(ekklesia),* the community *(plethos,* literally, "number") and the people *(laos),* which also spread and grow. Indeed the word of God, the gospel of Christ, received in faith, spreads and grows in and through the church, the community and the people. The word of God takes root in the Christian community, as a seed does in Jesus' parable of the sower and the seed (8:4 – 8, 11 – 15). The word of God is growing in the community and through the community, as it shares the word of God with others.

In this context, "the word *(logos)* of God" refers at once to the message, the messenger, the announcement, the recipient and the message's reception in faith. The word of God is the good news of Christ in deed and word, most especially Christ's death and resurrection, together with the call to repentance *(metanoia),* baptism and salvation — that is, everything essential to the mystery of Christ and the gospel. "The word of God" was embodied in the life, mission and ministry of the community. As such, it had to be nurtured. It had to be attended to.

To neglect the word of God would be to neglect Christ and his mission, the life of the church, the teaching of the apostles and the common-union, the breaking of the bread and the prayers (see Acts 2:42). To attend to the word of God meant being devoted "to prayer and to the ministry of the word." It also meant assuring the table of eucharistic ministry. As it was, the Twelve were neglecting the whole, the word of God *(ho logos tou theou),* while attending to a mere part, serving at tables *(diakonein trapezais).*

To Serve at Tables   In the beginning, when the Christian community assembled to break bread, serving at tables was very simple. The service was provided by the person or couple at whose home the community gathered. As the host or hostess (see 12:12; 16:14–16), that person or couple (see 18:1–3) welcomed everyone and attended to them, making sure that all were truly at home. In this, the host or hostess may have been assisted by some other members of the household.

Serving at tables was a matter of Christian hospitality, of creating an atmosphere for blessing and thanking, providing bread for breaking, a cup for sharing and time for praying, singing hymns and telling stories. Some of the hymns were psalms, taken from the psalter. Some were specifically Christian (see, for example, Luke 1:46–55, 68–79; 2:14; 19:38). Some of the stories were biblical. Some were of Jesus and some about the spread of the gospel, the church and its mission. All were stories of faith.

In the beginning, the community was small. There was no need to designate various members of the community for particular ministries. It was not very long, however, before the community grew (see Acts 1:15; 2:41; 4:4). It then became necessary to select and appoint members of the community for special ministries in the assembly.

Today, what began so simply as serving at tables covers a whole range of ministries. There are greeters, appointed to welcome the participants to the assembly. There are lectors, who are recognized as good public readers; they give flesh and blood to the word of God. And there is the priest, praying the eucharistic prayer in the name of the church, celebrating the sacrament of Christ's sacrifice in the midst of the assembly over which he presides. Besides these, there is a cantor, a choir and an organist, sometimes other musicians, transforming words into canticles and prayers into hymns. There are also eucharistic ministers, offering the body and blood of Christ, inviting each one to say, "Amen!" In Luke-Acts, there was just "serving at tables."

Instructions Regarding the Seven (6:3)   According to Acts, the first step toward diversifying the ministries was in serving at tables for the community meal, the breaking of the bread. When the Twelve recognized that they were neglecting the word of God, that is, the very life of the church in its common-union *(koinonia)* and mission, they made this proposal to the community: "Brothers *(adelphoi),* select from among you seven reputable men *(andras),* filled with the Spirit and wisdom, whom we shall appoint to the task" (6:3).

In Greek, the address *adelphoi,* literally, "brothers," is inclusive when it refers to a community comprising both men and women, as was surely the case in the primitive community in Jerusalem (see 1:14; 5:1 – 11). Greek, like many other languages, distinguishes between gender, which is a matter of grammar, and sex, which is a matter of biological difference and complementarity. Since this distinction does not exist in English, we need to compensate for it, rendering the address *adelphoi* as "brothers and sisters."

The Twelve presented the community with a twofold proposition, in which the community and the apostles would each have a role. First, the community would select seven men *(andras)* from among its members and present them to the apostles. These men should be of good repute. They should also be filled with the Spirit *(plereis pneumatos)* and wisdom *(sophia).* The apostles would then appoint those selected by the community to the task *(chreia),* that is, to fill the community's need (see 2:45; 4:35) for ministry *diakonia* at tables.

The specification that there should be seven selected suggests that there was already a group of seven who were recognized by the Greek-speaking members of the community (the Hellenists) as their leaders. If so, Acts was simply recognizing and ratifying a *de facto* situation. It is hard to know, otherwise, why the number proposed from the beginning would have been seven. Why not five? Or why not twelve? The tradition of the Seven would very likely have been preserved by the church of Antioch as part of the story of its origins.

Prayer and the Ministry of the Word (6:4)   With the Seven serving *(diakonein)* at tables, the Twelve would then devote themselves *(proskartereo)* to prayer *(he proseuche)* and the ministry of the word *(he diakonia tou logou).* In this way, they would attend to their larger responsibility of overseeing the word of God as expressed in the life of the church.

They would pray as Jesus taught them to pray (Luke 11:2 – 4; Acts 1:14; 2:42) and they would preach as they were commissioned to preach (Luke 24:46 – 49; Acts 2:42). They would be Christ's witnesses (Acts 1:8). A good summary of the apostolic preaching *(logos)* is presented in the discourses of Peter, especially his discourse after the Pentecost event (2:14 – 41), but also the one he gave in the temple area at the Portico of Solomon (3:12 – 26) and the two he gave before the Sanhedrin (4:8 – 12; 5:29 – 32).

Response and Implementation (6:5 – 6)

The body of the story opens with the Twelve calling the community of disciples together. The Twelve then address the community concerning their situation and they propose a solution (6:2 – 4). In the second part the story tells how their proposal was accepted and implemented (6:5 – 6).

> The proposal was acceptable to the whole community, so they chose Stephen, a man filled with faith and the holy Spirit, also Philip, Prochorus, Nicanor, Timon, Parmenas, and Nicholas of Antioch, a convert to Judaism. They presented these men to the apostles who prayed and laid hands on them.

The whole community *(pas ho plethos)* was pleased with the word *(logos)* of the Twelve (6:5; see 6:2). They selected Stephen, a man full *(pleres)* of faith and the holy Spirit. The Twelve had asked that the men be of good repute and full *(plereis)* of Spirit and wisdom (6:3). Stephen was filled with the wisdom of faith. Along with Stephen, the community selected six others, including Philip, Prochorus, Nicanor, Timon and Parmenas. There was also Nicholas of Antioch, a convert *(proselytos)* to Judaism.

The Twelve had asked that seven men be selected to serve *(diakonein)* at tables (6:3), and that is the task for which they were selected. The Seven, however, are never seen serving at tables.

In the context of 6:1 – 7, their role has to do with table ministry and the development of ministry in the early church (see 1:15 – 26; 13:1 – 3). In the greater context of 6:1 — 12:25, however, they serve as preachers in the tradition of the Twelve, providing a historical bridge between the Twelve and Saul Paul, Barnabas and many others.

So it is that Acts tells the stories of Stephen (6:8 — 8:3) and of Philip (8:4 – 40), both of whom were great preachers and teachers. About the other five, Acts says absolutely nothing, except that they belonged to the Seven. As with "the Twelve," the designation "the Seven" was significant in itself, quite apart from those who actually composed it.

After choosing the Seven, the community presented them to the apostles, "who prayed and laid hands on them" (6:6). Before choosing the Twelve, Jesus had spent the night in prayer (Luke 6:12–16). At the beginning of Acts, the community prayed before choosing Matthias to replace Judas in the apostolic ministry (Acts 1:24). Later, the prophets and teachers in the church at Antioch would do the same after setting aside Barnabas and Saul and imposing hands on them (13:1–3).

The apostles now did the same before imposing hands on the Seven (6:6; 13:3). The laying on of hands, a traditional Jewish gesture, invoked God's blessing and the bestowal of power that the Seven be able to fulfill the ministry *diakonia* or task *(chreia)* for which they were chosen.

The Seven all had Greek names, showing their relationship to the Hellenists and the diaspora, where Judaism and the church were mainly Greek-speaking. Coming from Hellenistic Judaism, the Seven provided the Christian community with a bridge to the Hellenistic world.

The last to be named, Nicholas of Antioch, associated the Seven with Antioch. Like the other six, Nicholas came to Christianity from Judaism. But unlike the others, Nicholas had been born a Gentile, not a Jew. It was only later that he became a Jew, entering Judaism as a convert.

Nicholas thus provided a special link to the Gentile world of Antioch, where Gentiles first became Christians in large numbers (11:21–22). Beginning in Jerusalem with Hebrew-speaking, that is, Aramaic-speaking Jews, Christianity first spread among Greek-speaking Jews, then among Gentile converts to Judaism. At Antioch it would spread among Gentiles directly, without their having to pass through Judaism.

Growth of the Word of God (6:7)

The story ends with a summary describing life in the community at Jerusalem. Now that the service at table was assured (6:3–6), the Hellenists had no cause to complain that their widows were neglected in the daily distribution (6:1), nor did the Twelve "neglect the word of God to serve at tables" (6:2). With the Twelve attending to the word of God (6:7),

> The word of God continued to spread, and the number of the disciples in Jerusalem increased greatly; even a large group of priests were becoming obedient to the faith.

The Twelve attended to the word of God by devoting themselves to prayer and to the ministry of the word (6:4).

"The word of God continued to spread" (*auxanein*, literally, "to grow"; 6:7a). The growth of the word is a new theme in Acts. The theme will reappear at the end of this entire section (6:1 — 12:25), and at the end of the next section (13:1 — 19:20), both times in a little summary (12:24; 19:20).

The growth of the word was through the church and its mission, in which the word found dynamic expression.[23] Here in 6:7, the theme is directly related to the number of disciples increasing *(plethunein)* greatly (6:7b). This second theme, that is, the growth in the number of disciples, was introduced at the end of a major summary (2:42 – 47; see 2:47) and in a further summary (5:14). It will reappear in the summary conclusion of the story of Saul's conversion (9:1 – 31; see 9:31; see also 11:21, 24; 16:5).

Concluding, the story indicates the background of some of the new disciples. Many of them were priests. Luke-Acts often indicates the humble social and religious background of those who came to Jesus. Luke-Acts also mentions those who were well-placed socially and religiously. Recall, for example, that Joanna, one of those who provided for Jesus and the Twelve out of her resources, was the wife of Chuza, Herod's steward (8:1 – 3).

This time the story notes that a good part of the growth in the community came from those who were priests. Like Zechariah, the father of John the Baptist, priests served in the worship in Jerusalem at the sanctuary of the Lord (Luke 1:5 – 9).

The Conversion of Saul (9:1 – 30)

Now get up
and go into the city
and you will be told
what you must do.
　　　　Acts 9:6

The second story that has implications for the development of the eucharist is the conversion of Saul (Acts 9:1 – 31).[24] The story shows that the eucharist is related to conversion, baptism and the ministry of evangelization. For the first time, we see how the eucharist affects the life of new members and their relationships with others.

The story of Saul's conversion provides a transition between the church's initial spread in Judea and Samaria and its spread among the Gentiles "to the ends of the earth" for which Saul would be the Lord's chosen instrument (9:15). The story is told after the stories of Stephen (6:8 — 8:3) and Philip (8:4 – 40) and just before that of Peter's ministry outside Jerusalem (9:32 — 11:18). Literarily, it is connected with each of those stories in various ways and must be read in relation to them.

After a brief introduction (9:1 – 2), the story begins with a blinding vision on the Damascus road (9:3 – 8), leaving Saul unable to see for three days, during which "he neither ate nor drank" (9:9). Then, while in Damascus, thanks to a disciple named Ananias, Saul regained his sight and was baptized (9:10 – 18), "and when he had eaten, he recovered his strength" (9:19a). Once strengthened, Saul stayed on in Damascus, preaching Jesus in the synagogues until a plot against his life forced him to escape (9:19b – 25). When the same thing happened in Jerusalem, he left for his native Tarsus, passing through Caesarea (9:26 – 30). After that, the church was at peace and it continued to grow (9:31).

In the course of Acts, Saul would repeat the story of his conversion on two occasions, the first while defending himself before the Jews who attacked him in Jerusalem (22:1 – 21), the second, while defending himself before King Agrippa at Caesarea just before his departure for Rome (26:1 – 23).[25]

The differences among the three versions of Saul's conversion stem from their literary form and context. The first is told in the third person by the narrator of Acts as part of the story of the church spreading beyond Judea and Samaria to the ends of the earth (9:1 – 31).

As told by the narrator, the story addresses Acts' Christian readers directly, stressing the role of the Lord Jesus appearing to Ananias as well as to Saul as well as Ananias' role as "a disciple in Damascus" in the conversion of Saul (9:10).

The second and third versions are told in the first person by Paul in the form of a discourse. The differences between these two versions stem from their respective context, from Paul's purpose in retelling the story, as well as from the particular audience he addressed. On both occasions, Paul reviewed his life up to his conversion, but with fewer details than the narrator included (9:1 – 31).

While defending himself in Jerusalem against Jews from the province of Asia (22:1 – 21), Paul spoke in Hebrew (21:40; 21:2). He also stressed his Jewish identity as one born in Tarsus in Cilicia but brought up in Jerusalem where he was educated strictly at the feet of Gamaliel in Jewish ancestral law. Like those listening to him that day, Paul too was zealous for God (22:3). Speaking to Jews, Paul presented Ananias not as "a disciple in Damascus" (9:10) but as "a devout observer of the law, and highly spoken of by all the Jews who lived" in Damascus (22:12). It is as such, as "a devout observer of the law," that Ananias came to Paul, and not because of a vision of the Lord Jesus commanding him to go to Paul (compare 9:10 – 16).

Later, while defending himself before King Agrippa (26:1 – 26) in the presence of the Roman governor Festus, Paul spoke of how fortunate he was to defend himself before Agrippa against charges made by the Jews, especially since Agrippa was "an expert in all the Jewish customs and controversies" (26:3). In his address to Agrippa, Paul made no mention of Ananias. Neither Agrippa nor Festus would have been impressed by Ananias, whether as "a disciple in Damascus" (9:10) or as "a devout observer of the law" (22:12). In the presence of Festus and Agrippa, Paul stressed his mission to the Gentiles as well as to the Jews.

All three accounts speak of Paul's conversion, but only the first (9:1 – 31) and second (22:1 – 21) tell of Saul's baptism by Ananias. And only the first (9:1 – 31) relates Saul's conversion to a period of fasting while he was blind for three days (9:9) and later to a meal (9:19) once he could see again and had been baptized (9:18).

The story of Saul's conversion (9:19) refers to a meal, "taking food," but does not describe the meal as eucharistic, nor does it use terms that were traditionally associated with the eucharist. It does not speak, for example, of "the breaking of the bread" or "breaking bread," as the summary in 2:42 – 47 and the story of the meal at Troas do (20:7 – 12). Nor does it refer to "service at table" *diakonia,* as in the choice of the Seven (6:1 – 7). Nor does it allude to a recognizable eucharistic formula, as does the story of when Paul "took bread, gave thanks to God . . . broke it, and began to eat" at the height of a storm at sea (27:35).

Acts does not say or suggest that historically Saul actually prepared for baptism by fasting for three days. Nor does it say or suggest that Saul's baptism was followed by a celebration of the eucharist. Direct evidence for such practices comes from outside the New Testament, in the first century from the *Didache*[26] and in the second century from the writings of Justin Martyr.[27] But the practices described in the *Didache* and by Justin Martyr had a history. Very likely, for Christians at the end of the first century and in the second, the story of Saul's conversion (9:1 – 31), together with other stories in Luke and Acts, represented a very early point, if not the very beginning, of that history.

The story of Saul's conversion in Acts was written many years after the event to help Christian communities understand and devote themselves anew to the teaching of the apostles, the *koinonia,* the breaking of the bread and the prayers in circumstances quite different from the days of Saul and his conversion. For Christian readers in the 80s of the first century, many of the terms and expressions in the story had acquired special meanings and connotations.

There is a big difference between what the story tells happened historically at the time of Saul's conversion and what it tells its readers about that conversion literarily. There is more to the story than what actually happened when Saul was struck blind, "neither ate nor drank" for three days (9:7 – 9), regained his sight, was baptized, took food and regained his strength (9:18 – 19). It is from a literary point of view that the story of Saul's conversion is related to the eucharist.

Not Eating and Drinking, Taking Food

In relation to the eucharist, the story contains two key expressions, *ouk ephagen oude epien* (9:9), meaning "he neither ate nor drank," and *labon trophen* (9:19), meaning "taking food."

The expression "to eat and to drink" is found some fourteen times in Luke's Gospel and three times in Acts, including here in Acts 9:9. Luke also refers eighteen times to eating with no mention of drinking. Acts does the same on four occasions. Twice Luke refers to drinking without eating, both times with special reference to wine (Luke 1:15; 5:39).

Sometimes eating refers to a meal, such as a symposium, which would not be a symposium without sharing wine. In such cases, drinking is implied and does not need to be indicated. Sometimes eating is an abbreviated reference to a meal that has already been described as eating and drinking.

We need to remember that in Luke-Acts, as in the world of the Old and New Testament, eating and drinking formed a communal event. People did not eat and drink by themselves but with others as an expression of solidarity with them, sometimes entering into a new relationship, sometimes reaffirming and nurturing an existing relationship. Most of the time, "to eat" and "to drink" mean "to eat with" and "to drink with" even when the preposition "with" *(syn)* is not expressed.[28]

The same applies to taking food *(trophe)* either with the verb *lambano* (to take, Acts 9:19), or the verb *metalambano* (to share in or partake of), as when "they ate their meals *(metalambanon trophes)* with exultation and sincerity of heart" (2:46; see also 27:33, 34). Another verb used with *trophe* (food) is *proslambanomai* (to eat or take) as when "they were all encouraged, and took some food *(proselabonto trophes)* themselves (27:36).

In the negative, the expression, "neither eating nor drinking," is found only once in Luke (7:33) and three times in Acts (9:9; 23:12, 21). There is also a reference to not eating with no mention of not drinking (Luke 4:2).

Again we need to remember that in Luke-Acts, as in the entire biblical world, fasting, like eating and drinking, is generally a communal event. In the Old Testament, the entire people together with the king and other leaders often undertook a fast in sign of their repentance and their dependence on God. Sometimes, fasting was undertaken to ensure the speedy outcome of a communal commitment, as when some Jews in Jerusalem "made a plot and bound themselves by oath not to eat or drink until they had killed Paul" (Acts 23:12; see 23:14, 21).[29] One might fast to show solidarity with others in a common cause or mission. But then, one might also fast to avoid showing solidarity with others in some common cause.

Overview of 9:1-31

Like the story of the Seven, the story of Saul's conversion has an introduction (9:1-2), a body (9:3-30) and a conclusion (9:31). Again like the story of the Seven, each unit plays a significant role in the story of Saul's conversion and in the greater context of Acts.

The introduction (9:1-2) describes Saul's life and activities at the time of his conversion, providing the setting for his conversion. Saul was "still breathing murderous threats against the disciples of the Lord" (9:1a). The expression "still *(eti)* breathing" connects Saul's conversion (9:1-31) with the stoning of Stephen (7:58) and his activities against the church in Jerusalem (8:3), when Saul began "breathing murderous threats against the disciples of the Lord" (9:1a).

Not content with persecuting the church in Jerusalem, Saul went to the high priest and obtained letters to the synagogues of Damascus, authorizing him to bring men and women who belonged to the Way back to Jerusalem in chains (9:1b-2). Those scattered by the persecution had gone preaching the word (see 8:4) as far as Damascus (9:2).

The body of the story (9:3-30) begins with the story of Saul's conversion (9:3-19a) and continues with his activities right after his conversion (9:19b-30). Our reflections will focus mainly on the conversion story itself (9:1-19a), which alone has implications for the eucharist.

The conversion (9:3-19a) is told in two units (3-9 and 10-19a), corresponding to the two stages in Saul's conversion. First, there was a vision on the Damascus road in which Jesus called out to Saul: "Saul, Saul, why are you persecuting me?" (9:4). In the second stage, Ananias, one of the disciples in Damascus, came to Saul, interpreted Saul's vision and laid hands on him, whereupon Saul was healed of blindness and was baptized.

The two stages are both christological and ecclesiogical. But the first stage, with its focus on the vision and the person of the risen Jesus, is mainly christological. The second stage, with its focus on the life of the community, is mainly ecclesiological.

Both units open with a vision: that of Saul on the Damascus road (9:3-6) and that of Ananias at home in Damascus (9:10-16). After each vision, each unit tells how Saul and Ananias responded to the message they received in the vision (9:7-9, 17-19a). The references to Saul fasting (9:9) and eating (9:19a) have implications for the development of the eucharist, which we shall consider in detail.

What Saul did after his conversion is also told in two units. At first Saul preached in the synagogues of Damascus (9:19b – 22). Then, after he was forced to flee Damascus (9:23 – 25), Saul was introduced to the community in Jerusalem (9:26 – 30). In Jerusalem, Saul spoke out boldly "in the name of the Lord" (9:28), especially to the Hellenists (9:29). Both units show that Saul, the persecutor, became Saul, the persecuted, first in Damascus, where his life as a persecutor came to an end, and then in Jerusalem, where his life as a persecutor had begun.

As in the story of the choice of the Seven (6:1 – 7), the conclusion is in the form of a summary of the life of the church (9:31). With Saul's conversion, the church was at peace "throughout all of Judea, Galilee, and Samaria" (9:31a). It was being built up *(oikodomoumene)* while walking in the fear of the Lord (9:32b). With the consolation of the holy Spirit, the church was also growing in numbers *(eplethunato* 9:31c). Growth in the number of the disciples is a recurrent theme in Acts (6:1, 7), closely related to the growth of the word (6:7; 12:24; 19:20; see also 2:47; 5:14; 11:21, 24; 16:5).[30]

Parallels in Luke-Acts

The most obvious parallel to the story of Paul's conversion is in the two discourses of Paul where he retells the story, first defending himself before the Jews in Jerusalem (22:1 – 21) and later defending himself before King Agrippa in Caesarea (26:1 – 23). There are differences between the story in 9:1 – 31 and the discourses, as well as between the discourses themselves.

These differences, as has already been shown, come from the difference between the primary narrative form in 9:1 – 31 and the secondary discourse form in 22:1 – 21 and 26:1 – 23. Both discourses presuppose that the reader already knows the story. Differences between the two discourses come from the difference in Paul's addressees. It was one thing for Paul to defend himself before the Jews in Jerusalem, another to defend himself before King Agrippa.

Neither of the discourses refers to Saul fasting for three days and eating after he was baptized. Those details are important for the Christian reader of Acts but were of no interest either to the Jews in Jerusalem or King Agrippa.

Another parallel to the story of Paul's conversion is the conversion of Cornelius, where the appearances to Cornelius (10:1–8) and Peter (10:9–16) correspond to the appearances to Paul (9:1–9) and Ananias (9:10–16). As in the appearance to Paul, both Cornelius and Peter received instructions whose full significance would be revealed only later. In the case of Paul, this would be done by Ananias (9:10–19). For Peter, it would be done by the messengers from Cornelius and what Peter witnessed at Cornelius' home (10:17–33, 44–47). For Cornelius, it would be done by Peter's discourse (10:34–43). Finally, both Paul and Peter had to prove the genuineness of their experience before the church in Jerusalem (9:26–27; 11:1–18).

The difference between the two stories is also significant. In the story of Saul's conversion, Saul himself, not Ananias, is the principal personage. In the story of Cornelius' conversion, the principal personage is not Cornelius but Peter.

Saul the Persecutor (9:1–2)

The introductory verses (9:1–2) continue the story of Saul as a persecutor of the Christians: Saul was "still breathing murderous threats against the disciples of the Lord" (9:1a). The persecution had begun in Jerusalem. Saul brought it as far as Damascus, in his search for men and women who belonged to what Acts calls "the Way" *(he hodos)*.[31]

> Now Saul, still breathing murderous threats against the disciples of the Lord, went to the high priest and asked him for letters to the synagogues in Damascus, that, if he could find any men or women who belonged to the Way, he might bring them back to Jerusalem in chains.

Saul had already been introduced at the end of Stephen's story (6:8–8:3) when the witnesses to the stoning of Stephen "laid down their cloaks at the feet of a young man named Saul" (7:58). Saul was personally consenting to the execution (8:1a). During the persecution that followed, and while the devout were still mourning the death of Stephen, Saul was intent on destroying the church,[32] dragging men and women from their homes and handing them over for imprisonment (8:1b–3; see also 22:20).[33]

Saul was not alone in persecuting those belonging to the Way. Those who accompanied him would later lead him by the hand to

Damascus, to a house on a street called Straight *(Eutheia),* where Saul received hospitality from a man named Judas (9:11). The fact that Saul "neither ate nor drank" while in the house of Judas is very significant for Acts' story of the development of the eucharist.

While at the home of Judas, Saul did not yet belong to the Way of the Lord. Still, he had seen and heard the Lord Jesus. No longer could Saul associate himself with those who had not seen and heard Jesus and who were still intent on persecuting Jesus' disciples. Eating and drinking with them would have shown solidarity with them.

Saul's Journey to Damascus (9:3 – 9)

After the introduction (9:1 – 2), the first part of the story tells of Saul's journey to Damascus (9:3 – 9). Very little, however, is said of the journey itself. The entire focus is on one event, Jesus' appearance to Saul at the end of the journey as he was approaching Damascus (9:3b – 7). Jesus' appearance would prove decisive for the rest of Saul's life.

> On his journey, as he was nearing Damascus, a light from the sky suddenly flashed around him.

The light from the sky[34] flashing around Saul was an extraordinary heavenly manifestation as in a theophany or an angelophany. For the moment, however, the manifestation remained clothed in mystery and was not identified as an appearance (see 9:17) of the Lord Jesus. This would be done later in the course of a dialogue (9:4 – 6).

> He fell to the ground and heard a voice saying to him, "Saul, Saul, why are you persecuting me?" He said, "Who are you, sir *(kyrie)*?" The reply came, "I am *(ego eimi)* Jesus, whom you are persecuting. Now get up and go into the city and you will be told what you must *(dei)* do."

The flashing light *(phos)* from the sky had an extraordinary effect on Saul. Surrounded by it, Saul "fell to the ground" (9:4a). The short but extremely significant dialogue that follows (9:4b – 6) is at the very heart of the appearance. All of it took place while Saul, overwhelmed by the light, remained on the ground with his eyes closed (see 9:8a).

The double invocation, "Saul, Saul," evokes a few stories in the Old Testament, such as when Abraham was called by name when he was tested (Genesis 22:1 – 2) or when God's messenger or God called Jacob, Israel, by name (31:11 – 13; 46:2 – 4). Besides these, there is the call of Moses, when the angel of the Lord called to him from a bush aflame without being consumed (Exodus 3:2 – 14). And, of course, there was the call of Samuel, announcing that God was about to do something in Israel (1 Samuel 3:4 – 14).

In each case, repeating the name calls attention to the person, the importance of the call and indirectly to the person issuing the call. Nowhere in the Old Testament, however, does the double call introduce a question, statement or reproach directly, let alone a dialogue. These come only after the person called has responded.

We have two examples in Luke-Acts, however, where the double call introduces a statement directly. The first introduces the Lord's response to Martha: "Martha, Martha, you are anxious and worried about many things" (Luke 10:41). The second introduces Jesus' announcement to Peter at the Last Supper: "Simon, Simon, behold Satan has demanded to sift all of you like wheat, but I have prayed that your faith may not fail; and once you have turned back, you must strengthen your brothers" (22:31 – 32).

Nowhere, however, in either Testament, is the double invocation associated with the person's conversion as it is in the case of Saul. The story of Saul's conversion (Acts 9:1 – 31) reflects a number of literary forms combining various elements from traditional call stories, commissioning stories and conversion stories[35] with an appearance of the risen Lord.

After calling, "Saul, Saul," the voice *(phone)* from heaven asked, "why are you persecuting me?" Before responding, Saul wanted to know who was calling him and describing himself as one Saul is persecuting: "Who are you, sir *(kyrie)*?" he asked.

From Saul's point of view, the voice came from a stranger. Hence the translation of *kyrie* as "sir." From the point of view of the author of Acts, however, and of his readers, Saul was addressing the stranger as "Lord," even before he recognized the Lord's voice (see 9:1). At this point, the story may be compared with that of the two disciples of Emmaus who spoke to Jesus on the way before recognizing him at home in the breaking of the bread (Luke 24:13 – 35).

The voice responded, "I am *(ego eimi)* Jesus, whom you are persecuting." In the response, Jesus identified himself both with the presence of the Lord God as "I AM" and with the disciples, those men and women belonging to the Way whom Saul was persecuting (Acts 9:1 – 2).

The voice from heaven was the voice of the risen Lord, who returned to God, his Father, on completing his mission (Luke 24:50 – 53). With God, the risen Lord could now speak in the name of God. Jesus was the sacrament of God in deed and word.

Eating salt with the apostles for forty days while present to them and appearing to them (Acts 1:3 – 4), the Lord Jesus had made them sacramentally one with him. And they became the sacrament of the Lord Jesus in deed and word (1:3 – 14). Therefore, to persecute the apostles and the apostolic church was to persecute the person of the Lord Jesus.

The voice from heaven, now identified as the voice of the Lord Jesus, then ordered Saul to get up and go into the city. There he would be told what he must *(dei)* do. In Luke-Acts, the expression *dei,* "it is necessary," is always associated with the great events of salvation. Paul's mission, including what he would have to suffer (9:16), like the mission of Jesus and his suffering (see Luke 2:49; 9:22; 19:5; 24:26), was inseparable from the history of salvation.

Those with Saul on the journey to Damascus heard of the voice *(tes phones)* but did not see anyone speaking. Nor did they join in the dialogue.

> The men who were traveling with him stood speechless, for they heard [of] the voice but could see no one.

Those with Saul did not see the flashing light from the sky. Nor did they see the person who addressed Saul and to whom Saul spoke. They heard the voice, at least through its effect on Saul, but apart from the mysterious manifestation, the voice had no effect on them.

The difference between the manifestation's effect on Saul and its having no effect on his companions set Saul apart from them. From the moment the light flashed around Saul, he was different from the others. Saul was not yet a Christian, but neither was he the person "trying to destroy the church" (8:3) and "breathing murderous threats against the disciples of the Lord" (9:1).

The flashing light (9:3) and the encounter with Jesus (9:4 – 6) left Saul unable to see. Those who were traveling with him had to lead him by the hand into Damascus. For three days Saul was unable to see. Nor did he take anything to eat (9:8 – 9).

> Saul got up from the ground, but when he opened his eyes he could see nothing; so they led him by the hand and brought him to Damascus. For three days he was unable to see, and he neither ate nor drank.

When the light flashed, Saul "fell to the ground." After the dialogue encounter with Jesus, "Saul got up from the ground." Literarily, the dialogue is framed by Saul falling *(peson)* to the ground and rising *(egerthe)* from the ground. The reference to falling and rising does not indicate that the event was baptismal. For Luke and the early Christian readers, however, Saul's falling and rising must have evoked the dying and rising of Christ as well as the baptismal symbolism of dying and rising with Christ. As such, at least for the reader, Saul's falling and rising announces his approaching baptism in Damascus.

The appearance rendered Saul completely helpless. Since he could see nothing, he had to be led by the hand to Damascus. Saul's blindness, like each expression in the story of the appearance, including the dialogue, is very symbolic.

Saul, Saul The heavenly voice called Saul by name, not only once but twice. Whenever that happens in Luke-Acts, it signals a very important announcement or message. In the Gospel, Jesus addressed Martha by name and repeated the name, "Martha, Martha" (Luke 10:41), calling her attention to his person and what he was about to say about the one thing necessary in the ministry *diakonia.*

Later, at the Last Supper, Jesus addressed Peter as Simon (see 24:34) and repeated his name, calling Peter's attention to an important announcement: "Simon, Simon, behold, Satan has demanded to sift all of you like wheat, but I have prayed that your own faith may not fail; and once you have turned back, you must strengthen your brothers" (22:31 – 32). Strengthened by the prayer of Jesus, Peter was to strengthen his brothers.

Now for Saul's conversion, the heavenly voice addresses Saul and repeats his name: "Saul, Saul *(Saoul, Saoul),* why are you persecuting me?" (Acts 9:4). As in the case of Martha and Simon, the repetition draws attention to the person addressed and the message that follows. The Hebraic form of Saul, *Saoul,* emphasizes the Jewishness of Saul. Later, when telling the story of his conversion, Paul would do the same (22:7; 26:14). While telling the story before King Agrippa, Paul even specified that the voice spoke to him "in Hebrew" *(te Hebraidi dialekto).*

He Could See Nothing   "Saul got up from the ground, but when he opened his eyes, he could see nothing" (9:8a). Like a blind man, Saul had to be led by the hand (9:8b).

Saul had become like those Jesus had described when the disciples asked him to explain the parable of the sower: "Knowledge of the mysteries of the kingdom of God has been granted to you; but to the rest, they are made known through parables so that 'they may look but not see, and hear but not understand'" (Luke 8:10). Saul had not yet been given "knowledge of the mysteries of the kingdom of God."

The words "they may look but not see, and hear but not understand" are from a passage from Isaiah 6:9–10. In the quotation, the words "look" and "hear" parallel and interpret one another. So do the expressions "not see" and "not understand." Being unable to see is the same as not being able to understand.

Paul himself would quote from the same passage from Isaiah while addressing the leaders of the Jews in Rome (28:26–27):

> Go to this people and say:
> You shall indeed hear but not understand.
> You shall indeed look but never see.
> Gross is the heart of this people;
> they will not hear with their ears;
> they have closed their eyes,
> so they may not see with their eyes
> and hear with their ears
> and understand with their heart and be converted,
> and I heal them.

It was different with Saul, who opened his eyes and did not see anything. For Saul, however, that would be only for a time. Unlike those who rejected his message, when Paul tried "to convince them about Jesus from the law of Moses and the prophets" (28:23), Saul did not close his eyes so that he might see with his eyes. He opened his eyes, but could not see. Saul was ready to understand with his heart and be converted. He was ready to be healed.[36]

For three days, Saul was unable to see (9:9a). Saul was like the disciples of Emmaus, who at one time could see, or at least thought they could see. On the way to Emmaus, they spoke of "the things that happened to Jesus the Nazarene, who was a prophet mighty in deed and word before God and all the people" (Luke 24:19). But now they could no longer see or understand "how our chief priests and rulers both handed him over to a sentence of death and crucified him. But we were hoping that he would be the one to redeem Israel; and besides all this, it is now the third day since this took place" (24:20–21).

What at one time the disciples could see and understand, they no longer could see and understand. But now it was the third day, and Jesus would open their eyes to see and their minds to understand: "'Oh, how foolish you are! How slow of heart to believe all that the prophets spoke! Was it not necessary that the Messiah should suffer these things and enter into his glory?' Then beginning with Moses and all the prophets, he interpreted to them what referred to him in all the scriptures" (24:25–27).

He neither Ate nor Drank　Like the light, the voice and Saul's blindness, the fact that Saul neither ate nor drank for three days is also symbolic. In the cultural context of the New Testament, one did not eat or drink by oneself but with companions. Eating and drinking was a community or family event, both expressing and strengthening the bond among those who ate and drank.

Sharing a meal together was a sign of solidarity and reconciliation. The Gospel of Luke developed these aspects in the stories of meals Jesus took with his disciples and others who responded to his call. See, for example, the story of Levi, when the Pharisees protested that Jesus' disciples ate with tax collectors and sinners (5:27–32). Recall, too, that the Pharisees and scribes complained that Jesus welcomed sinners and ate with them (15:1–2), and that the older brother in the parable of the lost son refused to partake of the feast when his brother was found (15:11–32). If eating together had not expressed solidarity, reconciliation and a common commitment, there would have been no reason to protest.

From the moment the light flashed around Saul and he fell to the ground, Saul was different from his former companions who had not seen the light. Unlike them, Saul was no longer the person who was "trying to destroy the church" (Acts 8:3). When Saul set out with his companions for Damascus, he was "still breathing murderous threats against the disciples of the Lord (9:1). When Saul was struck to the ground, that was no longer the case.

Cut off from his former companions, he could no longer eat and drink with them. But since Saul was not yet baptized, he was not yet one with those who would be his new brothers and sisters in Christ. In his blindness, Saul would be alone for three days. And very likely that explains why he neither ate nor drank. There simply was no one with whom he could eat.

The Baptism of Saul (9:10 – 19)

In Jerusalem, Saul had tried to destroy the church, "entering house after house and dragging out men and women" to hand them over for imprisonment (8:3). His intention was to do the same in Damascus (9:2), until he was stopped by the light of Christ (9:3 – 5) and made blind (9:8a). Jesus had told him: "Go into the city and you will be told what you must do" (9:6).

After that, Saul's former companions "led him by the hand and brought him to Damascus" (9:8b), where Saul stayed on the street called Straight at the home of a Jew named Judas (9:11). And that is where a Christian named Ananias was told to ask for him (9:10 – 12).

> There was a disciple in Damascus named Ananias, and the Lord said to him in a vision, "Ananias." He answered, "Here I am, Lord." The Lord said to him, "Get up and go to the street called Straight and ask at the house of Judas for a man from Tarsus named Saul. He is there praying, and [in a vision] he has seen a man named Ananias come in and lay [his] hands on him, that he may regain his sight."

Ananias[37] was one of those men and women belonging to the Way whom Saul had intended to drag out of his house (see 8:3) and bring back to Jerusalem in chains (see 9:3). Later, while defending himself before the Jews in Jerusalem, Paul described him as "a devout observer of the law, and highly spoken of by all the Jews who lived" in Damascus (22:12). Ananias was a member of the church in Damascus. As a Christian who continued to observe the law, he was highly regarded by the Jews in Damascus.[38]

Appearing to Ananias, the Lord told him to go to the home of Judas and ask for Saul, who was there praying. While praying, Saul had received a vision in which Ananias came in and laid his hands on him that he might regain his sight (9:11 – 12).

Blind and fasting, Saul prayed "for three days" (see 9:9). The expression "for three days," like "on the third day" and "after three days," is more theological than chronological. Early rabbinical tradition associated "three days" with the day God saves his people. Early Christian tradition applied that meaning to Jesus' resurrection (1 Corinthians 15:4).[39] The people were saved when God raised Jesus on the third day. Saul was now about to share in that salvation.

Ananias did not have to be told of Saul's blindness. Since Saul was not yet a disciple, he was still blind. As a Christian, Ananias participated in Jesus' mission to proclaim "recovery of sight to the blind" (Luke 4:18; see also 7:22). He would exercise that mission by laying hands on Saul. Before doing that, however, Ananias would have to be reassured (9:13 – 16).

> But Ananias replied, "Lord, I have heard from many sources about this man, what evil things he has done to your holy ones in Jerusalem. And here he has authority from the chief priests to imprison all who call upon your name." But the Lord said to him, "Go, for this man is a chosen instrument of mine to carry my name before Gentiles, kings and Israelites, and I will show him what he will have to suffer for my name."

As a member of the church in Damascus, Ananias had only heard of Saul and how Saul persecuted the Christians in Jerusalem and had authority to extend the persecution to Damascus.[40] In response, the Lord told Ananias to go and seek out Saul. Saul may have persecuted those who were calling upon the Lord's name (9:14), but he was the Lord's chosen instrument to carry the Lord's name to the Gentiles. In doing that, the former persecutor would also have to suffer for his name.

Saul had been surrounded by the light of Jesus, "a light for revelation to the Gentiles, and glory for your people Israel" (Luke 2:32). That light would shine in the mission of Saul, as Saul, now referred to by his Gentile name Paul, would recall at Antioch in Pisidia: "For so the Lord has commanded us, 'I have made you a light to the Gentiles, that you may be an instrument of salvation to the ends of the earth'" (Acts 13:47).

With that, Ananias did as the Lord told him and went to find Saul.

So Ananias went and entered the house; laying hands on him, he said, "Saul, my brother, the Lord has sent me, Jesus who appeared to you on the way by which you came, that you may regain your sight and be filled with the holy Spirit." Immediately things like scales fell from his eyes and he regained his sight. He got up and was baptized, and when he had eaten, he recovered his strength.

When Ananias laid hands on Saul, he became Ananias' "brother" in the Lord. And as a brother he could now see and understand in faith. What had prevented him from understanding had fallen from his eyes. Regaining his sight, Saul was filled with the holy Spirit and was baptized.

As a brother to the disciples in Damascus, as one who could see in faith, was filled with the holy Spirit and was baptized, Saul could once again eat. For three days, he had not eaten or drunk with his former companions. With the arrival of Ananias, he ate with his new brother in the Lord. Eating with Ananias, Saul expressed solidarity and reconciliation with him. Having so eaten, he was strengthened to carry the Lord's name before Gentiles, kings, and Israelites (see 9:15).

Read in this way, the story of Saul's conversion is a very eucharistic story. It is not that Paul's fast was a preparation for baptism, or that Paul's eating after being baptized was part of his initiation as a Christian. Later, in the second century, in the time of Justin Martyr that would have been the case.

As described by Luke, the conversion of Saul did not include a eucharistic meal. The story of his conversion did say a great deal, however, about the solidarity and reconciliation implied in eating and drinking with others. In the context of Luke-Acts, that eating and drinking surely included meals where the Christians gathered as a church for the breaking of the bread.

The Conversion of Cornelius (10:1 — 11:18)

This man God raised [on] the third day
and granted that he be visible,
not to all the people, but to us
the witnesses chosen by God in advance,
who ate and drank with him
after he rose from the dead.

Acts 10:40 – 41

The third story in this section of Acts (6:1 — 12:25) with implications for the development of the eucharist is the story of Peter and Cornelius (10:1 — 11:18).[41] The story tells how the church first reached out to the Gentiles. Doing so, it shows that the eucharist is related to the universality of the church.

Luke introduces Cornelius as the first Gentile convert. Prior to Cornelius, many Jews had become believers, joining the company of Jesus' disciples. At first, in Jerusalem, the Jewish converts were Hebrews, that is, Jews coming from Hebrew-speaking synagogues. They were soon joined by Jewish converts described as Hellenists, that is, Jews coming from Greek-speaking synagogues.

Many Samaritans also became believers through the ministry of Philip in Samaria (8:4 – 13). When the apostles in Jerusalem heard of this astonishing development, they sent Peter and John, who prayed that as believers the Samaritans might receive the holy Spirit. When Peter and John imposed hands on them, the Samaritans, like the apostles on Pentecost and many Jews in Jerusalem, received the holy Spirit (8:14 – 17). Then, as they returned to Jerusalem, Peter and John proclaimed the good news in many Samaritan villages on the way (8:25).

Later, Philip met an Ethiopian eunuch who had gone to Jerusalem to worship. The Ethiopian eunuch may have belonged to an ancient Ethiopian Jewish community, who, unlike the Samaritans, looked to Jerusalem as their spiritual center, or he also have been a convert *(proselyte)* to Judaism. After Philip interpreted the scriptures for him, showing how a passage from Isaiah was about Jesus, the eunuch asked to be baptized and Philip baptized him (8:26 – 39).

Besides the apostles and the original disciples, the community now included Hebrew-speaking Jews from Jerusalem, Greek-speaking Jews who had come to Jerusalem from the diaspora, Samaritans and the Ethiopian eunuch returning home to Ethiopia. Until now, however, the community did not include any Gentiles. Cornelius, with his entire household, would be the first.

The story of Saul told how he was converted to the Lord Jesus and the Way (9:1–31; see 9:2). The story of Peter and Cornelius tells how Cornelius was converted to "Jesus Christ, who is Lord of all" (10:36). As part of that story, Luke also tells how Peter was converted to the Gentile mission, providing the christological and ecclesiological grounds for the church's mission to the Gentiles.

The conversion of Cornelius also provided Paul's mission to the Gentiles with a precedent in the mission of Peter. Paul may have been the apostle to the Gentiles, but he did not initiate the mission to the Gentiles. It was Peter who initiated the mission to the Gentiles.

The mission to the Gentiles was announced at the beginning of Acts, when Jesus told the apostolic community, "But you will receive power when the holy Spirit comes upon you, and you will be my witnesses in Jerusalem, throughout Judea and Samaria, and to the ends of the earth" (1:8). The mission to the Gentiles was also symbolically announced at Pentecost by the crowd of "devout Jews from every nation under heaven staying in Jerusalem" (2:5). Peter himself spoke of the mission to the Gentiles in his discourse in the portico of Solomon: "You are the children of the prophets and of the covenant that God made with your ancestors when he said to Abraham, 'In your offspring all the families of the earth shall be blessed'" (3:25).

The mission to the Gentiles had also been prepared from the very beginning of the Gospel, with a reference to Augustus calling for a census of the whole world (Luke 2:1), with Simeon's canticle proclaiming Jesus as "a light for revelation to the Gentiles" (2:32) and with a reference to the reign of Tiberius Caesar and Pontius Pilate when the Word came to John in the desert (3:1–2). There was also the genealogy of Jesus reaching all the way back to Adam, the common ancestor of the entire human race (3:23–38), and the temptation of Jesus, in which the devil showed "him all the kingdoms of the world in a single instant" (4:5).

Then, when Jesus began his ministry with a discourse at the synagogue of Nazareth, he challenged his own people with the mission to the Gentiles. For that he invoked the example of Elijah, who was sent "to a widow in Zarephath in the land of Sidon," and of Elisha, who cleansed Naaman, a leper who was Syrian (4:16–30; see especially 4:25–27).

Both in the Gospel and Acts, the mission to the Gentiles had been well prepared and announced. The story of Peter and Cornelius, however, is the first time it is formally addressed. The Gospel and Acts had also provided the mission to the Gentiles with a biblical rationale, relating it to the role of our ancestor Adam, to the promises made to Abraham and to the example of Elijah and Elisha. The story of Peter and Cornelius provided the mission to the Gentiles with a christological and ecclesiological rationale.

Overview of 10:1 — 11:18

Like the stories of the Seven (Acts 6:1 – 7) and of Saul's conversion (9:1 – 31), the story of Peter and the conversion of Cornelius (10:1 — 11:18) can be divided into three units, including an introduction, a body and a conclusion. The introduction tells that an angel of the Lord appeared to Cornelius and told him to send for Peter (10:1 – 8). The body of the story tells that Peter also received a vision, accompanied the messengers from Cornelius, was converted to the Gentile mission and actually initiated it (10:9 – 49). To conclude, the story tells that Peter defended his action and the Gentile mission before the church in Jerusalem (11:1 – 18).

The story begins by introducing Cornelius, a centurion of the Cohort Italica who lived in Caesarea (10:1) and telling that an angel of God came to him with instructions to summon Peter, who at the time was staying with Simon the tanner in Joppa (10:1 – 18).

The body of the story shows that while the messengers from Cornelius were on the way, Peter too received a vision, telling him that what God had made clean he should not call profane (10:9 – 11). While Peter was pondering the vision, the men from Cornelius arrived, asked for him and gave him Cornelius' message (10:17 – 23a).

The following day, Peter and some of the Christians from Joppa went to Caesarea to the home of Cornelius. Peter now realized the significance of the vision he received at the home of Simon the tanner. Visiting and eating with Gentiles would not make Peter ritually unclean (10:23b – 29). Cornelius then told Peter about the vision he himself had received (10:30 – 37), and Peter responded with an extremely important discourse, showing the christological and ecclesiological basis for the mission to the Gentiles (10:34 – 43). As Peter was concluding the discourse, the holy Spirit fell on all who listened to the word, whereupon Peter ordered the entire household to be baptized (10:44–49).

The conclusion of the story tells that those in Jerusalem confronted Peter when they heard about his ministry to the Gentiles. In response, Peter told them about the vision he had received and how he was summoned to Caesarea. He also told them about the vision Cornelius had received, and that the holy Spirit fell upon him and his entire household. When those in Jerusalem heard Peter's report, they glorified God for granting "life-giving repentance to the Gentiles too" (11:1–18).

Parallels in Luke-Acts

For the story of Peter and the conversion of Cornelius, Luke's Gospel offers stories that are thematically parallel. Consider, for example, the story of the banquet at the home of Levi the tax collector (5:27–39) and the story of Jesus requesting hospitality at the home of Zacchaeus, the chief tax collector in Jericho (19:1–10). Both stories show Jesus entering the home of a Jew who was an outcast and eating with him. In both cases, people objected that Jesus' disciples and Jesus himself went to the home of a sinner.[42] Similar objections were directed at Peter when he went to the home of Gentiles and ate with them (Acts 11:1–3).

In the Book of Acts, the story of Peter and the conversion of Cornelius (10:1 — 11:18) parallels the story of Paul's conversion (9:1–31). Together the stories of Peter and Paul tell how the mission to the Gentiles actually began.

The mission to the Gentiles was very successful. As such, it drew the attention of the disciples in Jerusalem, who remained very close to their Jewish roots and continued to frequent the synagogue. To resolve any tension and to set a policy regarding the Gentiles, a great assembly was called in Jerusalem (15:1–35).

The story of Paul's conversion and that of Peter and the conversion of Cornelius are both related to the story of the great assembly. Peter participated in that assembly, as well as Barnabas and Paul. At the assembly, Peter recalled his experience at the home of Cornelius and what he learned from it (15:7–11).

The story of Peter and the conversion of Cornelius showed that the church had to reach out to the Gentiles and preach God's word to them. The story of the great assembly in Jerusalem told that the church had to welcome the Gentiles on an equal footing with the Jews without imposing Jewish law and religious practices on them. Both stories deal with hospitality, including eucharistic hospitality, and eating with Gentiles, including eating at the table of the Lord.

The story of Peter and the conversion of Cornelius deals with the universality of the church. The story of the assembly in Jerusalem deals with the unity of the church.

The story begins with the vision of Cornelius (10:1 – 8), the one who would be converted. It then continues with the vision of Peter (10:9 – 16), the one who would go to the home of Cornelius and baptize him (10:17 – 48). After staying a few days in Caesarea (10:49), Peter would go to Jerusalem, tell the story and defend what he did at Caesarea (11:1 – 18).

In many respects, it is the same in the story of Saul, which begins with the vision of Saul (9:1 – 9), the one who would be converted. It continues with the vision to Ananias (9:10 – 16), the one who would go to the home where Saul was staying and baptize him (9:17 – 19a). At this point, the parallel continues but in a different direction. It is not Ananias, but Saul, the one who was converted, who stayed a few days in Damascus (9:19b – 25), went to Jerusalem, told the story of his conversion and showed that he really was a disciple (9:26 – 30).

Although the story begins with the vision to Cornelius, the story is really about Peter welcoming a Gentile household to the church and the basis for his action. Peter is the principal personage in the story of the conversion of Cornelius. In the story of the conversion of Saul, Saul himself, not Ananias, is the principal personage.

The Vision of Cornelius (10:1 – 8)

The story begins by introducing the centurion Cornelius, known for his generosity to the Jewish people and as a person of prayer (10:1 – 2):

> Now in Caesarea there was a man named Cornelius, a centurion of the Cohort called the Italica, devout and God-fearing along with his whole household, who used to give alms generously to the Jewish people and pray to God constantly.

Cornelius is the third centurion *(hekatontarches)* with a role in Luke-Acts. The first was in Capernaum, where Jesus healed a centurion's slave. He too was noted for his generosity to the Jewish people and for his profound faith (Luke 7:1 – 10). The second was the one at the crucifixion who glorified God and declared Jesus an innocent *(dikaios,* righteous) man (23:47). In Luke-Acts, Roman centurions are always presented in a very favorable light.[43]

Cornelius, together with his whole household, is described as "devout and God-fearing *(phoboumenos ton theon)."* The expression describes a Gentile who is not a proselyte but appreciates the Jewish faith, who attends synagogue services and observes many Jewish practices.[44] Like the centurion in Capernaum, he was also very generous to the Jewish people (see Luke 7:1 – 10). Cornelius gave alms and he prayed to God constantly *(dia pantos).*[45]

Giving alms and praying constantly, Cornelius was also like the early Christians in Jerusalem (see Acts 2:42 – 47). The apostles themselves made prayer a priority and associated it with the ministry of the word (see 6:4). These last qualities introduce the vision, which Cornelius received while he was at prayer (10:3 – 6):

> One afternoon about three o'clock, he saw plainly in a vision an angel of God come in to him and say to him, "Cornelius." He looked intently at him and, seized with fear, said, "What is it, sir?" He said to him, "Your prayers and almsgiving have ascended as a memorial offering before God. Now send some men to Joppa and summon one Simon who is called Peter. He is staying with another Simon, a tanner, who has a house by the sea."

Cornelius was praying around three o'clock *(peri horan enanten tes hemeras,* around the ninth hour of the day), as Peter and John (3:1) and the whole community did in Jerusalem (see 2:42, 46). In the temple, the public prayer at the ninth hour was the hour of sacrificial incense offering (see Luke 1:8 – 10). As the angel of God said to Cornelius, his "prayers and almsgiving have ascended as a memorial offering before God" (Acts 10:4). God had remembered Cornelius, and his prayers were about to be answered. In view of that, he was told to summon Simon who is staying with a tanner in Joppa.

After the story of Saul's conversion, Acts resumes the story of Peter. After visiting Samaria, Peter had returned to Jerusalem, preaching in many Samaritan villages on the way (8:14 – 25). At the time,

Peter was accompanied by John, as he had been earlier in Jerusalem (see 3:1 — 4:31). Now he was going about the various regions visiting the Christian communities in Judea. After passing through Lydda and Sharon (9:32 – 35), he came to Joppa, at the request of the disciples in Joppa (9:36 – 42). There he stayed with Simon the tanner (9:43).

The tanning of leather was one of several occupations that a good Jew avoided, for it made one ritually unclean.[46] Within the context of Luke-Acts, Peter's staying at the home of someone who was considered ritually unclean is very significant. Just as Jesus had accepted hospitality from tax collectors (Luke 5:27 – 32; 15:1 – 2; 19:1 – 10), Peter accepted hospitality from a tanner of leather.

It may be that the home of Simon the tanner was already a home for the church, where the Christians of Joppa gathered for the prayers and for the breaking of the bread. As the home for the church in Joppa, the home of Simon the tanner would have offered hospitality to Christians traveling from other towns and cities.[47]

But if that was not already the case, the home of Simon the tanner became a home for the church with Peter's visit, when "he stayed a long time in Joppa with Simon, a tanner" (Acts 9:43). It was at the home of Simon the tanner that Peter welcomed visitors, including the Gentiles sent by Cornelius, and offered them hospitality (10:23a), making Simon's home a center in Joppa for Christian ministry and hospitality. Later, members of the community in Joppa would accompany Peter to Caesarea and the home of Cornelius (10:23b).

The Vision of Peter (10:9 – 16)

The story of Peter and Cornelius continues with the vision of Peter. The day after Cornelius' vision, while "two of his servants and a devout soldier from his staff" were on the way to Joppa, Peter went to the roof terrace at Simon's house to pray (10:9 – 10):

> The next day, while they were on their way and nearing the city, Peter went up to the roof terrace to pray at about noontime. He was hungry and wished to eat, and while they were making preparations he fell into a trance.

Like Cornelius, Peter was at prayer when he received the vision. The time of day and the fact that Peter was hungry and was looking forward to eating had a great deal to do with the content of his vision.

The reference to people making preparations *(paraskeuazonton de auton)* is also significant. Those preparing the meal were surely observing the Jewish kosher laws that regulated every aspect of the meal, including the choice of foods to be eaten and their preparation.[48] The verb "to prepare a meal" *(paraskeuazo)* refers to the vessels, dishes and containers *(skeuos)* used in the preparations. The same term, *skeuos,* is used to describe the large sheet in the vision containing the many foods that were not kosher.[49]

Peter's vision was very different from that of Cornelius. In the case of Cornelius, we saw that an angel of God came to him. Peter, however, simply fell into a trance (10:11 – 16).

> He saw heaven opened and something resembling a large sheet coming down, lowered to the ground by its four corners. In it were all of earth's four-legged animals and reptiles and the birds of the sky. A voice said to him, "Get up, Peter. Slaughter and eat." But Peter said, "Certainly not, sir. For never have I eaten anything profane and unclean." The voice spoke to him again, a second time, "What God has made clean, you are not to call profane." This happened three times, and then the object was taken up into the sky.

For Cornelius' vision of the angel of God, Luke uses the Greek word for "vision" *(horama,* 10:3). For Peter's vision, he uses the word *ekstasis* (10:10), literally, "a trance." While Cornelius' vision was objective, Peter's vision was a mental state somewhere between being fully awake and fully asleep. Later, however, Luke refers to what he saw in the trance as "a vision" *(horama,* 10:17, 19). Later yet, while telling the story in Jerusalem, Peter referred to the whole experience as seeing a vision in a trance: "I was at prayer in the city of Joppa when in a trance *(en ekstasei)* I had (literally, saw, *eidon*) a vision" *(horama,* 11:5).

In the vision, Peter saw something, a food container *(skeuos)* which was like a large piece of cloth *(othone)* coming down from heaven, held up by the corners. Three times it came down and three times it was taken up *(anelemphthe).*[50] The food container was clearly from heaven.

Of itself, such a vision would have been very striking. More striking still, however, was what Peter saw in the cloth: "all the earth's four-legged animals and reptiles and the birds of the sky" (10:12). Later, telling the story in Jerusalem, Peter added "the wild beasts" (11:6).

The vision evokes the fifth day of creation, when God created the winged birds that fly beneath the dome of the sky (Genesis 1:20 – 23) and the sixth day of creation, when God created creeping things, cattle and wild animals of all kinds (1:24 – 25).

Even more striking is what Peter heard: a voice addressing him by name and giving him a command, "Get up, Peter. Slaughter and eat" (Acts 10:13; see 11:7). Among "all the earth's four-legged animals and reptiles and the birds of the sky" (10:12), God had forbidden the Israelites to eat many of them. A summary of the laws governing clean and unclean foods is in Leviticus 11:1 – 47.

Among the land animals (Leviticus 11:1 – 8), they could eat "any animal that has hoofs . . . provided it is cloven-footed and chews the cud" (11:3), but none of the others. The camel, for example, and the pig were declared unclean. Among the creatures living in the water (11:9 – 12), they could eat "whatever in the seas or in river waters has both fins and scales" (11:9), but none of the others. Clams, for example, lobster and squid are unclean. Leviticus also names many birds that are not to be eaten (11:13 – 19). It even distinguishes between the insects that can be eaten and those that cannot be eaten (11:20 – 23). Among those that could be eaten were locusts and the various kinds of grasshoppers (11:22; see Mark 1:6).

Recognizing in the large piece of cloth many animals, reptiles and birds that were unclean, Peter protested, "Certainly not, sir. For never have I eaten anything profane and unclean" (Acts 10:14; see 11:8). Peter's protest recalls that of Ezekiel, when God commanded him to eat food that was unclean to symbolize how it would be for the Israelites dispersed among the nations, "Oh no, Lord God! . . . never has any unclean meat entered my mouth" (Ezekiel 4:14).

Responding to Peter, the voice said, "What God has made clean, you are not to call profane" (Acts 10:15). God has made all things clean. The laws regarding clean and unclean foods are now superseded. Like the vision, the voice evokes the fifth and sixth days of creation, when God saw how good the living creatures were and blessed them (Genesis 1:21 – 22, 25).

The story of Peter's vision and his reaction presupposes that until now Peter has been observing the Jewish kosher laws and practices. Given Peter's position in the church, the same is presupposed for the church in Jerusalem, Judea, Samaria and on the coast from Azotus (Ashdod) to Caesarea. That also means that Christians everywhere had been observing the kosher laws when they assembled as a church on the first day of the week for the breaking of the bread or when they broke bread daily in their respective homes.

The Christians, therefore, like the Jews, avoided many foods eaten by the Gentiles, who had no such kosher laws. Gentiles, for example, ate pork and ridiculed Jews for not eating it. Banquets at the home of Gentiles often included a variety of mollusks and crustaceans, creatures of the sea that were unclean for the early Christians and Jews, since they had neither fins nor scales.

Until now, adherence to the kosher laws prevented Christians from entering the home of Gentiles and eating with them. For that reason, Christians did not consider preaching the gospel of Jesus to Gentiles. Nor did they invite Gentiles into their common-union *(koinonia)* or to the breaking of the bread when they assembled as a church. Until now, the kosher laws were considered integral to the breaking of the bread. Peter's vision announced a major development regarding the eucharistic meal. The kosher laws were being abrogated in view of the mission to the Gentiles.

The Messengers from Cornelius (10:17 – 23a)

While Peter was pondering the meaning of the vision, the men sent by Cornelius arrived at the home of Simon the tanner and inquired whether Simon Peter was staying there. The Spirit told Peter about their arrival (10:19b – 20):

> There are three men here looking for you. So get up, go down-stairs, and accompany them without hesitation, because I have sent them.

Peter went down to them and introduced himself. They told him about Cornelius, the vision he had received and that the angel of God had told him to summon Peter to his home that he might hear what *(hremata)* Peter had to say. With that, Peter invited the two servants and the soldier (see 10:7) into Simon's home and showed them hospitality *(exenisen,* 10:23a).

Offering hospitality always included giving the guests something to eat (see Luke 11:5 – 8). This time, it included even more. People had already prepared a meal, and it was time for Peter to eat (Acts 10:10). Peter, who was hungry when he had the vision of the unclean foods, invited them to share the meal with him. He then gave them a place to stay for the night.

Peter was being shown the meaning of the vision. The unclean food he saw coming down from heaven in the food container *(skeuos)* was symbolic of the whole kosher law. If God made the food clean, he also made the Gentiles clean. If so, nothing prohibited Peter from sharing a meal with people who previously had been considered unclean but no longer were.[51]

At the Home of Cornelius (10:23b–49)

Accompanying the messengers from Cornelius, Peter and "some of the brothers from Joppa" went to Caesarea. In the meantime, Cornelius had invited his relatives and friends to hear Peter. On Peter's arrival, Cornelius fell at Peter's feet and paid him homage, but Peter raised him up, protesting that he too was "a human being" (*anthropos,* 10:25–26). Conversing with Cornelius, Peter entered and found the many who had come together to hear him. Addressing the household of Cornelius, Peter said (10:28):

> "You know that it is unlawful for a Jewish man to associate with, or visit, a Gentile, but God has shown me that I should not call any person profane or unclean."

With the coming of the messengers from Cornelius, Peter had understood the vision he had received and showed them hospitality. Understanding the vision even more clearly, he now accepted the hospitality offered by Cornelius.

Replying to Peter, Cornelius told him about the vision he himself had received (10:30–33). This is the third time we hear about Cornelius' vision. The first time, the story was told by the narrator (10:1–8). The second time, it was told by the messengers at the home of Simon the tanner when Peter asked why they had come (10:22). The third time, it was told by Cornelius himself (10:30–33).

Peter responded with a great discourse, giving the theological, christological and ecclesiological basis for the mission to the Gentiles and for inviting them to the table of the Lord (10:34–43). After hearing Cornelius tell about his vision, Peter now saw that God "shows no partiality" (10:34). The discourse ends with the baptism of Cornelius and his household (10:44 – 49)

The discourse to the household of Cornelius is the fifth and last of Peter's missionary, kerygmatic discourses. The first was on Pentecost when Peter had addressed a crowd representing "every nation under heaven," of whom some three thousand were baptized (2:14 – 41). The second was in the Portico of Solomon after Peter cured a man crippled from birth (3:11 – 26). The third was after he and the others were arrested and brought before the Sanhedrin (4:8 – 12). The fourth was also given before the Sanhedrin in the form of a response to the high priest (5:29 – 32).

Until now, Peter's discourses had addressed the Jewish people in Jerusalem and their leaders. For the first time, Peter now addressed a large number of Gentiles. All of Peter's discourses include a number of basic elements. Each of them also adapts the basic message to a particular audience and situation. So does the discourse at the home of Cornelius.

The discourse can be divided into three parts, including an introduction, a body and a conclusion. In the introduction, Peter directly addresses the situation (10:34 – 35). The body gives the basis for the mission to the Gentiles (10:36 – 43). The conclusion tells that Cornelius and his household were baptized (10:44 – 49).[52]

Introduction: "God Shows No Partiality" (10:34 – 35)   Introducing the discourse, Peter makes two statements, one about God in relation to people, the other about people in relation to God.

> "In truth, I see that God shows no partiality. Rather, in every nation whoever fears him and acts uprightly is acceptable to him."

The meaning of Peter's vision became gradually more clear to him. At first, Peter was in doubt about its meaning (10:17) and pondered what it could meant (10:19). After the messengers from Cornelius told him about Cornelius' vision, the meaning became clear enough for him to invite them in, show them hospitality (10:23a) and accompany them to Caesarea (10:23b) to the home of Cornelius (10:25).

After listening to Cornelius tell about his own vision, it became even clearer. "In truth, I see." Peter finally realized the meaning of the vision. It showed that "God shows no partiality" (*ouk estin pro-sopolemptes,* literally, "is not partial"). The meaning of Peter's vision unfolded gradually. Listening to Cornelius, he finally understood that God does not favor one nation over the others.[53]

In every nation, everyone who fears *(phoboumenos)* God and brings about justice *(ergazomenos dikaiosynen)* is acceptable *(dektos)* to God (10:35). Cornelius, who is "devout and God-fearing *(phoboumenos)* along with his whole household, who used to give alms generously to the Jewish people and pray to God constantly" (10:2), is surely acceptable to God (see Proverbs 12:22; 15:8). As the angel of God told Cornelius, "Your prayers and almsgiving have ascended as a memorial offering before God" (Acts 10:4, 31). In the Septuagint, the term *dektos* (acceptable) is often associated with sacrifices that are acceptable to God. See, for example, Isaiah 56:7:

> Them I will bring to my holy mountain
> and make joyful in my house of prayer;
> Their holocausts and sacrifices
> will be acceptable *(dektai)* on my altar,
> For my house shall be called
> a house of prayer for all peoples.

In light of Peter's vision, Cornelius and his household became an example for a general principle: In every nation everyone who fears God and does justice is acceptable to him.

Body: "Jesus Christ, Who Is Lord of All" (10:36–43)   The body of Peter's discourse deals with the christological and ecclesiological basis for the mission to the Gentiles, in particular, for inviting the Gentiles to the *koinonia* and the breaking of the bread. Cornelius and his household were already devoted to the prayers. Peter's discourse is a good example of "the teaching of the apostles" (Acts 2:42), but as applied to Gentiles. Peter's discourse on Pentecost, addressed to Jews, emphasized that Jesus was the Christ, their long-awaited Messiah (2:14–41). At the home of Cornelius, Peter emphasized that Jesus Christ is the Lord of all.

The body of the discourse summarizes the story of Jesus as presented by Luke, beginning in Galilee after John preached and ending with Jesus' appearances to the disciples after he rose from the dead.

Recalling the preface of Acts (1:1–2) and part of the prologue (1:3–8), the summary highlights the basic themes of the Gospel and applies them to the universal mission of the church.

Peter begins by showing that God, who shows no partiality (10:34), sent the word *(ton logon)* through Jesus Christ to the Israelites (10:36–38).

> "You know the word [that God] sent to the Israelites as he proclaimed peace through Jesus Christ, who is Lord of all, what has happened all over Judea, beginning in Galilee after the baptism that John preached, how God anointed Jesus of Nazareth with the holy Spirit and power. He went about doing good and healing all those oppressed by the devil, for God was with him."

Anointed by God, Jesus of Nazareth (10:38) is Jesus Christ, the Lord of all (10:36).

If Jesus Christ is the Lord of all *(panton kyrios),* the message *(ton logon)* God sent through him was meant not only for the Israelites but for all. So was the good news of peace God announced *(euaggelizomenos eirenen)* through him (10:36). Since Jesus Christ is the Lord of all, what *(to hrema)*[54] happened in the whole of Judea, beginning in Galilee "after the baptism John preached" (Luke 3:1–22; see Luke 16:16; Acts 1:5) had to happen among the nations and to the ends of the earth (Acts 1:8).

"The word" *(hrema)* included "how God anointed Jesus of Nazareth with holy Spirit and power" and all of Jesus' ministry (see Luke 4:16–19). In all that Jesus did and taught, God was with him (Acts 10:37–38). As the word *(hrema)* continued to spread through the message *(logos)* of his witnesses, among both Jews and Gentiles, God would also be with them.

> "We are witnesses of all that he did both in the country of the Jews and [in] Jerusalem. They put him to death by hanging him on a tree. This man God raised [on] the third day and granted that he be visible, not to all the people, but to us, the witnesses chosen by God in advance, who ate and drank with him after he rose from the dead."

After summarizing the story of Jesus' ministry, Peter included himself among the witnesses *(martyres)* "of all that he did in the country of the Jews and [in] Jerusalem" (see also 2:32; 5:32). At the home of

Cornelius, Peter was fulfilling his mission as a witness, not only to Jesus' ministry in Galilee and Judea (see 10:37–39a) but to his death, resurrection and appearances in Jerusalem (10:39b–40). They put Jesus of Nazareth (10:37) to death, but God raised him to be the Lord of all (10:36) and granted that he be visible *(emphane)* to Peter and the other witnesses whom God had chosen in advance (19:41a).

Peter's witness even included how those chosen by God in advance became Jesus' witnesses when they "ate and drank with him after he rose from the dead" (10:41b). In this, Peter was referring primarily to when Jesus "presented himself alive" to the apostles, "appearing to them during forty days and speaking about the kingdom of God" (1:3; see also Luke 24:36–53). Those appearances took place in the context of meals, when Jesus shared salt with them *(synalizomenos,* 1:4).

Sharing salt with the apostles, Jesus shared his life and mission with them. Eating and drinking with Jesus after he rose from the dead, the apostles expressed their solidarity with Jesus Christ, the Lord of all. In solidarity with the Lord of all, Peter had no choice but to reach out to all. Assembling Jews and Gentiles for the breaking of the bread, the table of the Lord of all was meant for all.

Theologically, the mission to the Gentiles is based on God's mission of salvation in Jesus. Christologically, it is based on Jesus' identity as the Christ and the Lord of all. Ecclesiologically, it is based on Jesus sharing salt with the apostles and their eating and drinking at the table of the Lord of all. It is also based on Jesus' word to the apostles while they were eating and drinking with him. Biblically, it is based on the witness of all the prophets (10:42–43).

> "He commissioned us to preach to the people and testify *(dia-martyrasthai)* that he is the one appointed by God as the judge of the living and the dead. To him all the prophets bear witness *(martyrousin)* that everyone who believes in him will receive forgiveness of sins through his name."

Jesus commissioned those who ate and drank at the table of the Lord of all to witness to him "as the judge of the living and the dead." In this Jesus made explicit what was already implicit in their joining him at table.

In Jesus' final appearance at the end of the Gospel, Jesus had addressed the disciples: "Thus it is written that the Messiah would suffer and rise from the dead on the third day and that repentance, for the forgiveness of sins, would be preached in his name to all the nations, beginning from Jerusalem. You are witnesses of these things" (Luke 24:46–48). Then, the last time he appeared to them at the beginning of Acts, he told them: "You will be my witnesses in Jerusalem, throughout Judea and Samaria, and to the ends of the earth" (Acts 1:8).

At the home of Cornelius, Peter showed that, as the Lord of all, Jesus is "appointed by God as the judge of the living and the dead," that is, of the whole human race, past, present and future. In view of that, the apostles were commissioned as his witnesses to the nations, indeed to the ends of the earth. Having eaten and drunk with Jesus after he rose from the dead, the apostles and the church have an awesome responsibility. All who believe in Jesus Christ, the Lord of all, "will receive forgiveness of their sins through his name." Such is the witness of all the prophets (see Luke 24:25–27; 44–48; Acts 2:25–36; 3:24–26).

Conclusion: "The Holy Spirit Fell Upon All" (10:44–49)   Peter was still speaking when "the holy Spirit fell upon all who were listening to the word *(ton logon),*" (Acts 10:44; see 10:36), to the astonishment of those who accompanied Peter. The holy Spirit had come upon the apostles on Pentecost (2:1–4), as well as on some three thousand who listened to Peter proclaiming the word (2:38–41) and on Saul (9:17). It had fallen also on the Samaritans when Peter and John imposed hands on them (8:14–17). What they witnessed at the home of Cornelius was like a new Pentecost, with Gentiles speaking in tongues as the apostles had on Pentecost (10:45–46; 2:4, 8, 11).

Peter responded dramatically:

> "Can anyone withhold the water for baptizing these people, who have received the holy Spirit even as we have?"

Peter's vision, the vision of Cornelius and the good disposition of his household showed Peter that he could accept the hospitality of Gentiles and eat with them. After all that, even if Peter had wanted to deny baptism to Cornelius and his household, the holy Spirit would have forced his hand. He therefore ordered that all be baptized in the name of Jesus Christ. Just as Paul had stayed some days with the disciples in Damascus (9:19b), Peter, invited by Cornelius and the new Christian community gathered at his home, stayed with them for a few days (10:48).

Back in Jerusalem (11:1 – 18)

The apostles and the community in Judea had heard that the Gentiles had accepted the word *(ton logon)* of God through the witness of Peter (11:1 – 3; see 10:36, 44).

> So when Peter went up to Jerusalem the circumcised believers confronted him, saying, "You entered the house of uncircumcised people and ate with them."

What Peter had come to understand through his experience at the home of Simon the tanner and at the home of Cornelius the centurion was anything but clear to the other apostles and the Judean community. Peter had not only entered the home of people who were uncircumcised, he actually had eaten with them. In their eyes, associating with Gentiles made Peter himself unclean. Besides that, Peter had also eaten food that was unclean and profane.

Their reaction was similar to that of Peter when he fell into the trance and the voice told him to slaughter and eat what he saw in the vision. Peter was horrified and protested that he had never done that (10:13 – 14). Too, as Peter implied when he spoke to Cornelius, he had not previously associated with or gone to the home of a Gentile (10:28). In Jerusalem, the apostles and the Christians in Judea were now protesting that Peter had done both, visiting with Gentiles and eating food that was unclean.

Peter told them what happened step by step *(kathexes,* 11:4), first about his trance, what he saw, what he heard, what he answered and what he was told (11:5 – 10). Continuing step by step, he told them about the men sent from Caesarea, that the Spirit told him to accompany them without discriminating *(meden diakrinanta),* that he accompanied them with six others from the community in Joppa, that they entered the man's house and that the man told him about his own vision and what the angel had told him (11:11 – 14). In all this, Peter never referred to Cornelius by name. This was not about a particular case. At issue was the idea of Christians relating to Gentiles.

Peter then told them what happened afterward, that the holy Spirit fell on them, as it had on the apostles in the beginning, and that he remembered the word of the Lord: "John baptized with water but you will be baptized with the holy Spirit" (11:15 – 16; see 1:5; Luke 3:16). Concluding, Peter argued (11:17):

"If then God gave them the same gift he gave to us when we came to believe in the Lord Jesus Christ, who was I to be able to hinder God?"

There was no withholding the water for baptizing them. It would have been like trying to hinder God and his plan for salvation in Jesus Christ, the Lord of all.

When the apostles and the communities in Judea heard Peter's response,

they stopped objecting and glorified God, saying, "God has then granted life-giving repentance to the Gentiles too."

They no longer objected that Peter "entered the house of uncircumcised people and ate with them" (11:3). God, who exalted Jesus "as leader and savior to grant Israel repentance *(metanoian)* to Israel" (5:31), had granted the Gentiles the same "life-giving repentance" *(metanoian eis zoen)*.

Luke presents the story of Peter and Cornelius as a pivotal point in the development of the church as universal. With the precedent set by Peter, all was in place for the arrival of Christianity in Antioch (11:19–12:25). For that, Luke takes up the section's main story line, showing that the Word spread from Jerusalem to Antioch as a result of "the persecution that arose because of Stephen" (11:19; see 8:1–4).

At first, the ones who scattered spread throughout the countryside of Judea and Samaria (8:1). Philip went as far as Caesarea (8:40). Eventually, they "went as far as Phoenicia, Cyprus, and Antioch" (11:19).

It was at Antioch that Christians, notably Cypriots and Cyrenians among them, began to speak to the Greeks as well as to the Jews, "proclaiming the Lord Jesus" (11:20). Upon hearing that a great number of Greeks believed and turned to the Lord, the church in Jerusalem sent Barnabas to Antioch.

Recognizing that the grace of God was at work in the new community, Barnabas brought Saul to Antioch. Together the two met with the church, teaching for a whole year. It was at Antioch that the church first embraced both Jews and Gentiles. For that they had the precedent set by Peter at Caesarea. Realizing that their community was neither Jew nor Gentile (see Galatians 3:28), the disciples at Antioch needed a new name. "It was in Antioch that the disciples were first called Christians" (Acts 11:26).

The second section of Acts (6:1 — 12:25), devoted to the spread of the church from Jerusalem to Antioch, includes three stories with important implications for the eucharist.

The first showed that growth of the community and its growing ethnic and linguistic diversity required that the ministry *diakonia* be diversified (6:1 – 7). In a general assembly held in Jerusalem, the apostles appointed the Seven to minister at tables (*diakonein trapezais,* 6:2). That ministry would be exercised especially at the breaking of the bread, when the community gathered as a church on the first day of the week.

The second, the story of Paul's conversion, showed that faith and baptism required one not to eat with those who were opposed to the gospel. Eating and drinking with them would have expressed Saul's solidarity with them. On the other hand, to show solidarity with other Christians, one had to join them at table. If that was true for breaking bread daily in the home, it applied, a fortiori, to the breaking of the bread when the community assembled as a church on the first day of the week.

The third story, that of Peter and Cornelius' conversion (10:1 — 11:18), gave the basis for including the Gentiles in the church, making it a universal church. Since the breaking of the bread is an essential and constitutive element of the church, the presence of Gentiles had major implications regarding the observance of the Jewish kosher laws. God made everything clean so that Christians of Jewish background might go into the homes of Gentiles and eat and drink with them. Regarding the breaking of the bread, what was at stake primarily was the universality of the church.

In the fifth chapter, we shall see that the church at Antioch matured to the point of sending missionaries to other cities and regions, preaching to both Jews and Gentiles. After hearing Peter in Jerusalem, the Christians there accepted that the church was for both Jews and Gentiles. That meant that those who came from Judaism were free to eat and drink with those who came from the Gentile world.

But there were other questions. For example, did the Gentiles themselves have to observe the kosher laws? And were the Gentiles, like the Jews, expected to host the community at the breaking of the bread? Luke addressed these questions in the third section of Acts, telling the story of the missions from Antioch (13:1 — 19:20). At stake in the next section is primarily the unity of the church.

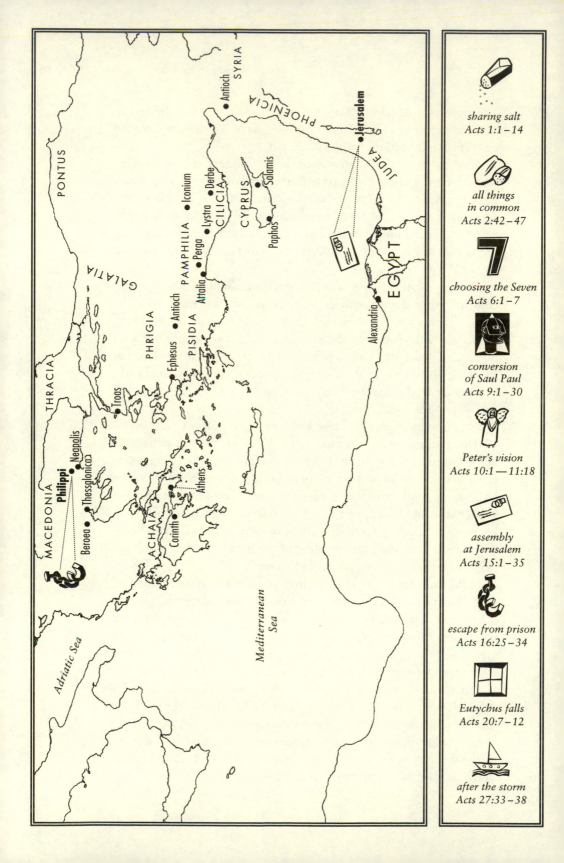

Map labels

PONTUS

GALATIA

THRACIA

MACEDONIA

Neapolis

Philippi

Thessalonica

Beroea

ACHAIA

Athens

Corinth

Troas

PHRIGIA

Ephesus • Antioch

PISIDIA

Attalia

Perga

PAMPHILIA

• Iconium

Lystra

Derbe

CILICIA

Antioch

SYRIA

PHOENICIA

Jerusalem

JUDEA

CYPRUS

Salamis

Paphos

EGYPT

Alexandria

Adriatic Sea

Mediterranean Sea

Side panel

sharing salt
Acts 1:1 – 14

all things
in common
Acts 2:42 – 47

choosing the Seven
Acts 6:1 – 7

conversion
of Saul Paul
Acts 9:1 – 30

Peter's vision
Acts 10:1 — 11:18

assembly
at Jerusalem
Acts 15:1 – 35

escape from prison
Acts 16:25 – 34

Eutychus falls
Acts 20:7 – 12

after the storm
Acts 27:33 – 38

Chapter V

The Missions from Antioch (13:1 — 19:20)

It is the decision of the holy Spirit and of us
not to place on you any burden
beyond these necessities,
namely, to abstain
from meat sacrificed to idols,
from blood,
from meats of strangled animals,
and from unlawful marriage.
If you keep free of these,
you will be doing what is right.
                    Acts 15:28 – 29

The first section of the Book of Acts presented the primitive community in Jerusalem as an ideal for all Christian communities (1:15 — 5:42). The second section described how the church spread from Jerusalem to Antioch, proclaiming the gospel to Gentiles as well as Jews (6:1 — 12:25). The third section tells about the missions from Antioch (13:1 — 19:20). Like the church in Antioch itself, the communities that sprang from its missions included both Jews and Gentiles.

Writing for the communities in the Pauline world three to four decades after Paul's missions from Antioch,[1] Luke emphasized aspects of the life of the church that would be most helpful for them. Luke wrote as a historian but also as a theologian: a historical theologian and a pastoral theologian.

In the first section of Acts (1:15 — 5:42), Luke's historical, theological and pastoral intentions find concrete expression in various stories, beginning with the choice of Matthias to replace Judas among the Twelve (1:15–26) and the descent of the Spirit on Pentecost (2:1–13). Luke's intentions are also revealed in several discourses given by Peter, beginning with the one on Pentecost (2:14–41). And they are revealed in a special way in three major summaries describing the life of the church in Jerusalem (2:42–47; 4:32–35; 5:12–16).

The first summary (2:42–47) follows immediately after the Pentecost event (2:1–13) and Peter's discourse (2:14–41). It describes the church, filled with the Spirit of Pentecost, responding to Peter's proclamation of the gospel.

Opening with a summary of its own, the first major summary (2:42–47) lists four elements that are essential for the life of a local church and for the church as a whole. The Christians in Jerusalem "devoted themselves to the teaching of the apostles and to the communal life, to the breaking of the bread and to the prayers" (2:42). Every other aspect of the life of the church flows from these four.

Each of the four elements, including "the breaking of the bread," had its roots in the life of Jesus and in the apostolic church. After Jesus broke bread with the apostles, he gave them a command: "Do this in memory of me" (Luke 22:19). As followers of Jesus, Peter and the Twelve obeyed his command, breaking bread with those who accepted the gospel of salvation and were baptized (Acts 2:41–42). As the apostle to the Gentiles, Paul also broke bread with the many communities formed by his preaching, such as the little church at the port of Troas (20:7–12).

Addressing Christianity's third generation, Luke reminded them that the breaking of the bread, like the teaching of the apostles, the *koinonia* and the prayers, was an essential element in the life of the church from the very beginning. The church in Jerusalem showed future generations how to devote themselves to the breaking of the bread as a primary expression of their life as Christians.

The second section of Acts (6:1–12-25) told how the church, with the teaching of the apostles and the common-union *(he koinonia),* the breaking of the bread and the prayers, spread from Jerusalem to Antioch. Heirs to the Pauline missions from Antioch, the church in Philippi, Thessalonica, Beroea, Corinth, Ephesus and many other cities had to know how the gospel and the church first came to Antioch and how the church in Antioch was related to the church in Jerusalem. For that, Luke told about the origin of the Seven, who were appointed by the apostles (6:1–7) and how they were related to the Twelve who were appointed by Christ (Luke 6:12–16).

Luke's readers needed to hear that the church in Antioch was born of a persecution that had scattered the Jerusalem community as far as Antioch. That same church in Antioch had sent Barnabas and Paul (Acts 13:1–3) and later Paul and Silas (15:36–41) on mission to them (13:1–3). Some of the Pauline communities also had experienced persecution, some of them from the very beginning, some later, some even as they were reading Luke's story of persecution in Acts.

While the growth of the church and its increasing ethnic diversity were a great blessing for the church, they also brought problems. Like persecution from without, conflict from within was also part of the life of the church from the beginning. That is why Luke introduced the second part of Acts (6:1—12:25) with a story of conflict in the community at Jerusalem (6:1–7). The conflict centered on ministry *(diakonia)*, including the ministry at tables *(diakonein trapezais)* when the community assembled as a church for the breaking of the bread.

The Pauline communities had to hear the story of Paul's conversion (9:1–31) and how the appearance of the Lord Jesus made a radical difference in Paul's life. Blinded by the light of Christ, Paul could not eat and drink with his former companions. Breaking bread and sharing life with them no longer had meaning for Paul. Once Paul heard the gospel of Jesus, regained his sight and was baptized, he ate with those who brought the gospel to him and shared the breaking of the bread with the community of the disciples in Damascus.

Conversion to Christ affects a person's relationships. *Koinonia* and the breaking of the bread are not without their demands. As Paul wrote to the Corinthians, "You cannot partake of the table of the Lord and of the table of demons" (1 Corinthians 10:21). Nor could Paul join Christians for the breaking of the bread and continue to break bread with those who persecuted them.

Finally, Luke's readers had to hear the story of Peter and Cornelius (Acts 10:1—11:18). Dying and rising, Jesus of Nazareth became the Lord of all. Those who ate and drank with Jesus as the Lord of all had to preach the gospel to all, to Gentiles as well as Jews. They also had to join at table with those who accepted the gospel and were baptized. Luke's readers also had to know that Peter had set a precedent for Paul in his mission to the Gentiles, and that the church in Jerusalem put its stamp of approval on what Peter had done at the home of Cornelius (11:1–18).

The third section of Acts now tells the story of Paul's missions from Antioch (13:1—19:20). The section can be divided into three parts. The first part tells about the first mission from Antioch, when Barnabas was the leader and Saul his associate (13:1 — 14:28).

The second part tells about the council of Jerusalem, and how it dealt with internal disunity over what should be expected of Gentile converts (15:1 – 35). The third part tells about the second mission from Antioch, when Saul was the leader and Silas his associate. This third part shows how the decisions made at the council of Jerusalem were implemented and bore fruit for the development of the church (15:36 — 19:20).[2]

Two stories in this third section have important implications for the eucharist. The first is the story of the council of Jerusalem, which settled a serious dispute regarding the obligation of Gentiles to observe the Jewish dietary laws (15:1 – 35). The second is a story about Gentile converts in Philippi who set a table and broke bread with Paul and his companions (16:25 – 34).

Overview of 13:1 — 19:20

Luke's story of the missions from Antioch shows that many churches had a common history and were part of a larger history of the church. All heard the same gospel. All responded to its call for repentance *(metanoia)*. All were baptized in the name of Jesus, and all received the same Spirit. Thanks to these missions, the church now included ecclesial communities in much of the eastern Mediterranean, all of them assembling for the breaking of the bread on the first day of the week (see 20:7 – 12) and all of them breaking bread daily in their homes (see 2:42 – 47).

As at Antioch, the gospel they received was addressed first to the Jews and then to the Gentiles, so that each church included members of Gentile as well as Jewish birth. As a result, the church at Antioch and the churches that sprang from its missions were very different from the church in Jerusalem, which stayed close to the synagogue and remained very Jewish in many respects.

Throughout this third section, Paul is the major figure. In the second section, we saw that when Peter went to Jerusalem he was confronted by those from Judea for entering the homes of Gentiles and eating with them (11:1 – 18). In the third section, we see that many went down to Antioch from Judea, demanding that the Gentiles in

Table VI

Setting for the Council of Jerusalem and the Meal with Gentiles at Philippi

13:1—19:20 The missions from Antioch

    The first mission from Antioch (13:1 – 28)
        The choice of Barnabas and Saul (13:1 – 3)
        In Cyprus, Perga, Antioch in Pisidia, Iconium, Lystra
          and Derbe (13:4 — 14:20)
        Return to Antioch (14:21 – 28)

    The Council of Jerusalem (15:1 – 35)
        Dissension and debate in Antioch (15:1 – 5)
        The council of Jerusalem (15:6 – 29)
            Discourse of Peter (15:6 – 11)
            Report of Paul and Barnabas (15:12)
            Discourse of James (15:13 – 21)
            The letter of the apostles (15:22 – 29)
        The delegates, Paul and Barnabas back in Antioch
        (15:30 – 35)

    The second mission from Antioch (15:36 — 19:20)
        Paul and Barnabas separate; Paul chooses Silas (15:36 – 41)
        In Lycaonia and Asia Minor (16:1 – 10)
        In Philippi (16:11 – 40)
            The conversion of Lydia (16:11 – 15)
            Paul and Silas imprisoned in Philippi (16:16 – 40)
                Imprisonment (16:16 – 24)
                Deliverance from prison (16:25 – 34)
                    Prayer and theophany (16:25 – 28)
                    Salvation, faith and the word of the Lord
                    (16:29 – 32)
                    Baptism followed by a meal (16:33 – 34)
                Official release (16:35 – 40)
        In Thessalonica, Beroea, Athens, Corinth, Antioch
          and Ephesus (17:1 — 19:20)

the community had to be circumcised and observe the Mosaic law. When Paul and Barnabas went to Jerusalem, they were confronted by many who objected to their missionary practice regarding the Gentiles (15:5).

The First Mission from Antioch   Opening the third section, Luke introduces a group of five prophets and teachers, prophetic teachers, in the church at Antioch. Among the five were Barnabas and Saul.[3] When the five were together, worshiping and fasting, the holy Spirit inspired them to set apart Barnabas and Saul for the work for which the holy Spirit had called them (13:2). When they finished fasting and praying, the prophetic teachers imposed hands on Barnabas and Saul and sent them on mission (13:3). In their mission Barnabas and Saul represented the whole church at Antioch.

According to Acts, this was the first time the church sent some of its members on mission to other cities and regions. Until now, the church had spread because of persecution (8:1, 4; 11:19–26; 12:1–19) or in response to a request for the word of God (10:5, 22–23, 33). Such circumstances would continue to be factors, but henceforth the church itself would take the missionary initiative to proclaim the gospel of Jesus.[4]

Luke introduces Barnabas as "Joseph, also named by the apostles Barnabas (which is translated 'son of encouragement'), a Levite, a Cypriot by birth" (4:36). As a member of the church in Jerusalem, he had sold a piece of property and placed the proceeds at the feet of the apostles (4:36–37). Barnabas was also the one who had introduced Saul to the community in Jerusalem (9:26–30) and brought Saul to Antioch, where the two met with the church and taught a large number of people (11:25–26). Later, Saul accompanied Barnabas on a relief misson to Judea (11:29–30; 12:25).

In the first mission, Barnabas was the leader and Saul his associate. The mission began in Cyprus,[5] where no less than the proconsul, Sergius Paulus, asked to hear the word of God and came to believe (13:4–12). While telling the story of Saul in Cyprus, Luke notes that Saul was also known by the name Paul (13:9). From that point on in the story of Acts, Saul is always called Paul, except when he himself tells the story of his conversion (22:7; 26:14).[6]

From Cyprus, Barnabas and Paul went on to Perga in Pamphylia and Antioch in Pisidia, where Paul addressed the synagogue on the sabbath. Like the discourse Jesus gave on a sabbath at the synagogue in Nazareth (Luke 4:16 – 30) and the discourse Peter gave in Jerusalem on Pentecost (Acts 2:14 – 40), the inaugural discourse Paul gave to the synagogue at Antioch in Pisidia is a keynote address, setting out Paul's basic message for the Jews (13:13 – 43). The following sabbath, Paul continued the discourse, adapting his message for the Gentiles (13:44 – 52), declaring: "For so the Lord commanded us, 'I have made you a light to the Gentiles, that you may be an instrument of salvation to the ends of the earth'" (13:47; see 1:8).

From his conversion in Damascus, Paul the persecutor (7:58; 8:1, 3, 9:1 – 2) became Paul the persecuted (9:23 – 25). Persecution continued to be part of his life, first in Antioch in Pisidia (13:50 – 51), then in Iconium (14:1 – 7). After Paul and Barnabas spoke to a large number of Jews and Greeks in the synagogue at Iconium (14:1), many Jews and Greeks were converted, but others, both Jews and Greeks, began persecuting them (14:2 – 7).

From Iconium, Paul and Barnabas went to Lystra, where Jews from Antioch in Pisidia and Iconium followed them and incited the crowd. After stoning Paul,[7] the crowd dragged him out of the city and left him for dead. But when the community gathered around him, Paul got up *(anastas)* and returned to the city. The following day, Paul and Barnabas went on to Derbe (14:8 – 20; see 14:6b – 7).

From Derbe, the two retraced their steps back to Lystra, Iconium and Antioch in Pisidia, appointing presbyters *(presbyteroi)*[8] in each church. With prayer and fasting,[9] they commended the churches to the Lord (14:21 – 23). From Pisidia, they returned to Perga in Pamphylia and went down to Attalia, the port from which they sailed to Antioch, "where they had been commended to the grace of God for the work they had now accomplished" (14:26; see 13:2 – 3).

Calling the church in Antioch together, Paul and Barnabas reported "what God had done with them and how he had opened the door of faith to the Gentiles" (14:27). So ended the first mission from the church at Antioch. Paul and Barnabas stayed with the disciples for a considerable time (14:28).

The Council of Jerusalem   After the first mission from Antioch (13:1 — 14:28), Luke tells about a great assembly in Jerusalem (15:1 – 35), often referred to as "the council of Jerusalem." Looking back, we may consider it a forerunner of the ecumenical councils that began with the Council of Nicaea (AD 325) and have characterized the history of the church down to our own time and the Second Vatican Council (AD 1962–1965). Historically, however, the council of Jerusalem was very different from an ecumenical council, since it was not an assembly representing all the churches.

While Paul and Barnabas were in Antioch, some Christians came from Judea teaching that circumcision according to the Mosaic practice was necessary for salvation (15:1). The ensuing dissension necessitated a consultation with the apostles and presbyters in Jerusalem (15:2–4). When Paul and Barnabas reported what God had done with them on behalf of the Gentiles, some of the Pharisees who had become believers demanded that Gentile converts had to observe the Mosaic law (15:5).

This was the occasion for the council of Jerusalem, as it is commonly called (15:6–21). At the end of the council, the assembly sent representatives with Paul and Barnabas back to Antioch with a letter for the Christians of Gentile origin in the church in Antioch, Syria and Cilicia (15:22–33). Returning to Antioch, Paul and Barnabas continued to teach and proclaim the word of the Lord (15:35; see 14:28).

The Second Mission from Antioch   After the apostolic council (15:1–35), Luke tells about the second mission from Antioch (15:36 — 19:20). Paul and Barnabas had stayed in Antioch, "teaching and proclaiming with many others (see 13:1) the word of the Lord" (15:35). But after some time, Paul spoke to Barnabas about visiting the cities where they had proclaimed the word of the Lord on their first mission. A dispute over taking John Mark[10] led them to follow separate ways. Barnabas left with Mark for Cyprus. Paul left with Silas, after being commended by the community to the grace of the Lord (see 13:3; 14:23), and traveled through Syria and Cilicia (15:36–41).

So began the second mission from Antioch (15:36 — 19:20). After the introduction (15:36–41), the story of the second mission focuses on Paul and Silas, who returned to Derbe and Lystra, where a disciple named Timothy joined them,[11] and then went on to Iconium. Traveling from city to city, "they handed on to the people for observance the decision reached by the apostles and presbyters in Jerusalem" (16:1–4; see 15:28–29). Summarizing the effects of their teaching, Luke adds that "day by day the churches grew stronger in faith and increased in number" (16:5; see 2:47; 6:7; 12:24).

The mission took them through Phrygian and Galatian territory and eventually to Troas, where Paul saw a Macedonian in a vision calling him to cross over into Macedonia (16:6 – 11). From Troas, Paul, Silas and Timothy then headed for Neapolis, the port of Philippi (16:11 – 12). Then follows the story of Paul's preaching and the beginning of the church in Philippi (16:13 – 40) and in Thessalonica (17:1 – 9). After that, it would be Beroea (17:10 – 15), Athens (17:16 – 34), Corinth (18:1 – 18) and Ephesus (18:19 – 20, 24 – 28; 19:1 – 20). Paul traveled to Ephesus with Priscilla and Aquila (18:18)[12] and left them there for a time while he paid a visit to Antioch (18:21 – 22).

Throughout the second mission, in practically every city, Paul encountered persecution, beginning at Philippi (16:19 – 40), but also at Thessalonica (17:5 – 9), Beroea (17:13 – 15) and Corinth (18:6, 12 – 17). At Athens, Paul was greeted with indifference (17:32 – 33). At the beginning of his great journey to Rome (19:21 — 28:31), Paul also encountered persecution at Ephesus (19:23 – 40).

In Relation to the Eucharist

Two stories in this third section of Acts have important implications for the eucharist: the story of the council of Jerusalem (15:1 – 35) and the story of Paul and Silas in Philippi when they were delivered from prison (16:25 – 34). The first story tells that an assembly of the whole church decided that the Gentiles were not bound by the Mosaic law and other Jewish laws and practices, many of which pertained to meals. The second story shows that, after being converted, a jailer welcomed Paul and Silas into his home and provided a meal, or more literally "set a table" *(paretheken trapezan)* for them, rejoicing with his whole household at having found faith in God (16:34).

In the story of Peter and Cornelius, we saw that Jews and Gentiles, once baptized, extended hospitality to one another, welcomed one another to their homes and joined one another at table for the breaking of the bread (10:1 — 11:18). For Christians whose roots were Jewish, this was an extraordinary development. It meant that they, Christians of Jewish background, could join Christians of Gentile background at the same table, most especially at the eucharistic table.

As the table of the Lord of all, the eucharistic table was meant for Gentiles as well as for Jews. For that, the story showed that food that God had made clean should not be called profane and unclean (10:14–15).

Jews and Gentiles who accepted the teaching of the apostles were baptized and welcomed into the church, and shared in the same *koinonia* (common-union). Assembling as a church, Jews and Gentiles also joined in the breaking of the bread. But did that mean that those with Gentile backgrounds were exempted from Jewish laws and practices regarding meals? In accepting baptism, did Gentiles also accept Judaism? Ultimately, when a Gentile became a Christian, did he also become a Jewish proselyte? If so, male Gentiles had to be circumcised.

In Jerusalem, where the Christians continued to observe Jewish laws and practices, many thought that Gentile converts should be circumcised and, like them, observe Jewish laws and practices, including those that regarded meals and their preparation. At issue was the very nature of Christianity. Was Christianity a form of Judaism, or did Christianity fulfill and transcend Judaism? These questions were critical when Christians gathered as a church for the breaking of the bread (see Galatians 2:11–14).

By Luke's time, the issue had already been resolved. Unlike the Pharisees, the Sadducees and the Essenes, the Christians were not just "a sect" *(hairesis)* within Judaism. The Jews in Jerusalem may have thought of them as "the sect of the Nazoreans" (*he ton Nazoraion hairesis,* see Acts 24:5; 14), but they were actually "the Way" (*he hodos,* see 18:26; 24:14), assuming Judaism within itself and transforming it. As a historian, Luke wanted to show how that came to be.

The section devoted to the missions from Antioch (13:1—19:20) raises the issue and addresses it from two points of view. After hearing a number of views, the council of Jerusalem decided that Gentile converts were not subject to laws that were specific to Jewish life, including those regarding meals. This decision applied to the meals they took in their homes as well as to the breaking of the bread on the first day of the week when they assembled as a church (15:1–35).

The story of the deliverance of Paul and Silas from jail shows how the decision of the council was implemented. Gentile converts were not subject to the Jewish dietary laws, and Jewish converts were able to join Gentiles and eat at their table. The decision of the apostolic council applied to meals taken on ordinary days as well as to the breaking of the bread on the first day of the week. The story also shows that Gentile converts, after baptism, hosted the whole community, including converts from Judaism, for the breaking of the bread. In the breaking of the bread, as in other expressions of Christian life, "there is neither Jew nor Greek" (see Galatians 3:28). All were now Christians (see 11:26).

The Council of Jerusalem (15:1 – 35)

And when they arrived,
they called the church together and reported
what God had done with them
and how he had opened the door of faith
to the Gentiles.
                Acts 14:27

In the first mission from Antioch, many Gentiles became members of the church, thanks to the work of Barnabas and Paul (13:1 — 14:28). Before this, Gentile converts may have been considered exceptional. At Caesarea, there was Cornelius and his household (10:1 — 11:18). At Antioch, a large number of Greeks had believed and turned to the Lord (11:20 – 21). After the first mission from Antioch, there were also Sergius Paulus, the Roman proconsul at Paphos in Cyprus (13:4 – 12) and many Gentiles who heard Barnabas and Paul proclaiming Jesus in Antioch in Pisidia (13:46 – 49) and in Iconium (14:1).

While at Antioch in Pisidia, Paul and Barnabas decided to focus their mission on the Gentiles: "For so the Lord has commanded us, 'I have made you a light to the Gentiles, that you may be an instrument of salvation to the ends of the earth'" (13:47). At the end of the first mission, Barnabas and Paul returned to Antioch and "reported what God had done with them," announcing that God "had opened the door of faith to the Gentiles" (14:27).

By the end of the first mission (circa AD 49), the mission to the Gentiles was accepted in principle and in fact, at least in Antioch and wherever Barnabas and Paul preached the gospel. It was God's doing that the community at Antioch and the communities established during the first mission included Gentiles and Jews.

In Jerusalem, however, there had always been a great deal of resistance to the Gentile mission. Even by this time, while Gentile converts to the Lord were becoming more and more numerous in the diaspora, the church in Jerusalem remained exclusively made up of converts who came from Judaism and continued to observe the Mosaic law and the Jewish practices including the ancient dietary laws (see 21:20).

Recall that after the conversion of Cornelius, when Peter went up to Jerusalem, he was confronted by circumcised believers for entering the home of uncircumcised people and eating with them. In response, Peter told them about his vision and explained to them step by step how he had pondered the vision and how he finally came to understand what it meant. After hearing him, the circumcised believers stopped objecting and glorified God: "God has then granted life-giving repentance to the Gentiles too" (11:1–18). The implications of that "life-giving repentance," however, were far from clear.

Recall, too, how the church in Jerusalem responded when they heard that a large number of Greeks in Antioch were turning to the Lord. At first, those who had been scattered by the persecution in Jerusalem spoke the word only to Jews, even when they reached Antioch. Eventually, however, some Christians from Cyprus and Cyrene began to speak also to Greeks, and many Greeks were converted. With that, the mission to the Gentiles began in earnest (11:19–21). When news reached Jerusalem, the church sent Barnabas to investigate (11:19–22).

When Barnabas arrived at Antioch "and saw the grace of God, he rejoiced and encouraged them all to remain faithful to the Lord in firmness of heart" (11:23). After that, he went to seek out Saul, brought him back to Antioch and together "they met with the church and taught a large number of people" (11:25–26a).[13]

Barnabas rejoiced at seeing the grace of God in the Christian community at Antioch, and, surely, many in Jerusalem also rejoiced at seeing so many Gentiles embrace the faith. They rejoiced as any good and righteous Jews would have done. Jewish communities also were welcoming a growing number of Gentile proselytes to the synagogue. Like them, the Christians in Jerusalem thought of Gentile converts as proselytes. And like the Jewish communities, the church in Jerusalem expected the Gentiles to observe the Mosaic law.

Earlier, when the church had sent Barnabas to investigate what they heard about the community in Antioch, Barnabas approved of what he saw and, with the help of Saul, took an active part in the formation of the new community. Now, as the Antiochene community continued to grow, with more and more Gentiles, other members of the church came to see for themselves. Unlike Barnabas, however, they did not see the grace of God. Nor did they rejoice or encourage the community "to remain faithful to the Lord in firmness of heart" (11:23).

We must remember that the form of Christianity that was developing at Antioch was very new. The members of the community came from the Gentile as well as from the Jewish world, and they formed one community, participating in the same common-union *(koinonia)* enjoyed by the primitive community in Jerusalem (2:42). After hearing the word, being baptized and receiving the holy Spirit, a member of the community was neither Jew nor Gentile, but Christian. As Christian, the believing community represented a new reality, one that was spreading beyond Antioch through the missions from Antioch.

It was not by accident that the disciples in Antioch were the first to be called Christians (11:26). The term "Christian" was closely tied to the experience of Antioch, where both Jews and Gentiles assembled as a church and broke bread together on an equal basis and without distinctions. A new experience and a new reality called for a new name. At Antioch, the name chosen was "Christian."

While Paul and Barnabas were at Antioch, adherents of the old observance and proponents of the new dispensation met and clashed. This led the community at Antioch to send Paul and Barnabas and some others to Jerusalem. Some of the believers in Jerusalem, those who had come from the party of the Pharisees, brought the matter to a head. The apostles and the presbyters then called what is known as the council of Jerusalem.

The story begins with an introduction, showing the circumstances that led Paul, Barnabas and the others from Antioch to go to Jerusalem (15:1 – 5). The body describes the council itself and how it resolved the "Gentile question" (15:6 – 29). The conclusion shows that Paul, Barnabas and the others returned to Antioch (15:30 – 35).

Dissension and Debate in Antioch (15:1 – 5)

The introduction opens with some "brothers" from Judea coming to Antioch, insisting that circumcision is necessary for salvation (15:1).

> Some who had come down from Judea were instructing the
> brothers, "Unless you are circumcised according to the Mosaic
> practice, you cannot be saved."

The view of the brothers from Judea was straightforward. It was
not that the Gentiles were excluded from the church, but if the
Gentiles wanted to be members, they had first to become Jews. The
gospel of salvation was for the Jewish people, including Jewish proselytes. If Gentiles wanted to be saved, they had to be circumcised.
Their position was that there was no salvation without circumcision.

Salvation is a basic theme at the very heart of "the teaching of
the apostles" (2:42). For the apostles, salvation came through the
person of Jesus: "There is no salvation through anyone else, nor is
there any other name under heaven given to the human race by
which we are to be saved" (4:12). But did that mean that Gentiles
were exempted from the Mosaic practice of circumcision? Was not
Jesus himself circumcised when he received the name Jesus, eight
days after his birth (2:21)?

The instruction given by those who came from Judea led to dissension and debate, pointing to serious disunity not in the community of Antioch itself but between them and those who came from
Judea (15:2).

> Because there arose no little dissension and debate by Paul and
> Barnabas with them, it was decided that Paul, Barnabas, and
> some of the others should go up to Jerusalem to the apostles
> and presbyters about this question.

To resolve the dissension and debate and bring about unity, the
community sent Paul and Barnabas on an embassy to Jerusalem.
Those who accompanied them were of like mind. On the way Paul
and Barnabas passed through Phoenicia and Samaria, spreading the
good news of the conversion of the Gentiles (15:3).

> They were sent on their journey by the church, and passed
> through Phoenicia and Samaria telling of the conversion of the
> Gentiles, and brought great joy to all the brothers.

Those who had scattered because of the persecution in Jerusalem
(see 8:1–4) had gone "as far as Phoenicia, Cyprus, and Antioch,
preaching the word to no one but Jews" (11:19). Later, Paul returned
to Phoenicia on his way to Jerusalem when his ship put in at Tyre,
and he spent a week with the disciples there. The account assumes

that the Christians in Tyre knew Paul very well (21:3 – 6).[14] The story of the evangelization of Samaria is told after the martyrdom of Stephen, as part of Philip's mission (8:5 – 25).[15]

In Jerusalem, Paul and Barnabas were welcomed by the church, together with the apostles and the presbyters (15:4).

> When they arrived in Jerusalem, they were welcomed by the church, as well as by the apostles and the presbyters, and they reported what God had done with them.

After hearing Paul and Barnabas, the community as a whole apparently accepted what they had done regarding Gentile converts. But there were exceptions, namely those who had come from the party of the Pharisees (15:5).[16]

> But some from the party of the Pharisees who had become believers stood up and said, "It is necessary to circumcise them and direct them to observe the Mosaic law."

The disagreement of those who had come from the party of the Pharisees was the immediate occasion for the council of Jerusalem.

The Council (15:6 – 29)

To resolve the question the apostles and the presbyters came together as a church (15:6; see 15:22).

> The apostles and the presbyters met together to see about this matter.

Besides the apostles and the presbyters,[17] Paul and Barnabas and those who came with them from Antioch, the council included the whole church in Jerusalem (*pan to plethos,* 15:12; *syn hole te ekklesia,* 15:22).

The story of the council unfolds in three phases. Beginning with a discourse by Peter (15:7 – 12), the story continues with a discourse by James (15:13 – 21) and concludes with the decision of the church (15:22 – 29).

Discourse of Peter   In his discourse, Peter reminded the community in Jerusalem that Cornelius and his household were converted (15:7b – 9) and that they should learn from it (15:10 – 11).

First, Peter addressed the assembly concerning the mission to the Gentiles (15:7–12), recalling how Cornelius and his household were converted when God first granted the holy Spirit to the Gentiles as God had done to the Jews (see 2:1–4). In the conversion of Cornelius, God made no distinction between Gentiles and Jews, purifying *(katharisas)* the hearts of the Gentiles by faith *(te pistei)* as God did for the Jews (15:5–9).

With the emphasis on faith, Peter now had an even fuller understanding of what God had revealed to him in prayer at the home of Simon the tanner. Peter's growth in understanding came progressively, in four steps.

- In his vision at Joppa, Peter was told: "What God has made clean *(ekatharisen),* you are not to call profane" (10:15).

- Before the household of Cornelius in Caesarea, he understood that "what God has made clean" applied not only to food but to persons: "God has shown me that I should not call any person profane or unclean *(akatharton)*" (10:28). Then, when Cornelius' household received the holy Spirit, Peter understood that nothing prevented them from being baptized (10:44–48) just as nothing prevented him from staying with them (10:49).

- Telling the story in Jerusalem, Peter saw those who God made clean *(ekatharisen,* 11:9) and received the holy Spirit. If so, God had granted them "life-giving repentance" (11:18).

- Now, at the council of Jerusalem, Peter understood even better that it is through faith *(te pistei)* that God purified *(katharisas)* their hearts (15:9).

Concluding the address, Peter then argued (15:10–11):

"Why then, are you now putting God to the test by placing on the disciples a yoke that neither our ancestors nor we have been able to bear?

On the contrary, we believe that we are saved through the grace of the Lord Jesus, in the same way as they."

Peter referred to Jesus as the Lord, that is, the Lord of all, as he had at the household of Cornelius (10:36). Salvation comes through the grace of the Lord Jesus, not through circumcision.

In the Gospel, Jesus had addressed much the same question while dining at the home of a Pharisee (Luke 11:37–54).[18] When people observed that Jesus "did not observe the prescribed washing before the meal" (11:38), Jesus challenged the Pharisees (11:39 – 44) and the scholars of the law (11:45 – 52).

Addressing the Pharisees, Jesus accused them of cleansing "the outside of the cup and the dish," while inside they remained filled with plunder and evil (11:39). Addressing the scholars of the law, he accused them of imposing "on people burdens hard to carry," that they themselves did "not lift one finger to touch them" (11:46).

In this first phase, Peter addressed the matter in general, showing that, like Jews, Gentiles "are saved through the grace of the Lord Jesus" (Acts 15:11). In that, Peter recapitulated what he had learned from his experience at Joppa, Caesarea and Jerusalem, emphasizing that God did not make distinction between "us and them" (see 10:34 – 35; 11:12, 17 – 18).

On leaving Caesarea, Peter had gone up to Jerusalem (11:1 – 18). Meeting with the community, he told them why he had gone to the home of Gentiles and had eaten with them: "If then God gave them the same gift he gave to us when we came to believe in the Lord Jesus Christ, who was I to be able to hinder God?" (11:17). Now, addressing the full assembly of the church in Jerusalem, Peter went further. Since God made no distinction, they should not impose a burden on the Gentiles, especially one that they themselves could not bear. That would be testing God (11:10).

Before Peter began to speak, there had been much debate (15:7a). After he finished, "the whole assembly fell silent" (15:12a). The assembly then listened "while Paul and Barnabas described the signs and wonders God had worked among the Gentiles through them" (15:12b). When Paul and Barnabas finished speaking and the whole assembly again fell silent, James began to speak.

The Discourse of James   In the second phase of the council, James addressed some specific matters (15:13 – 21), bringing the discussion a step further in light of the debate in Antioch and the demands made by the believers from the party of the Pharisees.

James had been first introduced in Acts when Peter went to the home of Mary, "the mother of John who is called Mark" (12:12), where many were gathered in prayer. Explaining how "the Lord had led him out of the prison," Peter had asked that they "report this to

James and the brothers" (12:17). Now, at the council of Jerusalem, James appeared as the leader of the whole church in Jerusalem.

In his discourse, James began by concurring with what Peter had said in the opening discourse (15:13 – 14) and by supporting Peter's position with words from the prophets (15:15 – 19).

> "My brothers, listen to me. Symeon has described how God first concerned himself with acquiring from among the Gentiles a people for his name."

In his discourse, Peter had attributed the conversion of the Gentiles to God. So did James. Note that James referred to Peter as Symeon, not as Simon (see Luke 24:34). Simon was a Hellenized version of the Hebrew name Symeon. In this we recognize a delicate rhetorical touch emphasizing Peter's Jewish and Hebrew-speaking background (see Acts 6:1). Recall that the assembly included many who took their Jewish background very seriously and clung tenaciously to Jewish customs and laws.

James then supported Symeon's description of what God had done, with "words of the prophets."

> "The words of the prophets agree with this, as is written: 'After this I shall return and rebuild the fallen hut of David; from its ruins I shall rebuild it and raise it up again, so that the rest of humanity may seek out the Lord, even all the Gentiles on whom my name is invoked. Thus says the Lord who accomplishes these things, known from of old.'"

It is not that the will of God concerning the Gentiles is revealed or finds proof in the fulfillment of the prophets. Rather, the meaning of the words of the prophets and their fulfillment is revealed by what God had done and what Peter had described.

James' position was not based on the fulfillment of prophecy. He began with what God had done, as told by Peter. He then showed that the prophets concur with what God had done and with Peter's description of it (Acts 15:7 – 11).

In the process, James applied "the words of the prophets" to the conversion of the Gentiles. "The words of the prophets" refer to several prophetic passages (Jeremiah 12:15; Amos 9:10 – 12; Isaiah 45:21, all from the LXX) and present them in a theological synthesis. The main passage is from Amos 9:11 – 12. The introduction, however, "After then I shall return," is from Jeremiah 12:15, and the conclusion, "known from of old," is implied in Isaiah 45:21.

The words of the prophet Amos are extremely well chosen. Quoting Amos 9:11 – 12 from the Septuagint, James interpreted the passage messianically, applying it to the restoration of the kingdom of David and its transformation into a kingdom for all peoples. In Jesus the kingdom of David is fulfilled in the kingdom of God (see Luke 1:32 – 33).

James began by giving the rationale for his decision, allowing the community and Luke's readers to consider the same evidence (Acts 15:13 – 18). He then gave his decision (15:19 – 21). Peter had proceeded in the same way, giving the rationale (15:7 – 9) and offering his decision (15:10 – 11).

From what God had done, what Peter described and from the words of the prophets, James' conclusion began by reaffirming Peter's conclusion (15:19). He then added four important stipulations, indicating what Gentile converts to Christianity must avoid (15:20 – 21).

> "It is my judgment, therefore, that we ought to stop troubling the Gentiles who turn to God, but tell them by letter to avoid pollution from idols, unlawful marriage, the meat of strangled animals and blood. For Moses, for generations now, has had those who proclaim him in every town, as he has been read in the synagogues every sabbath."

Gentile converts must avoid pollution from idols, unlawful marriage, eating meat from animals slaughtered by strangling and eating or drinking blood.

The laws that continued to apply to the Gentiles were considered more basic than circumcision and the other dietary laws. Like Christians of Jewish origin, Christians of Gentile origin should not participate in pagan religious meals held at a temple honoring a particular god. *Koinonia* and solidarity with those devoting themselves to an idol are incompatible with Christian *koinonia* and solidarity.

Paul would deal with idols and the religious meals that were part of their worship in 1 Corinthians: "The cup of blessing that we bless, is it not a participation *(koinonia)* in the blood of Christ? The bread that we break, is it not a participation *(koinonia)* in the body of Christ? . . . I do not want you to become participants *(koinonous)* with demons. You cannot drink the cup of the Lord and also the cup of demons. You cannot partake of the table of the Lord and of the table of demons" (1 Corinthians 10:16 – 21).[19]

The Gentiles, then, should not be subject to ordinary Jewish dietary laws, nor to the various ritual purifications connected with preparing a meal. In Mark's Gospel, Jesus had dealt with dietary laws and the whole matter of ritual purifications in a very similar context (7:1–23). In Mark, as in Acts, it was a matter of objections made by Pharisees regarding ritual purifications. In both, it was also a matter of the mission to the Gentiles and its implications for the eucharist.

In the context of Mark, Jesus had just broken bread for a crowd of five thousand (6:34–44) and made the disciples get into a boat to cross over to Bethsaida, a Greek city in the Decapolis (6:45–52). The disciples, however, failed to cross over. Instead, they came to land at Gennesaret, not far from where they left (6:53). Jesus then addressed what had become a basic problem, the traditional ritual purifications (7:1–23), preventing those of Jewish backgound from going to the Gentiles and breaking bread with them (see 8:1–10).

An Embassy with a Letter to Antioch (15:30–35)

As in the two previous assemblies of the church, the decision was made with the church. For the choice of Judas's successor, Peter had proposed to the assembly that one of those who had been with them from the baptism of John to the day Jesus was taken up should become a witness to the resurrection (see Luke 24:48; Acts 1:8; 10:41). That assembly of 120 persons proposed two candidates. After this, they prayed and drew lots (Acts 1:15–26).

Later, to resolve a complaint from the Hellenists in the community at Jerusalem, the Twelve had assembled the community and presented a proposal to them. They should select "seven reputable men, filled with the Spirit and wisdom" to minister at tables. The proposal was accepted, seven were selected by the assembly and the Twelve "prayed and laid hands on them" (6:1–7).

Now, after hearing Peter (15:6–11), Paul and Barnabas (15:12) and James (15:13–21), the church in Jerusalem accepted the proposals made by James (15:22).

> Then the apostles and presbyters, in agreement with the whole church, decided to choose representatives and to send them to Antioch with Paul and Barnabas. The ones chosen were Judas, who was called Barsabbas, and Silas, leaders among the brothers.

Silas later became Paul's companion in the second mission from Antioch. As a member of the Christian community in Jerusalem

(15:22), he delivered the letter from the church in Jerusalem to the church in Antioch. Spending time in Antioch, Judas and Silas "exhorted and strengthened the brothers with many words" and were sent back to Jerusalem with greetings of peace from the community at Antioch. "After some time" (15:36), Silas must have returned to Antioch (see 15:40).

Here is the letter that the church in Jerusalem sent to the church in Antioch (15:23 – 29):

> "The apostles and the presbyters, your brothers, to the brothers in Antioch, Syria, and Cilicia of Gentile origin: greetings. Since we have heard that some of our number [who went out] without any mandate from us have upset you with their teachings and disturbed your peace of mind, we have with one accord decided to choose representatives and to send them to you along with our beloved Barnabas and Paul, who have dedicated their lives to the name of our Lord Jesus Christ. So we are sending Judas and Silas who will also convey this same message by word of mouth: 'It is the decision of the holy Spirit and of us not to place on you any burden beyond these necessities, namely, to abstain from meat sacrificed to idols, from blood, from meats of strangled animals, and from unlawful marriage. If you keep free of these, you will be doing what is right. Farewell.'"

The decision was that the Christians of Gentile origin did not have to observe the Mosaic law (see 15:5), in particular the laws regarding food and its preparation. The letter mentioned the same four stipulations that James mentioned in his address to the assembly (15:20), but in a different order[20] and in one case with a different wording (see also 21:25). James had proposed that the letter ask them "to avoid pollution from idols." The letter specifies further that they should "abstain from meat sacrificed to idols."[21]

In the second mission from Antioch, Paul implemented the decision that had been made in Jerusalem. As Paul, Silas and Timothy "traveled from city to city, they handed on to the people for observance the decisions reached by the apostles and presbyters in Jerusalem" (16:4).

At Table with Gentiles (16:25–34)

And God, who knows the heart,
bore witness by granting them the holy Spirit
just as he did us.
He made no distinctions
between us and them,
for by faith he purified their hearts.
                    Acts 15:8–9

The church now had a general policy concerning Christians of Gentile origin. For years, many Gentiles had been part of the church, at least in the diaspora. At Jerusalem, at least in the eyes of some, the status of Christians of Gentile origin was now comparable to that of Gentiles who embraced the Jewish faith.

If Gentiles could become Jews, Gentiles surely could become Christians. But the question remained: To become Christians did Gentiles first have to become Jews and follow the Mosaic law? The question had major implications for the celebration of the eucharist. At the breaking of the bread, did the Christians of Gentile origins have to observe the Jewish dietary laws? The letter from the church in Jerusalem addressed the question directly. No, Christians of Gentile origin did not have to observe the Jewish dietary laws. But they did have to observe those basic laws which they applied to all human beings.

Another question remained: Could Christians of Jewish origin who did observe the dietary laws eat with Christians of Gentile origin who were not bound by these laws and did not observe them? That question also had major implications for the celebration of the eucharist. Could Christians of Jewish and Gentile origin gather at the same table for the breaking of the bread? At stake was the unity of the church.

Implicitly, the council of Jerusalem had answered the question. The story of Paul eating at the tables of Gentile converts at Philippi made it explicit. Philippi was the first major stop on Paul's mission after the great assembly in Jerusalem, the first opportunity to carry out the assembly's decision concerning the Gentiles. Paul did this at the home of Lydia, a Gentile woman, who offered hospitality to Paul and his companions, and at the home of the jailer, who invited them to his home and set tables for them.

Early in the second mission, Paul had a vision in which a Macedonian pleaded with him to come to Macedonia and help them. At the time, Paul was at Troas (Acts 16:8 – 9). Accompanied by Silas, Timothy and possibly Luke,[22] Paul set sail for Neapolis, the port of Philippi, where they stayed for some time.

Philippi, a Roman colony, was the first city in Macedonia that Paul evangelized. At a place of prayer *(proseuche)*[23] outside the city, he spoke to a group of women, including one named Lydia, a Gentile woman but a God-fearer, that is, one who associated herself with the Jewish community and Jewish worship (see 13:16).

Lydia was the first convert in Philippi. After she and her household were baptized, she extended hospitality to Paul and his companions (16:13 – 15).[24] Later, when Paul and his companions were released from prison, they returned to her home, where the fledgling Christian community of Philippi assembled (16:40). The early Christian community assembled at the home of Lydia. Offering hospitality, of course, included offering something to eat.

On the way to the place of prayer *(eis ten proseuchen)*, Paul drove out an oracular spirit from a slave girl. The girl had brought a fortune to her owners by her power of divination (16:16). But without the oracular spirit, "their hope for profit was gone" (16:19), and so the owners had Paul and his companions put in prison.[25]

The story of Paul's deliverance from prison (16:25 – 40) is significant for the development of the eucharist. The story of Lydia's baptism and her offer of hospitality suggests that Paul may have broken bread at her home (16:15, 40), but that story does not use any of the terms associated with the breaking of the bread. The story of Paul's deliverance from prison does.

The story can be divided into two parts. The first begins at midnight (16:25 – 34). It tells that a great earthquake set Paul and his companions free and how the jailer reacted (16:25 – 27). It continues with the jailer's conversion and a meal at his home (16:28 – 34).[26] The second part begins the following morning, when Paul and his companions were formally released from prison (16:35 – 40). Only the first part concerns us. The second tells how Paul and Silas were released by the city magistrates.

Prayer and Theophany (16:25–28)

It was around midnight (*kata de to mesonyktion,* see 20:7 and 27:27, 33) and Paul and Silas were at prayer, when suddenly a severe earthquake shook the prison (16:25–26).

> About midnight, while Paul and Silas were praying and singing hymns to God as the prisoners listened, there was suddenly such a severe earthquake that the foundations of the jail shook; all the doors flew open, and the chains of all were pulled loose.

The severe earthquake came while Paul and Silas were at prayer, singing hymns to God. An ordinary earthquake would have collapsed the roof and crumbled the walls of the prison, killing everyone inside. In this case, the earthquake simply opened the doors of the prison and loosened the shackles of the prisoners.

This was not an ordinary earthquake, but a theophany, an extraordinary manifestation of God's presence, responding to the prayer of Paul and Silas. The earthquake is reminiscent of the manifestation at Sinai, when Moses led the people to meet God and the whole mountain trembled violently (Exodus 19:16–19). It also evokes the call of Isaiah, when the frame of the door of the temple shook (Isaiah 6:1–13, see 6:4).

> When the jailer woke up and saw the prison doors wide open, he drew [his] sword and was about to kill himself, thinking that the prisoners had escaped. But Paul shouted out in a loud voice, "Do no harm to yourself; we are all here."

Awakened by the earthquake, the jailer saw that the doors of the prison were wide open. Thinking that the prisoners had escaped, he drew his sword to kill himself (16:27). But Paul shouted out to him that all of them were there (16:28), including those who had listened as "Paul and Silas were praying and singing hymns to God" (16:25)

The story has parallels with a later story, that of the breaking of the bread at Troas (20:7–12). That story is in the last part of Acts, at the beginning of Paul's final journey (19:21–28:31) when he returned from Macedonia to Troas. Proclaiming the word to the community in Troas, Paul spoke until midnight (*mechri mesonyktion,* 20:7). In the prison at Philippi, Paul and Silas were praying with hymns to God around midnight (*kata de to mesonyktion*).

At Troas, as Paul prolonged the word, a young man fell asleep and fell to his death (20:9). At Philippi, the prayers of Paul and Silas brought on the earthquake, and the jailer picked up the sword to kill himself. At Troas, Paul went down, threw himself on the boy and declared that he was alive (20:10). At Philippi, Paul shouted out and stopped the jailer from killing himself.

Prayer and the ministry of the word (see 6:4) do not bring death to anyone but life and salvation.

Salvation, Faith and the Word of the Lord (16:29 – 32)

The jailer then came to Paul and Silas. Bringing them out, he asked what he had to do to be saved (16:29 – 32).

> He asked for a light and rushed in and, trembling with fear, he fell down before Paul and Silas. Then he brought them out and said, "Sirs, what must I do to be saved?" And they said, "Believe in the Lord Jesus and you and your household will be saved." So they spoke the word of the Lord to him and to everyone in the house.

Having witnessed the saving power of God (16:27 – 28) and finding everyone still inside, the jailer was filled with fear *(entromos)*. The earthquake was not an ordinary earthquake, but a manifestation of God's presence. His fear was not an ordinary fear, but a response to the divine manifestation. Seeing Paul and Silas still in the prison along with the other prisoners, he associated them with the theophany and fell before them. Surely there was something extraordinary about these prisoners.

Taking them outside, he said to them, "Sirs, what must *(dei)* I do to be saved *(sotho)*?" Like the earthquake and the jailer's fear, the question was extraordinary. Worded in the Christian vocabulary developed in the early church, it speaks of prophetic necessity *(dei)* and salvation *(sotho)*,[27] alerting us that the story is to be read from the point of view of faith. The jailer's question makes sense only in a Christian environment with a long tradition.

In Luke's Gospel the themes of prophetic necessity and salvation were brought together in the story of Zacchaeus: "Zacchaeus, come down quickly, for today I must *(dei)* stay at your house" (Luke 19:5); "Today salvation *(soteria)* has come to this house" (19:9). Later in

Acts, in Paul's journey to Rome, they were again brought together when Paul broke the bread on a ship at the height of a storm (see Acts 27:24 and 31, 33–38).

Responding to the jailer's question, Paul and Silas told him to believe *(pisteuson)* in the Lord Jesus. Believing, he and his household *(ho oikos)* will be saved *(sothese)*. Belief in the Lord Jesus leads to salvation. Paul and Silas then spoke the word of the Lord *(ton logon tou kyriou)* to him and to all in his house.

Baptism Followed by a Meal (16:33–34)

After Paul and Silas spoke the word of the Lord to the jailer and his household, the jailer attended to their wounds. The rest of the episode tells that they were baptized (16:33) and that they provided a meal for Paul and Silas (16:34).

> He took them in at that hour of the night and bathed their wounds; then he and all his family were baptized at once. He brought them up into his house and provided a meal and his household rejoiced at having come to faith in God.

The sequence of events began with Paul and Silas praying and singing hymns around midnight. That is when God manifested himself in the earthquake. Awakened, the jailer saw the doors open and drew a sword to kill himself. Stopped by Paul, he asked for a light and ran to them.

The story does not tell how long the dialogue among Paul, Silas and the jailer lasted. Nor does it tell how long Paul and Silas spoke the word of the Lord to the jailer and his household. Normally it would have taken quite a long time.

Here in the story Luke provides a short summary of the dialogue (16:30–31):

> "Sirs, what must I do to be saved?"
> "Believe in the Lord Jesus and you and your household will be saved."

The summary presupposes that the jailer knew about the Lord Jesus, about having faith in him and about Christian salvation. Such a summary would have been appropriate after a period of evangelization and catechesis, as part of a baptismal liturgy.

The period of evangelization and catechesis is also given in summary form:

> So they spoke the word of the Lord to him and to everyone in his house.

Such a summary might refer to the final word and catechesis at a baptismal liturgy.

In the story, everything is presented as taking place in the same night during the hours after midnight. Having heard the word of the Lord, the jailer reached out to the prisoners, took them in at that hour of the night and bathed their wounds. For that, the jailer did not wait until it was day (16:35).

After the jailer reached out to them and bathed their wounds, he and his whole family were baptized immediately. Hearing the word of the Lord prompted his gesture. Having bathed their wounds, the jailer and his family received their baptismal bath.

Having heard the word of the Lord, the jailer and his whole family *(hoi autou pantes)* were baptized. For this, Acts has parallels in the story of Pentecost (2:1–41), the story of Cornelius (10:1–11:18) and the story of Lydia (16:13–15). After the jailer and his family were baptized, he brought Paul and Silas into his home where he placed a table before them *(paretheken trapezan)* and the whole household *(panoikei)* rejoiced, having come to believe in God.

The expression *paretheken trapezan,* that is, placing or setting a table before them, is based on the practice in the Hellenistic world of placing a small table before each guest. The story assumes that the whole household joined them for the feast. Having believed the word of the Lord, the jailer was baptized. As baptized, as a Christian, he then offered hospitality and ministered to Paul and Silas at tables (see 6:2).

Baptism is associated with the breaking of the bread at Pentecost (2:41, 42). Baptism is followed by a meal in the story of Paul's conversion (9:18–19). Baptism is followed by an offer of hospitality in the story of the conversion of Cornelius (10:48–49) and in the story of the conversion of Lydia (16:15). In the case of Cornelius and of Lydia, as here in the case of the jailer, the entire household was involved.

Here in the story of the jailer at Philippi, as elsewhere, the meal has implications for the eucharist in the context of Christian initiation. This does not mean that historically, the jailer and his household at the time of their conversion celebrated the eucharist with Paul and Silas. It does mean that when Luke told the story, he had the eucharist, the breaking of the bread, in mind. For Luke and Luke's listeners and readers, it referred to the eucharist, to Christian hospitality and table ministry *(diakonia)*.

A story can refer to the eucharist in different ways: historically, or literarily and symbolically. A meal that was not eucharistic historically can be presented symbolically as eucharistic as part of a story. Throughout the story of Paul, Silas and the jailer, Luke has a baptismal celebration in mind. That celebration is followed by the breaking of the bread.

The jailer, Gentile in origin, and his household offered Christian hospitality, ministered at the table of the Lord and broke the bread with Paul and Silas, both of whom were Jewish in origin. The story of Acts shows that Christians of Gentile origin took their place alongside Christians of Jewish origin in the eucharistic ministry. It also shows that Christians of Jewish origin could join Christians of Gentile origin who did not observe the traditional dietary laws.

In this fifth chapter, we have seen that the eucharist developed in the missions from Antioch (13:1 — 19:20). We analyzed two passages for their implications for the celebration of the eucharist.

The first was the story of what is popularly called the council of Jerusalem, where the assembly in Jerusalem decided that Gentiles did not have to observe the Jewish dietary laws, except those laws considered so basic that they applied to all human beings (15:1 – 35). That means that the Jewish dietary laws did not apply to the breaking of the bread celebrated in Gentile communities.

The second was the story of Paul's evangelization at Philippi (16:11 – 40), in particular, the story of his deliverance from prison (16:25 – 34). The story tells how the decree of the council of Jerusalem was implemented, showing that Christians of Gentile origin, who did not have to observe the dietary laws, did not have to assemble separately. Christians of Gentile origin could invite Christians of Jewish origin to their assembly for the breaking of the bread, and those of Jewish origin could join them at the same table of the Lord.

In the sixth chapter, we shall see how the understanding of the eucharist developed in Paul's great journey to Rome, to the ends of the earth (19:21 — 28:31). For this we shall study two stories. The first is the story of an assembly for the breaking of the bread at Troas

(20:7 – 12). The story shows that the proclamation of the word is life-giving. The second is the story of Paul breaking the bread aboard a ship at the height of a storm (27:33 – 38). The story shows that the breaking of the bread brings salvation.

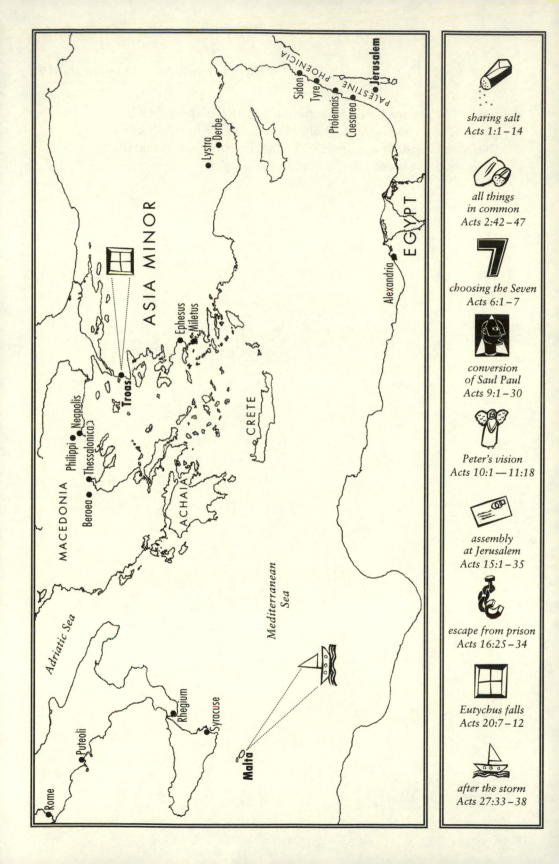

sharing salt
Acts 1:1–14

all things
in common
Acts 2:42–47

choosing the Seven
Acts 6:1–7

conversion
of Saul Paul
Acts 9:1–30

Peter's vision
Acts 10:1—11:18

assembly
at Jerusalem
Acts 15:1–35

escape from prison
Acts 16:25–34

Eutychus falls
Acts 20:7–12

after the storm
Acts 27:33–38

Jerusalem

Sidon
Tyre
PHOENICIA
Ptolemais
Caesarea
PALESTINE

EGYPT

Alexandria

ASIA MINOR

Lystra
Derbe

Ephesus
Miletus

CRETE

Troas

Neapolis
Philippi
Thessalonica
Beroea

MACEDONIA

ACHAIA

Mediterranean
Sea

Adriatic Sea

Rhegium
Syracuse

Malta

Puteoli

Rome

Chapter VI

The Great Journey to Rome (19:21—28:31)

When this was concluded,
Paul made up his mind
to travel through Macedonia and Achaia,
and then to go on to Jerusalem, saying,
"After I have been there,
I must visit Rome also."

Acts 19:21

The first section of Acts (1:15 — 5:42) told how the church began in Jerusalem and how it grew from a small nucleus (see 1:13 – 14) to a community of some five thousand (4:4), devoting themselves "to the teaching of the apostles and to the communal life, to the breaking of the bread and to the prayers" (2:42). In those very early days, the Christians broke bread on the first day of the week when they assembled as a church. They also broke bread daily in their respective homes (2:46).

The second section (6:1 — 12:25) told how the church spread from Jerusalem to Antioch and how it dealt with growth and cultural diversity, geographical expansion and the implications of conversion for Jews as well as for Gentiles. In the process, it showed that the church in Jerusalem selected the Seven to serve at tables (6:1 – 7), that when Jesus appeared to Saul on the Damascus road, Saul could no longer eat and drink with his former colleagues (9:1 – 31) and that Peter came to see that the Christian table had to include both Jews and Gentiles (10:1 — 11:18).

The third section (13:1 — 19:20) told how the church spread through various missions from Antioch and that it continued to integrate members from increasingly diverse backgrounds into one church. In the process, it showed how the church came to see that Gentiles did not have to be circumcised or follow the Jewish dietary laws. It also showed that Gentile converts, like Jewish converts, could and should host the community at the Christian table.

No doubt, there were other missions from Antioch that Luke did not include in the story of Acts. For Luke, it was enough to show how the church developed as a missionary church and how it dealt with the issues of growth, universality, diversity and unity.

Everything is now ready for the fourth and last section of Acts, the story of Paul's great journey to Rome (19:21 — 28:31).

Jews came to Jerusalem from everywhere in the diaspora, making Jerusalem a symbol for the whole Jewish world (see 2:8 – 11). People came to Rome from every nation under the sun, and that made Rome an apt symbol for the whole world, in biblical terms, "the ends of the earth."

With the story of Paul's journey to Rome, the structure of Acts continues to parallel that of Luke's Gospel. The Gospel told about the origins of the church in Jesus' Galilean ministry (Luke 5:1 — 9:50), when he called the first disciples (5:1 — 6:11), formed them as the Twelve (6:12 — 8:56) and sent them on mission (9:1 – 50). It then told about the destiny of the church in the story of Jesus' great journey to Jerusalem, where Jesus fulfilled his mission and was taken up (9:51 — 24:53). Blessing the disciples as he was taken up (24:50 – 51), Jesus fulfilled the promises made to Abraham: "In your offspring all the families of the earth shall be blessed" (Acts 3:25; see Luke 1:55).

The Book of Acts told about the development of the church (1:15 — 19:20) from its beginning in Jerusalem (1:15 — 5:42), as it spread from Jerusalem to Antioch (6:1 — 12:25) and in the missions from Antioch (13:1 — 19:20). It now tells about the mission of the church "to the ends of the earth" (1:8) in the story of Paul's great journey to Rome (19:21 — 28:31). For two full years "with complete assurance and without hindrance [Paul] proclaimed the kingdom of God and taught about the Lord Jesus Christ" (28:30 – 31), witnessing to the mission of Jesus in whom all the families of the earth would be blessed (Luke 24:50 – 51; Acts 3:25).

Table VII

Setting for the Breaking of the Bread at Troas

19:21 – 20:38 Through Macedonia and Achaia

> Introducing the journey to Jerusalem and Rome (19:21 – 22)
>
> In Ephesus, the riot of the silversmiths (19:23 – 40)
>
> In Macedonia and Achaia (20:1 – 3)
>
> Return to Troas (20:4 – 6)
>> The breaking of the bread at Troas (20:7 – 12)
>>> Assembling to break bread (20:7a – c)
>>> Eutychus and the breaking of the bread (20:7d – 11)
>>> They took the boy away alive (20:12)
>
> The journey to Jerusalem with a major stop at Miletus
> (20:13 – 38)

Overview of Acts 19:21 — 28:31

The section begins with a brief introduction (Acts 19:21–22), giving Paul's plans for the journey:

> When this was concluded, Paul made his mind to travel through Macedonia and Achaia, and then to go on to Jerusalem, saying, "After I have been there, I must visit Rome also." Then he sent to Macedonia two of his assistants, Timothy and Erastus, while he himself stayed for a while in the province of Asia.

This introduction recalls the introduction of Jesus' great journey to Jerusalem (Luke 9:51 – 52a), when he too sent messengers ahead of him:

> When the days for his being taken up were fulfilled, he resolutely determined to journey to Jerusalem, and he sent messengers ahead of him.

Like Jesus, Paul went to Jerusalem, but only as an intermediate destination. Paul's ultimate destination was Rome. To emphasize that destination, Luke quoted Paul directly: "After I have been there, I must *(dei)* visit Rome" (Acts 19:21).

Just as it was necessary *(dei)* for Jesus to fulfill his mission in Jerusalem (Luke 13:33), it is now necessary *(dei)* for Paul to fulfill his mission in Rome. In the story of the journey, Acts underlines its necessity three times, whenever its continuation seemed to be threatened (Acts 23:11; 25:10; 27:24).

- The night before Paul was taken from Jerusalem to Caesarea, "the Lord stood by him and said, "Take courage. For just as you have borne witness to my cause in Jerusalem, so you must *(dei)* also bear witness in Rome."

- Then at Caesarea, defending himself before Festus, Paul appealed to Caesar: "I am standing before the tribunal of Caesar; this is where I should be tried," that is, "where it is necessary *(dei)* for me to tried."

- Again in the midst of a violent storm, threatening everyone with destruction, Paul told everyone that an angel had appeared to him, saying: "Do not be afraid, Paul. You are destined *(dei)* to stand before Caesar."

In Greek and Roman literature, necessity is a matter of blind fate, which no one can escape.[1] In Virgil's *Aeneid,* for example, Aeneas was driven by fate *(fato profugus)* to the shores of Lavinia (Book I, line 2). In the scriptures, necessity is a matter not of blind fate, but of divine providence, bringing all of creation and human history to fulfillment.

Throughout Luke-Acts, necessity *(dei)* is always associated with the history of salvation, the fulfillment of the scriptures and the prophetic message of Jesus Christ. The theme of necessity shows that God, present in history, guides it to fulfillment according to a divine salvific plan.[2]

In the gospel, that salvific necessity *(dei)* referred to Jesus' passion and resurrection: "The Son of Man must *(dei)* suffer greatly and be rejected by the elders, the chief priests, and the scribes, and be killed and on the third day be raised" (Luke 9:22; see also Luke 24:7, 26, 44). The same necessity applied to Jesus' journey to Jerusalem: "Yet I must *(dei)* continue on my way today, tomorrow, and the following day, for it is impossible that a prophet should die outside of Jerusalem" (13:33).[3]

Everything associated with the work of salvation was under the same necessity, including the ascension (2:49). So was Paul's journey to Rome, proclaiming the kingdom of God and witnessing to Jesus to the ends of the earth.

The introduction (Acts 19:21–22) divides Paul's journey into three stages: First, Paul traveled through Macedonia and Achaia; he then went on to Jerusalem; after that he visited Rome. The three stages of the journey correspond to the story's literary structure.

First Stage   In the first stage (19:23 — 20:38), Paul traveled through Macedonia and Achaia. At the time his journey began, Paul had been in Ephesus, the capital of the Roman province of Asia (19:26; see 19:1–20). After visiting Macedonia and Greece (Achaia), Paul returned to the province of Asia, but not to Ephesus. Sailing past Ephesus (20:16), he continued to Miletus, where he met the presbyters of the church of Ephesus (19:17–38).

Second Stage   In the second stage (21:1 — 23:11), Paul traveled to Jerusalem via Tyre (21:1–6), Ptolemais (21:7) and Caesarea (21:7–14), visiting the Christians at each stop. At Caesarea, he stayed at the home of Philip the evangelist *(euaggelistos),* one of the Seven *(ek ton hepta).* From there, Paul went to Jerusalem (21:15 — 23:12), where he was arrested and imprisoned. Arrested (21:27–40), Paul defended himself before the Jews of Jerusalem (22:1–21). Imprisoned (22:22–29), he defended himself before the Sanhedrin (22:30 — 23:11).

Third Stage   In the third stage (23:12 — 28:31), Paul was transferred to Caesarea (23:12–35), where he was tried before Felix, the governor (24:1–27). Two years later, when Felix' successor, Porcius Festus (25:1–12), wanted to bring Paul back to Jerusalem to stand trial before him there, Paul appealed to Caesar (25:21, 25). Finding no charge against Paul, Festus had him appear before King Agrippa (25:13 — 26:32), who also found nothing with which to charge Paul: "This man could have been set free if he had not appealed to Caesar" (26:32).

After that, Paul was sent by ship for Rome. After surviving a storm at sea (27:1–44), Paul wintered in Malta, where he was bitten by a viper, but the snake did no harm to him (28:1–11). Finally, Paul arrived in Rome, where he stayed for two years (28:11–31).

Throughout the journey, we never lose sight of Paul's ultimate destination, Rome, the imperial capital. Paul's goal was to preach the gospel "to the ends of the earth" (1:8). Indeed, it was necessary for him to do that. Such was his mission. But at every stage, everything and everyone conspired against Paul reaching Rome and fulfilling his mission.

Even before Paul even got under way, while he was still in Ephesus, a riot broke out over the effects of Paul's teaching on the local economy,[4] and Paul had to be dissuaded from going before the rioting crowd (19:23–40). Then, in Greece, Paul had to change his plans because of a plot against his life. Instead of sailing to Syria, he returned to Macedonia and back to the province of Asia (20:3–38), whence he left for Jerusalem (21:1–15).

On the way to Jerusalem, the disciples in Tyre "kept telling Paul through the Spirit not to embark for Jerusalem" (21:4). At Caesarea, a prophet showed that Paul would be bound by his own belt and handed over to the Gentiles (21:10–11). Hearing that, Paul's traveling companions as well as the disciples in Caesarea "begged him not to go up to Jerusalem" (21:12).

In Jerusalem, a riot broke out over reports that Paul was bringing Gentiles into the temple (21:15–30). Paul was rescued by Roman soldiers (21:31—22:21), imprisoned (22:22–29) and after an appearance before the Sanhedrin (22:30—23:11), transferred back to Caesarea (23:12–35).

In Caesarea, Paul was held captive by the governor, Felix (24:1–27). Two years later, when Felix' successor, Festus, threatened to transfer Paul back to Jerusalem, Paul appealed to Caesar (25:1–12). Neither Festus nor King Agrippa found any cause for Paul to appear before Caesar (25:13—26:32), but they respected Paul's appeal: "This man could have been set free if he had not appealed to Caesar" (26:32).

On the sea journey to Rome, a huge storm arose, wrecking the ship and threatening Paul's life. Clinging to planks and other debris, Paul and others reached shore safely (27:1–44). They landed on the island of Malta, where a final threat to Paul's reaching Rome came from a serpent. While Paul was putting a bundle of brushwood on a fire, a viper bit his hand. Unharmed, Paul threw the serpent off into the fire (28:1–10). Overcoming that final threat, Paul continued to Rome (28:11–29).

Paul remained in Rome for two full years, welcoming all who came to him, "and with complete assurance and without hindrance he proclaimed the kingdom of God and taught about the Lord Jesus Christ" (28:33–31).

Paul's journey recalls the epic journeys told by Homer and Virgil, where everything conspires to keep the hero from reaching his ultimate destination.

- In Ephesus, a riot of the pagan silversmiths endangered Paul's life (19:23–40).

- In Tyre and Caesarea, the Christians tried to dissuade Paul from going on to Jerusalem (21:4, 10–14).

- In Jerusalem, the Jews tried to kill him (21:27–31) and the Romans took him into custody (21:32—23:11), eventually transferring him to Caesarea (23:12–35).

- In Caesarea, two successive governors, Felix and Festus, and King Agrippa found Paul innocent. There was no reason for him to go to Rome (24:1—26:32).

- At sea, the very elements, the winds and the waves, rose up against Paul (27:6–44).

- In Malta, a serpent, evoking the primeval mythic serpent of Eden (see Genesis 3:1–24), tried to destroy him (Acts 28:1–10).

Overcoming every obstacle, Paul finally reached Rome. It was necessary that Paul proclaim the kingdom of God and teach about the Lord Jesus Christ to the ends of the earth.

In Relation to the Eucharist

Two stories in Paul's great journey to Rome (19:21—28:31) have special implications for the development of the eucharist according to Acts. The first of these is the story of the breaking of the bread at Troas (20:7–12). The second is the story of the breaking of the bread at the height of a storm at sea (27:33–38).

The assembly for the breaking of the bread at Troas (20:7–12) took place in the first stage of Paul's journey, when Paul bade farewell to the community on his return from Macedonia and Achaia. The breaking of the bread aboard the ship (27:33–38) takes place at the climax of the third stage of Paul's journey before the shipwreck on Malta.

Both stories are significant for their theology. The breaking of the bread shows that death is powerless in the eucharistic assembly. The breaking of the bread is a source of life. The breaking of the bread in the midst of the storm shows that the eucharist is a source of salvation.

Both stories are also significant for the development of liturgical roles. Elsewhere in Acts, when there is reference to the breaking of the bread, the action is attributed to the community or the household (2:42 – 47), and we are not told who actually broke the bread. Both at Troas and on the ship, we are told explicity that Paul broke the bread.

Breaking Bread at Troas (20:7 – 12)

Don't be alarmed;
there is life in him.
Acts 20:10

Paul was no stranger to Troas, a port city near the ancient city of Troy. Earlier, after separating from Barnabas (15:36 – 39), Paul had traveled through Syria and Cilicia, accompanied by Silas (15:40–41).[5] From city to city, they made their way through Asia Minor until they came to Troas (16:6 – 8).[6]

At Troas, Paul had a vision. In the vision, a Macedonian stood before him, imploring him, "Come over to Macedonia and help us" (16:9). Troas was the embarkation point for Neapolis,[7] the port of Philippi, a Roman colony in eastern Macedonia (16:11 – 12).

Acts does not record whether Paul planned or actually made a special effort to evangelize Troas. After the vision, Paul, Silas and Timothy had concluded that God called them to proclaim the gospel to the Macedonians, and they immediately sought passage to Macedonia (16:10).[8]

But while awaiting the boat in Troas, Paul surely shared the gospel with everyone who was willing to listen. From that spontaneous sharing, a small community sprang up. The same must have happened in various places where Paul stopped on his way to other places. Later, Paul may have stopped at Troas again on his way from Ephesus to Macedonia (20:1 – 2), but Acts gives no record of it.[9]

Returning from Macedonia, Paul spent a full week at Troas. In Macedonia, Paul had been accompanied by seven Christians from various communities in Macedonia and Asia Minor (20:4).

Three of Paul's companions were from Macedonia. First, there was Sopater, the son of Pyrrhus, who was from Beroea (see 17:10 – 15), where many had become believers, including not a few influential Greek women and men (17:12). There were also Aristarchus and Secundus from Thessalonica (17:1 – 9). Later, Aristarchus accompanied Paul on the journey to Rome (27:2). He must have been present when Paul broke the bread in the midst of the storm (27:35).

Four of Paul's companions were from Asia Minor. First, there was Gaius from Derbe, a city near Lystra (see 16:1).[10] There were also Timothy, who came from Lystra (16:1), Tychicus and Trophimus. Timothy (see 16:1 – 3) had gone ahead with Erastus to Macedonia while Paul had stayed for a time in the province of Asia (19:22). Trophimus was an Ephesian. He accompanied Paul all the way to Jerusalem (21:29).

The seven who had accompanied Paul went ahead and waited for Paul and the other companions at Troas. One of the companions may have been Luke himself, the author of Acts (20:5, 13).[11] Paul and his companions left Philippi after the feast of Unleavened Bread and joined the others at Troas five days later, where they spent a full week.

Luke shows that Paul observed the feast of Unleavened Bread, which coincided with the feast of Passover. Paul also wanted to be in Jerusalem for the feast of Pentecost (20:16). The seven who had gone ahead did not observe the feast. Indeed, as Greeks, there was no need for them to observe it (16:4). That had been decided at the great assembly in Jerusalem (see 15:22 – 29).

The assembly for the breaking of the bread at Troas was not an ordinary assembly. Together with the local community, Paul's companions were there, personally representing many of the other communities. And of course, Paul himself, from whom they had first received the word, was there. By itself, that would have made the assembly an extraordinary one. For Paul and the local community, it was also a farewell meal.

Overview of Acts 20:7 – 12

The story of the breaking of the bread at Troas is tightly knit. It tells about a particular assembly for the breaking of the bread, not a typical assembly but a singular assembly for two reasons. The assembly was a farewell assembly for Paul. It was also marked by an extraordinary event, the death and resurrection of a young man named Eutychus.

The story begins as a farewell celebration for Paul. But while Paul talked on and on, a young man named Eutychus, sitting on a window sill, fell asleep and dropped from the fourth floor to the ground. When they picked him up, he was dead. Going down, Paul threw himself on the boy and raised him to life. Returning upstairs, Paul broke the bread. What had begun as a farewell celebration became a celebration of life.

Some stories are easily divided into sections. For this story, it is more difficult. Still, it helps the reader to follow the development of the story when the story is divided into three parts, an introduction (20:7a – c), a body (20:7d – 11) and a conclusion (20:12).

- The story opens with a little introduction, giving the setting for the event at the community's breaking of the bread on the first day of the week, when Paul spoke to them until midnight because he was leaving the next day (20:7a – c).
- The body of the story is framed by Paul's speaking to and with the assembly (20:7c, 11). As very often in a story, the end of the introduction (20:7c) at the same time can be considered as the beginning of the body, and the end of the body (20:11c) can be considered as the beginning of the conclusion.[12]
- After a long conversation (20:11c), the story concludes with the community taking the boy away alive (20:12).

From the point of view of Paul's journey to Jerusalem and Rome (19:21 — 28:31), the story tells about Paul's farewell visit to Troas. Before coming to Troas, Paul had bid farewell to the community of Ephesus (20:1 – 3). Later he presented a major farewell discourse at Miletus before the elders of the church at Ephesus (20:17 – 38). After that, there was a farewell visit to the communities at Tyre (21:1 – 6), Ptolemais (21:7) and Caesarea (21:8 – 14).

Paul's farewell visit to the community at Troas was part of a series of such visits as Paul made his way to Jerusalem (21:15 – 26), where Paul was arrested in the midst of a riot at the temple (21:27 – 36). Thereafter, Paul was in the custody of the Romans.

The reason it is so difficult to take apart the structure of the story is that Paul's farewell visit to Troas actually includes two stories. The first tells about Paul's farewell when the community at Troas assembled for the breaking of the bread. The second tells about the extraordinary event that occurred while the community was assembled for the breaking of the bread. A young man named Eutychus fell from a window to his death but was revived by Paul.

The two stories are intertwined and are presented as one. Some of the details in the story flow from the motif of the farewell visit. Some flow from the event involving Eutychus, with its motif of death and life. The setting, the breaking of the bread at which Paul spoke, unites the two motifs.

Assembling to Break Bread (20:7a–c)

The introductory verse places the event temporally, describes the setting and presents it as a special occasion. The event took place "on the first day of the week," when the community "gathered to break bread." Since Paul was to leave the next day, Paul spoke to the community.

> On the first day of the week when we gathered to break bread, Paul spoke to them because he was going to leave on the next day.

The main statement in the verse says that Paul spoke to the assembly and adds the reason why he spoke (20:7c). The two previous statements describe the time and setting. Paul spoke on a particular day, "the first day of the week" (20:7a), and in a particular setting, "when we gathered to break bread" (20:7b). All three statements have important implications for the development of the eucharist according to Acts.

On the First Day of the Week   Very early on, "the first day of the week" *(he mia ton sabbaton)* was observed by Christians everywhere as a very special day.[13] A related expression appears in 1 Corinthians, when Paul gives instructions for the collection for the holy ones: "On the first day of the week *(kata mian sabbatou)* each of you should set aside and save whatever he can afford, so that collections will not be going on when I come" (1 Corinthians 16:2).

That passage refers to each *(kata)* first day of the week. That presupposes that the Christians regularly assembled on the first day of the week. The verse also presupposes that the assembly on the first day of the week served several purposes. For example, it was a time to collect money for the poor. That, however, would not distract from more important functions. When Paul came to the community, they would have other pressing things to attend to, including the way they celebrated the Lord's Supper (see 11:17–34).

The gospels associate the resurrection of Jesus with the first day of the week. In each of the four gospels, the expression "the first day of the week" introduces the women's visit to the tomb of Jesus (Mark 16:2; Matthew 28:1; Luke 24:1; John 20:1). In various ways, each of those stories proclaims the resurrection of Jesus of Nazareth, the one who was crucified.

In Luke, the first day of the week is also the day Jesus appears to the disciples of Emmaus (Luke 24:13–35), to the community in Jerusalem (24:36–49) and ascends to heaven, fulfilling the promise to Abraham that through his progeny all the families of the earth would be blessed (24:50–53). In John, the first day of the week is the day Jesus appears to Mary Magdalene (20:11; see 20:1) and to the disciples (20:19, 26).

In Acts, the first day of the week was the day when Christians proclaimed the resurrection of Jesus and celebrated his presence to them as risen Lord. They did that at their assembly for the breaking of the bread.

The first day of the week is more than a temporal designation. Using the cardinal number *(mia)* instead of the ordinal number *(prote),* the expression evokes the first day of creation in Genesis 1:5. Hebrew does not have an ordinal number for "one," only a cardinal. Greek has both the cardinal (one) and the ordinal (first), but the Septuagint rendered the Hebrew very literally, using the cardinal instead of the ordinal. The New Testament expression "the first *(mia)* day of the week" is a transparent reference to the first day of creation.

Although using the cardinal number in that context represented a barbarism in Greek, the early Christians never corrected it. Only in the second century, in the alternate ending of Mark, do we find the ordinal number *prote* (first) for the first day of the week (Mark 16:9).

Using the cardinal number instead of the ordinal, the expression "the first *(mia)* day of the week" is a theological statement, associating Jesus' resurrection, its proclamation and the experience of the risen Lord with the first day of the new creation. Assembling on the first day of the week for the breaking of the bread, the early Christians celebrated the new creation manifested in Jesus' risen life. In the breaking of the bread, they also participated in the new creation.

When We Gathered to Break Bread From the start, the story focuses on the assembly: "when we gathered" *(synegmenon hemon)*. For the early Christians, assembling was very important. That is when they came together as a church. The Christians assembled for many reasons. As we saw in 6:1 – 7 and 15:1 – 35, they sometimes assembled to discuss and solve a major problem. Mainly, as here in 20:7 – 12, they assembled to break bread. But that does not mean they did not do anything else. Principal activities included prayer, listening to the word, telling stories about Jesus, evangelization, catechesis, even collecting money for the poor.

Note that the introduction is in the first person plural. The story of the breaking of the bread at Troas is told as part of one of the "we-passages" in Acts (20:5 – 15; see 16:10 – 17; 21:1 – 18; 27:1 — 28:16). The "we-passages" reflect a natural literary tendency that is quite typical of sea stories in the ancient world. Using the first person plural, the author, narrator or a personage in the story identifies with the others on the journey. On a ship, everyone moves as one.

In the *Odyssey* and the *Aeneid,* when Odysseus and Aeneas tell about a sea journey, they tell it as an experience in which they participated. In those cases, the epic "we-passage" does not come from the main narrator or author, but is attributed to a personage in the story.

In the same way, when a story is told by the narrator or the author, as here in Acts, the narrator or the author also tells it as a personal experience. For that reason, recognizing what may be a literary device used in stories of sea journeys, the "we-passages" also presuppose that Luke, the author of Luke-Acts, present here as the narrator, was actually traveling with Paul.[14]

We recognize the expression "to break bread" from the summary describing life in the community at Jerusalem (2:42, 46). The introductory verse in the summary refers to "the breaking of the bread"

(2:42). Later, the summary refers to the Christians in Jerusalem "breaking bread in their homes" (2:46).

Here in the story of Troas, the expression "breaking bread" *(klasai arton)* is used without the definite article, as in 2:46. Later in the story, when Paul broke the bread (20:11), the expression includes the definite article *(klasas ton arton)* as in 2:42. In Acts, breaking bread and breaking the bread can refer to "the breaking of the bread" as well as to "breaking bread in their homes" (see 2:42, 46).

Paul again broke bread at the height of the storm at sea (27:35). Introducing the story of the assembly at Troas, the expression "when we gathered to break bread" is a direct reference to the eucharist. Its function is to describe the setting and identify the occasion. Later in the story, the expression "he . . . broke the bread" refers to and evokes the liturgical formula used in the celebration of the eucharist. The same is true in the summary of life in the Jerusalem community (2:46). The same is also true when Paul broke bread in the midst of the storm (27:35), when Jesus broke bread for the five thousand (Luke 9:16), for the apostles at the Last Supper (22:19) and for the disciples of Emmaus (24:30).

Only twice in the whole of Luke-Acts do we find the expression "the breaking of the bread" used as a name for the eucharist. We find it first in the Gospel, in Luke's summary of the Emmaus event (24:35). We then find it in the Acts of the Apostles, in Luke's summary of life in the community at Jerusalem (2:42).

The story of the assembly at Troas is the only story in the entire New Testament that describes an actual eucharistic assembly in the early church. Because of what happened during the celebration, Eutychus falling from the window sill to his death, the story was included in Luke's narrative of Paul's journey to Jerusalem and Rome. Except for that, we would not have a description of an actual eucharistic celebration in New Testament times. For that reason alone, the story is important to the history of the eucharist.

Elsewhere in the New Testament, Paul tells about abuses at the Lord's Supper in Corinth (1 Corinthians 11:17–34; see all of chapters 11–14). While responding to the abuses, Paul also provides an early liturgical formula used at the Lord's Supper at Corinth and, presumably, in other communities where Paul preached. Paul also reflects on the implications of the Lord's Supper for the life of the community. Paul describes how it was in general when the Corinthians assembled as a church for the Lord's Supper. He does not describe a particular celebration of the Lord's Supper.

The Gospels also refer to the Lord's Supper, but in relation to the mission and ministry of Jesus before the passion, especially at the Last Supper, and after the passion, after Jesus rose from the dead. The Gospel of Luke tells the stories of ten meals with Jesus, all of them with implications for the eucharist. These stories tell a great deal about the eucharist in the first century, but they do not describe a particular assembly of Christians gathering to break bread.

Until now, Acts has referred to the breaking of the bread beginning with a summary describing life in the community at Jerusalem (2:42 – 47). But this is the first time Acts tells about a particular Christian assembly for the breaking of the bread. The story describes a eucharistic event on the first day of the week when the entire community at Troas, together with Paul and visitors from other communities, assembled as a church.

Paul Spoke to Them   On the first day of the week, when a community gathered to break bread, the members surely spoke to one another. When Paul was visiting, it would have been normal for him to speak to the community. It would have been abnormal if he had not spoken to them. The introductory verse, however, seems to imply otherwise.

The story says that Paul spoke *(dielegeto)* to them because he was leaving the next day. Does that mean that he would not have spoken to them if he had not intended to leave the next day?

First, we should note that Paul spoke to them before the breaking of the bread. In the Gospel, Jesus addressed the participants (Luke 5:33 – 39) not before but after a banquet (5:27 – 32). At the Last Supper, he gave his farewell discourse (22:21 – 38) not before but after the breaking of the bread (22:14 – 20).[15] Such was the pattern for a symposium, a formal dinner where the participants reclined.

The breaking of the bread at Troas was not a symposium, but it may have been influenced by the structure of a symposium. If that was the case, Paul took advantage of the gathering to address the community before the breaking of the bread. He did that precisely because he was leaving the next day.

The breaking of the bread, the eucharist, was the main purpose of the assembly. But prior to the breaking of the bread, the assembly served another purpose. It allowed Paul to address the community. We note that, as at a symposium, Paul also would have a long conversation *(homilesas)* with the community after the breaking of the bread (Acts 20:11).

The reference to the next day *(te epaurion)* refers to the following morning. That means that "the first day of the week" did not begin at sunset in the Jewish way, but at dawn in the Greek and Roman way. Accordingly, in Acts 20:7 – 11, the first day of the week began on what is now Sunday morning. The breaking of the bread, then, took place in the early hours of what is for us Monday morning.

Eutychus and the Breaking of the Bread (20:7d – 11)

The body of the story begins with the story of Eutychus, who fell to his death from a third-story window and was restored to life by Paul (20:7d – 10). It then tells that Paul broke the bread and kept speaking until his departure at daybreak (20:11).

The body of the story can then be divided into two little units. One tells what happened to Eutychus (20:7d – 10), whose story is closely connected with Paul's speaking to the community (20:7c). The other focuses on the breaking of the bread (20:11), the main reason for the assembly (20:7b)

The first unit begins by giving the circumstances that led to Eutychus' fall.

> Paul kept on speaking until midnight. There were many lamps in the upstairs room where we gathered, and a young man named Eutychus who was sitting on the window sill was sinking into a deep sleep as Paul talked on and on.

Paul spoke *(dielegeto)* to the community because he was to leave the next day. And he spoke for a long time. Christian communities, like others in the Hellenistic world, came together to eat at the end of the day. Inviting Jesus to their home, the disciples of Emmaus had said to him, "Stay with us, for it is nearly evening and the day is almost over" (Luke 24:29). That evening, Paul spoke *(pareteinen te ton logon)* to them from early evening until midnight (Acts 20:7d).

We understand why Paul spoke so long. This was the last time he would address the community at Troas.

Addressing the community, Paul prolonged *(pareteinen)* the word *(ton logon)* until midnight, announcing and teaching the word to them. While the ministry of the word is related to the ministry at tables, it is also different (see 6:1 – 7).

If Paul had not prolonged the word until midnight, Eutychus would not have fallen asleep. Paul's preaching and teaching, however, were but the occasion. The cause lay in the many lamps lit in the upstairs room where they gathered *(hou emen synegmenoi,* see 20:7b). The story's reference to the lamps is more than a colorful detail. The many lamps consumed the oxygen in the room and made the air stale. If Eutychus fell asleep, it was not Paul's fault, even if Paul spoke *(dialegomenou)* to them on and on *(epi pleion)*. It was the lamps' fault.

Giving the name of the young man, Eutychus, makes the story very concrete. He appears for the first time in this story and has no further role. At Troas, however, Eutychus must have become a significant member of the community. That he was sitting on the window sill while Paul proclaimed the word shows that the assembly for the breaking of the bread was quite informal.

The breaking of the bread at Troas was not held in a formal dining room, as would have been the case for a symposium. The breaking of the bread at Troas was not a symposium. Sitting on the window sill, a young man like Eutychus must have felt at home.

The assembly took place in an upstairs room *(en to hyperoo)*, evoking the upstairs (upper) room *(hyperoon)* where the apostolic community gathered in Jerusalem after the ascension (1:13 – 14). This room, however, was a different kind of room, as we are about to see.

Having described the circumstances that led to Eutychus' death, the first unit (20:7d – 10) goes on to describe how he died.

> Once overcome by sleep, he fell down from the third story and when he was picked up, he was dead.

It was bad enough that Eutychus fell into a deep sleep, but once asleep, he fell *(epesen)* from the window sill to his death. Acts says that he fell from the third story *(apo tou tristegou)*. Many buildings in a city like Troas could have had as many as six stories.

The community did not meet in a family's personal dwelling, which in Jerusalem often had an upper room that was used as a dining area. The community met in an apartment house, in the apartment of one of the members. In such a house, only wealthy people could afford to live on the first floor, close to facilities. Poor people lived on the upper floors, where there were no facilities and where there was more danger from fire. Since they were assembling on the third floor, the community must have been fairly poor.

When Eutychus was picked up, he was dead. What is significant here is that the story says he was dead. Whether he was actually dead, or as good as dead, does not matter. The message of the story requires that we think of him as falling to his death as the community was gathered for the breaking of the bread. Eutychus died while listening to Paul's proclamation of the word of the Lord, the source of the community's life.

After the death of Eutychus, the first unit (20:7d – 10) ends, once again focusing on Paul.

> Paul went down, threw himself on him, and said as he embraced him, "Don't be alarmed, there is life in him."

Paul's action is reminiscent of prophetic acts of Elijah and Elisha in First and Second Kings when the son of a widow in Zarephath and the son of a Shunammite died. Addressing a widow of Zarephath in Sidon, Elijah said: "Give me your son." He then "carried him to the upper room where he was staying, and laid him on his own bed." After a short prayer, "he stretched himself out upon the child three times and called out to the Lord: 'O Lord, my God, let the life breath return to the body of this child.' The Lord heard the prayer of Elijah; the life breath returned to the child's body and the child revived" (1 Kings 17:19 – 22).

At Shunem, Elisha used to stay at the home of a Shunammite and her husband. When their young son died suddenly, Elisha revived him. Arriving at the house, "he found the boy lying dead." After praying, "he lay upon the child on the bed, placing his mouth upon the child's mouth, his eyes upon the eyes, and his hands upon the hands. As Elisha stretched himself over the child, the body became warm." After restoring him to life, he presented the woman with her son alive (2 Kings 4:32 – 36).

Paul's gesture was much more simple: Falling *(epepesen)* on the young man who had fallen *(epesen)* from the third-floor window, Paul embraced him. Paul then declared that the young man's soul *(psyche)* was in him. The story does not say that Paul restored the young man to life. The life that was in him may have come from the word Paul proclaimed.

The story's emphasis is on life. As Paul said, "There is life in him." Eutychus, who had fallen to his death, was now alive. Nothing would prevent Paul from achieving his goal, proclaiming the word in Rome. Nor would anything harm anyone associated with him (see Acts 27:22–24). As a member of the community that gathered on the first day of the week to break bread and heard Paul proclaim the word, Eutychus had life in him.

The second little unit in the body of the story (20:11) tells about the breaking of the bread.

> Then he returned upstairs, broke the bread, and ate; after a long conversation that lasted until daybreak, he departed.

The first unit (20:7d–10), the story of Eutychus, flowed from Paul's speaking to the assembly because he was to leave the next day (20:7c). The second unit (20:11), the breaking of the bread, develops the main purpose of the assembly, "when we gathered to break bread" (20:7b).

This is one of only two times in the New Testament that the story specifies who broke the bread. Both are in the Acts of the Apostles. And in both cases, Paul was the one who broke the bread. The second is when Paul broke the bread on a ship at the height of a huge storm (27:35).

Jesus, of course, broke the bread in the course of his life, one time for five thousand people, and very solemnly at the Last Supper (Luke 22:19). Jesus also broke bread after he rose from the dead (24:31). For the rest, it is not clear who actually broke the bread. Someone must have done it, but excepting the two cases where Paul broke the bread, we are not told.

We know that various people served as host for Jesus, the disciples and other people. In such cases the host may have broken the bread, unless Jesus was expected to break the bread as he was expected to speak to the participants as the special guest at a symposium. We also know that serving *(diakonein)* at table was a special ministry well before Luke wrote Luke-Acts in the mid-eighties of the first century (see Acts 6:1–7).

Did serving at table, ministering at table, include breaking the bread? Probably. When Jesus broke the bread, he asked the apostles (see Luke 22:14) to do this in memory of him (22:19). When the apostles imposed hands on the Seven, they shared their ministry with them (Acts 6:1 – 7). But who broke the bread when the Twelve or the Seven were not present?

In Acts' summary of life in the Jerusalem community, the breaking of the bread is attributed to the whole community or the household without specifying who actually broke the bread. "They devoted themselves . . . to the breaking of the bread" (2:42). And "every day they devoted themselves . . . to breaking bread in their homes" (2:46). That does not mean that no one was designated to break the bread for the other participants. Nor does it mean that breaking the bread was done every time by the same person.

Here at Troas, it is very clear that Paul, the special guest, the one who first shared the word at Troas and repeatedly visited the community, broke the bread (20:11). In our terms, Paul celebrated the eucharist in the midst of the community, and the community joined him in the breaking of the bread.

The breaking of the bread was a community event. From the story of Troas (20:7 – 12), we conclude that a designated person broke the bread in the name of Christ for the community (see Luke 22:19). Like Paul, the designated person had a special position in the community and acted in the name of the church (Acts 6:1 – 7).

After breaking the bread, Paul had a long conversation with the assembly. The conversation lasted until daybreak, when Paul departed. The term used to describe the conversation is different from the terms used to describe Paul's speaking before he broke bread with them.

In the introduction (20:7a–c) and the first part of the body (20:7d–10), the Greek verb used, *dialegomai,* has a wide range of meanings. In general, it means that Paul spoke *(dielegeto)* to the assembly *(autois)* and spoke *(dialegomenou)* on and on *(epi pleion)*. Speaking (20:7c, 9a), he could have been discussing or debating with the community. He could also have been addressing the community.

Fortunately, the story further specifies Paul's speaking as prolonging the word *(pareteinen te ton logon)*. Proclaiming the word, Paul was addressing the community. That does not exclude comments or questions from the community.

In the second part of the body (20:11), the verb used, *homileo,* means that Paul spoke to them in the sense of conversing with the community. The Greek noun *homilia* designates a company, an association, a community. A Christian *homilia* refers to a community based on a common-union *(koinonia)* to the Lord Jesus. The members of the community were *koinonoi,* united not by blood but by bread. Those who broke bread together were *koinonoi* and formed a Christian *homilia.* The verb *homileo* (to homilize) describes a manner of speaking for people who have broken bread together.

Paul's addressing the community from early evening to midnight was loosely tied to the breaking of the bread. The gathering of the community to break bread on the first day of the week provided an occasion for Paul to address the community. Paul's conversation with the community until daybreak was closely tied to the breaking of the bread. Today, we would speak of it as the liturgy of the word, an integral part of the eucharistic liturgy.

They Took the Boy Away Alive (20:12)

After the breaking of the bread and Paul's conversation with the community, Paul departed and the local community took the boy *(paida)* away alive *(zonta).* Those who took the boy were greatly comforted.

The same term, *zonta* (alive or living), was used to describe Jesus in the story of the women's visit to the tomb. Entering the tomb, the women did not find the body of the Lord Jesus (Luke 24:3). While they were wondering about this, two men in dazzling white stood before them: "Why do you seek the living one *(zonta)* among the dead?" (Acts 24:5).

For the reader, the question to the women raises another question: "Where then should we seek the living one, if not among the dead?" The answer is obvious: "Among the living!" In Mark, the women's visit to the tomb is the final climax of the Gospel (Mark 16:1–8). Luke transforms Mark's climactic story into an introduction (Luke 24:1–12) for two appearances of Jesus (24:13–35, 36–53). In the first, the story of Emmaus, two disciples found and recognized Jesus in the breaking of the bread (24:13–35). We find Jesus, not among the dead, but among the living in the breaking of the bread.

At the beginning of Acts, the prologue (1:3–14) says that Jesus presented himself alive *(zonta)* after the passion, appearing to the apostles for forty days, speaking to them about the kingdom of God and taking salt with them. As we have seen, taking salt with someone is closely related to breaking bread with someone.

The end of the Gospel and the beginning of Acts both present Jesus as the living one in relation to the meals with him after he rose from the dead. We should not be surprised that the community took the boy alive *(zonta)*. In his fall from the window sill, he died. But having heard the word and having participated in the breaking of the bread, the community was able to take him away alive. On the first day of the week, he participated in the new creation. There was no reason to grieve. He was alive. The community was comforted beyond measure.

Breaking Bread in a Great Storm at Sea (27:33 – 38)

I urge you, therefore,
to take some food;
it will help you survive.
                                  Acts 27:34

Paul was finally on his way to Rome. At Caesarea, Paul could have been set free, except that he had appealed to Caesar (26:32). Along with other prisoners, Paul had been handed over to a centurion[16] named Julius, who was of the Cohort Augusta (27:1).[17] Paul was in the hands of the same centurion throughout the journey (see 27:3, 6, 11, 31, 43).

Accompanying Paul was Aristarchus, the Macedonian from Thessalonica (27:2). Aristarchus was one of those who had been with Paul in Macedonia (20:4) and had gone ahead and waited for Paul at Troas (20:5). He was also present on the first day of the week when the community had gathered to break bread (20:7).

The sea voyage told in 27:1 – 44, along with the episodes in Malta (28:1 – 10) and the final leg of the journey to Rome (28:11 – 15), form the fourth and last of the "we-passages" in Acts. As such, Luke himself, the author and narrator of Acts, may also have been present as a companion of Paul.[18] The second "we-passage" included the breaking of the bread at Troas (20:7 – 12). The fourth includes the breaking of the bread on the ship in the midst of a violent storm (28:33 – 38).

Mark's Gospel, one of Luke's principal sources, includes two crossings of the Sea of Galilee (Mark 4:35 – 41; 6:45 – 52). In both cases, the crossing was from Galilee, on the Jewish side of the sea, to the Decapolis, the ten Greek cities, on the Gentile side of the sea. Both

---

Table VIII

Setting for the Breaking of the Bread in the Storm at Sea

23:12 — 28:31 On the way to Rome

    Paul's transfer to Caesarea (23:12 – 35)

    Trials before Felix, Festus and King Agrippa (24:1 — 26:32)

    The journey to Rome (27:1 — 28:10)
        Departure for Rome (27:1 – 5)
        A great storm and shipwreck (27:6 – 44)
            The storm (27:6 – 32)
            The breaking of the bread (27:33 – 38)
                Paul's exhortation (27:33 – 34)
                The breaking of the bread (27:35 – 37)
                Lightening the ship (27:38)
            Shipwreck (27:39 – 44)
        The winter in Malta (28:1 – 10)
        Arrival in Rome (28:11 – 16)
        Paul proclaims the word in Rome (28:17 – 31)

---

crossings were turbulent. In the first, the disciples encountered a great storm. In the second, they faced strong contrary winds.

The first crossing (4:35 – 41) is related to the universality of the church. After healing the Gerasene demoniac, Jesus and the disciples returned to the Jewish shore (5:21). The second (6:45 – 52) is related to the universal mission of the church. After breaking the bread for four thousand people, Jesus and the disciples again returned to the Jewish shore (8:14 – 21).

Mark includes two stories of the breaking of the bread, the breaking of the bread for the five thousand (6:34 – 44) and the breaking of the bread for the four thousand (8:1 – 9). Both are related to the crossing of the sea (6:52; 8:14 – 21).

Luke's Gospel retains only the first of Mark's two crossings (8:22 – 25), the one that concerns the universality of the church. Luke does not include the second crossing. Nor does he include the breaking of the bread in the Decapolis. In Luke, therefore, unlike Mark, the breaking of the bread (9:10 – 17) is not related to the crossing of the sea.

In Luke, the disciples were not sent on mission to the Gentiles during Jesus' life and ministry. In the section of the Gospel that is devoted to the mission of the Twelve (9:1–50), the apostles remained in Galilee. The mission of the Twelve to the Gentiles is told in the Acts of the Apostles.

The Acts of the Apostles often refers to sea journeys,[19] all related to the mission of the church. Scattered by the persecution in Jerusalem, members of the community in Jerusalem went as far as Phoenicia, Cyprus and Antioch. Among those who came to Antioch were Cypriots and Cyrenians (Acts 11:19–20). That presupposes at least two sea journeys, but the story of Acts does not allude to them.

In the section devoted to the missions from Antioch (13:1—19:20), several sea journeys are noted (13:4, 13; 14:26; 15:39; 16:11; 18:18). In the great journey to Rome (19:21—28:31), several more are noted. Paul sails from Ephesus to Macedonia (20:1), from Macedonia to Troas (20:6), from Troas to Miletus (20:13–16), from Miletus to Tyre (21:1–4) and on to Ptolemais (21:5) and Caesarea (21:8). Acts simply refers to the journeys but does not tell stories about them.

The first sea story in Acts is Paul's journey from Caesarea to Rome (27:1–44), when Paul reached for the ends of the earth. In Mark, the universal mission of the church was related to crossing the sea of Galilee from the Jewish shore of Galilee to the Gentile shore of the Decapolis. Mark related the breaking of the bread to that crossing. In Luke, the universal mission of the church is related to Paul's sea journey to Rome (27:1–44), the climax of his great journey to Jerusalem and on to Rome (19:21—28:31).

Like the crossing of the sea in Mark 4:35–41 and Luke 8:22–25, Acts tells that a great storm arose. As Mark relates the breaking of the bread to the sea crossing told in Mark 6:45–52 (see 6:34–44, 6:52; 8:1–9, 14–21), Luke relates the breaking of the bread to that final storm threatening Paul and the word on the way to Rome (27:33–38).[20]

The first leg of the journey took Paul and the others from Caesarea to Myra in Lycia, on the southwestern point of Asia Minor (27:1–5). For the second leg, they were put aboard an Alexandrian ship that was sailing to Italy (27:6–44). Egypt was the granary of Rome, and Alexandria was its port. Alexandrian ships carried grain to Rome until late in the season when the weather became treacherous.

From the start, the sailing was slow and difficult, so they aimed for Phoenix, a port in Crete, where they would spend the winter

(27:6–12). But a severe storm, a northeaster of hurricane force, drove the ship off course. At one point they lost all hope of surviving (27:13–20). The situation became more and more desperate (27:21–32) until Paul broke the bread (27:33–38). The breaking of the bread is the turning point in the story. After that, the ship itself was lost, but all on board survived (27:39–44).

Overview of Acts 27:33–38

This last story of the breaking of the bread (27:33–38) comes at the climax of the great storm at sea (27:6–38). Keeping that in mind, we can further divide the segment into three parts, including an introduction (27:33–34), body (27:35–37) and conclusion (27:38).

- The introduction begins by situating the event some time before dawn (27:33a) and tells about an exhortation from Paul (27:33b). It then quotes Paul's exhortation directly (27:33c–34).
- The body (27:35–37) tells that Paul broke the bread (27:35) and that the others also took some food (27:36). It ends by giving the number of those who ate (27:37).
- The conclusion (27:38) tells that after eating they lightened the ship by throwing the wheat overboard.

Interpreting the story, we have to ask why Luke made the breaking of the bread part of the story. We note that the others on board did not partake of the breaking of the bread, but inspired by Paul, they did take some food. Seen as a historical event, it makes no sense. Theologically, the story does not require it. Without it, however, the story would be quite different.

In the context of 27:33–38, what then is the function of the breaking of the bread? What significance does it have in the context of the great storm at sea? Why did the others on board not participate in the breaking of the bread? Answering those questions should tell us how the breaking of the bread is related to Christian life and salvation.

Paul's Exhortation (27:33–34)

The story opens by situating the event in time (27:33a). Then it introduces Paul's exhortation (27:33b) and summarizes the exhortation in Paul's own words (27:33c–34).

> Until the day began to dawn, Paul kept urging all to take some food. He said, "Today is the fourteenth day that you have been waiting, going hungry and eating nothing. I urge you, therefore, to take some food; it will help to survive. Not a hair of the head of any one of you will be lost."

It was the fourteenth night of the storm, toward midnight *(kata meson tes nyktes)*,[21] while they were still being driven on the Adriatic Sea. When the sailors suspected they were nearing land, they tried to abandon ship (27:27–30). Paul stopped them by addressing the centurion and the soldiers: "Unless these men stay with the ship, you cannot be saved" *(sothenai,* 27:31–32).

Paul's warning and implicit request can be understood on two levels. The first level is that of human survival. Unless the sailors stay with the ship, the passengers will perish. They would not be saved, that is, they would not survive. The second level is that of spiritual salvation. Referring to survival at sea, the story uses the Christian vocabulary of salvation. That is why Paul uses a passive form of the verb "to save," namely, *sothenai,* "to be saved." As Christians, we do not save ourselves. We are saved by the Lord Jesus.

Earlier, Luke had done the same thing, using language on two levels in describing the storm: "Neither the sun nor the stars were visible for many days, and no small storm raged. Finally, all hope *(elpis pasa)* of our surviving *(tou sozesthai hemas)* was taken away" (27:20). Hope *(elpis)* and being saved *(sozesthai)* can be understood as natural human hope and physical survival. It can also be understood as Christian hope and spiritual salvation. Like Paul in the warning (27:31–32), Luke as the narrator also uses the passive.

This use of the vocabulary of survival and salvation suggests that survival at sea is symbolic of Christian salvation. If that is so, the storm itself is symbolic of the evil forces that threaten salvation. But how are those on the ship to be saved? The story of the breaking of bread answers the question (27:33–38).

From midnight *(kata meson tes nyktes,* 27:27) until the day began to dawn *(achri de hou hemera emellen ginesthai,* 27:33, see also 27:39), Paul kept urging all to take some food *(metalabein trophes,*

27:33). To survive, those who were on the ship had to eat. For days (27:20), many had not been able to eat (*polles te asitias hyparchouses* 27:21). Now it was the fourteenth night (27:27) since they had left Myra in Lycia for Italy, and they had encountered difficulties from the start (27:5 – 8).

The food should be understood as ordinary food taken from the provisions of the ship or which the passengers had brought for themselves. Like Paul after his baptism (9:19), by eating they would recover their strength. But would ordinary food suffice to overcome the evil forces that threaten salvation? Would ordinary food bring salvation? The story invites us to think of another kind of food.

In the story of Paul's conversion, we read that "when he had eaten, he recovered his strength," stayed with the disciples in Damascus "and began at once to proclaim Jesus in the synagogues" (9:19 – 20). Paul's newly-recovered strength was for proclaiming the word.

In the summary of Paul's exhortation, Paul reminds all on the ship that it is the fourteenth day that they have waited, continuing to be hungry (*asitoi diateleite,* see 27:21) and taking nothing. Paul exhorts them to take some food (*metalabein trophes,* 27:34; see 27:33). Taking food would help them to survive, literally, taking food will be (*hyparchei*) for their salvation (*pros tes hymeteras soterias*). The food that Paul has in mind is not ordinary food. Such food would help them to survive at sea. But ordinary food would not bring them spiritual salvation.

Concluding the exhortation, Paul applies an old saying to those on the ship: "Not a hair of the head of any one of you will be lost" (27:34b; see 1 Samuel 14:45; 2 Samuel 14:11; 1 Kings 1:52).

In the Gospel, Jesus referred to the same saying on two occasions. While on the journey to Jerusalem, Jesus exhorted his disciples to have courage when they are persecuted: "Even the hairs of your head have all been counted. Do not be afraid" (Luke 12:7a). God, who takes care of little sparrows, would surely take care of them (12:6, 7b) Later, while teaching in the temple, Jesus told the people to expect persecution: "You will be hated by all because of my name, but not a hair on your head will be destroyed. By your perseverance you will secure your lives" (21:17 – 19).

Speaking to the passengers on the ship, Paul uses the saying in a similar way, suggesting that the storm is symbolic of persecution. In spite of the storm, not a hair of their head would be lost. None of the passengers would be lost. Earlier Paul had assured them that he had received a message from an angel of God: "Do not be afraid, Paul. You are destined to stand before Caesar; and behold, for your sake, God has granted safety to all who are sailing with you" (Acts 28:22 – 24).

The Breaking of the Bread (27:35 – 37)

After the introduction (27:33 – 34), the story continues with the body (27:35 – 37). After exhorting those on board to take some food in view of their salvation (27:33 – 34), Paul followed up his exhortation with his personal example, showing concretely that they would be saved.

> When he said this, he took bread, gave thanks to God in front of them all, broke it, and began to eat. They were all encouraged, and took some food themselves. In all, there were two hundred seventy-six of us on the ship.

The body of the story includes three elements. First, Paul took bread and broke it after giving thanks (27:35). Encouraged by his example, the others also ate (27:36). In conclusion, we are told the number of people who ate (27:37).

The body opens with a reference to a liturgical formula used when the community assembled to break the bread, especially on the first day of the week (see 20:7, 11). In the Gospel, Luke referred to the formula several times, beginning in Galilee when Jesus broke five loaves for a crowd of about five thousand (Luke 9:16), again in Jerusalem in the upper room at the Last Supper (22:19) and again at the home of the disciples of Emmaus (24:30, 35).

Acts introduced the breaking of the bread as an integral aspect of the church in Jerusalem, presenting the community in Jerusalem as an ideal for all the churches (2:42, 46). In a previous passage in Paul's journey to Rome, Acts included a story of an actual assembly for the breaking of the bread (20:7 – 12).

Earlier in the storm, Paul had introduced the theme of salvation and related it to taking food (27:20 – 21, 33 – 34). Eating something is necessary for salvation. Now, dramatically, he showed what kind of food is necessary for salvation. The bread that Christians break is the bread of salvation. For that he evoked the entire context of the breaking of the bread.

The story says that Paul "gave thanks to God in front of them all" (*enopion panton,* 27:35). What seems to be an insignificant detail recalls the meal that Jesus took with the community in Jerusalem at the end of the gospel: "They gave him a piece of baked fish; he took it and ate it in front of them" (*enopion autom,* Luke 24:43). Jesus gave them an example. As the living one, Jesus showed them that they too have to take food and eat. For Paul, giving thanks to God is integral to the breaking of the bread. Christians give thanks to God for the bread of salvation.

Having witnessed Paul, the others on the ship took food themselves (Acts 27:36). The story does not say that they partook of the bread Paul broke. But for Luke's readers, the food they took pointed to another kind of food. Just as the food they took assured their survival at sea, participating in the breaking of the bread would assure Luke's readers of their own Christian salvation.

In the gospel, when Jesus broke bread for a crowd, the story specified the number of those who ate as five thousand (Luke 9:14). Here the number is specified as 276. Most ships in the Mediterranean world were quite small, much smaller than this. Only Egyptian ships carrying grain were large enough for 276 passengers.

Lightening the Ship (27:38)

The conclusion says that they then lightened the ship.

> After they had eaten enough, they lightened the ship by throwing the wheat into the sea.

Passengers lived on the deck. The cargo was carried in the hold. Lightening the ship would allow it to get closer to the shore.

The story implies that they had eaten of the wheat stored in the hold. After eating, they had no further need of the wheat. For Christians, the bread broken in the breaking of the bread was sufficient for salvation. Paul had assured them of salvation if they took some food. Assured of their salvation, they threw the rest of the wheat into the sea.

In general, Alexandrian ships were large, carrying many passengers along with a great deal of cargo. To carry 276 passengers (27:37), the ship bringing Paul to Rome had to be very large. At the end of the season, it also must have had an exceptionally large cargo.

As they got nearer to land, the sea became shallower and shallower (27:28). As they approached the rocky coast (27:29), there was a real danger that the ship would strike rocks below the surface. They had already lightened the ship (27:18) by jettisoning some cargo and even the ship's tackle (27:19). It was now time to lighten it further.

They had quite a few bags of wheat left in the hold, most probably to serve as ballast. Throwing the rest of them overboard would give the ship less draft, allowing it to go over any rocks unscathed.[22]

When day came, they could make out a bay with a beach, and they headed for it, hoping to run the ship ashore. But even after throwing the rest of the cargo into the sea, the ship still had too much draft and ran aground on a sand bar.

They had lost the wheat but at least everyone could go ashore safely. They had reached the island of Malta, where the islanders welcomed Paul and the others and gave them hospitality (28:1 – 2).

In this sixth chapter, we saw that the understanding of the eucharist developed as part of Paul's journey to Rome. In the story of Troas, Luke showed that the breaking of the bread is related to the proclamation of the word and that the two are life-giving. Doing that, Luke also gave a good example of how the breaking of the bread could be celebrated (20:7 – 12).

In the story of the great storm, Luke showed that the breaking of the bread is salvific. Doing that, Luke also gave a good example of literature that is theological (27:33 – 38), providing a wonderful ending to his story of the development of the eucharist in the Book of Acts.

The Breaking of the Bread

It was over 50 years since the day Jesus "was taken up, after giving instructions through the holy Spirit to the apostles whom he had chosen" (Acts 1:2), over 50 years since the holy Spirit had come upon them (1:8) when they were together in Jerusalem on Pentecost (2:1 – 4).

At the very beginning, the church was very small, little more than three thousand people (2:41) living in Jerusalem. By birth, those first Christians were Jewish. Like Jesus, they observed the Sabbath, attended the synagogue, read the scriptures in Hebrew and worshiped at the temple. As Christians, they also broke bread in memory of Jesus (see Luke 22:19).

Since those early days, the church had grown by leaps and bounds. There was no stopping the gospel, as "the word of the Lord continued to spread with influence and power" (Acts 19:20). In the time of Luke, the church numbered many thousands throughout the Roman Empire and beyond.

That spread is reflected in Luke's description of the crowd at Pentecost, when "devout Jews from every nation under heaven" (2:5) heard the apostles, including Parthians, Medes and Elamites, inhabitants of Mesopotamia, Judea and Cappadocia, Pontus and Asia, Phrygia and Pamphylia, Egypt and the districts of Libya near Cyrene, as well as travelers from Rome" (2:9 – 10). The world of Luke-Acts stretched even to Africa and beyond Mesopotamia, deep into the Parthian Empire, Rome's giant rival to the east, to the very boundaries of India.

By Luke's time, Christians of Gentile origin had become a growing majority in the church, and the church was developing independently from Judaism and the synagogue. Christians of Gentile origin now broke bread at the same table with those of Jewish origin.

Luke wrote some fifteen years after the destruction of the temple (AD 70), when the church in Antioch-on-the-Orontes replaced Jerusalem as the center of the church. In the world of Luke-Acts, Christians assembled in various homes designated as homes for the church. They assembled as a church on the first day of the week, when they read the scriptures in Greek, listened to stories of Jesus, his followers and the early church.

They even had a name for themselves as followers of Christ. They called themselves Christians (see Acts 11:25). They also had a name for what Paul called the Lord's Supper (*to kyriakon deipnon,* 1 Corinthians 11:20). They called it "the breaking of the bread" (*he klasis tou artou,* Luke 24:35; Acts 2:42).[1]

In the Gospel, Luke had told the story of the origins of the church in Jesus' Galilean ministry (Luke 4:14 — 9:50) and in Jesus' journey to Jerusalem, when "the days for his being taken up were fulfilled" (9:51; see 24:50 – 53). He included the origins of the eucharist as part of the origins of the church.[2]

In the Acts of the Apostles, Luke told the story of the growth and development of the church. As in the Gospel, he included the development of the eucharist as part of the development of the church first in Jerusalem (1:15 — 5:42), then from Jerusalem to Antioch (6:1 — 12:25), and after that in the missions from Antioch (13:1 — 19:20). He also showed that the eucharist developed in Paul's journey to Rome, where Paul "proclaimed the kingdom of God and taught about the Lord Jesus Christ" (28:31).

The church and the assembly for the breaking of the bread are inseparable. Everything that affects the life of the church, for good or ill, affects the assembly for the breaking of the bread. Vice versa, everything that affects the assembly for the breaking of the bread affects the life of the church. Eucharistic issues are ecclesial issues, and ecclesial issues are eucharistic issues. In the Gospel, Luke showed that the eucharist is integral to the following of Christ. In the Acts of the Apostles, he showed that the eucharist is integral to the mission of the church.

In Luke-Acts, Luke was responding to the ecclesial and eucharistic issues that the church experienced in a time of rapid change in the middle of the ninth decade.[3] His response has important messages for us, as we too experience rapid change at the twilight of the 20th century and the dawn of the 21st. The Acts of the Apostles has much to teach us.

A Covenant of Salt

Before beginning the story of the church, Luke summarized the story of Jesus: "In the first book, Theophilus, I dealt with all that Jesus did and taught until the day he was taken up, after giving instructions through the holy Spirit to the apostles whom he had chosen" (1:1–2). The church springs from the life and mission of Jesus. As an integral element in the life of the church, the eucharist also springs from the life and mission of Jesus.

At the beginning of the prologue of Acts, Luke described how Jesus presented himself to the apostles after the passion, when he appeared to them for a period of forty days, speaking to them about the kingdom of God while sharing meals with them (1:3–4a). In those meals, the Lord Jesus shared salt with the apostles, bonding them to himself and to one another in a covenant of salt, assuring that the covenant would endure. Having shared salt with them for forty days, Jesus continued to be present to them and through them to the church, particularly when they assembled for the breaking of the bread. Having shared salt with Jesus, they would act and speak in his name, doing what Jesus did in memory of him.

The Breaking of the Bread

In the first section of Acts (1:15 — 5:42), Luke described the primitive church in Jerusalem as an ideal for all the communities: "They devoted themselves to the teaching of the apostles and to the communal life, to the breaking of the bread and to the prayers" (2:42).

The Christians broke bread when they assembled as a church on the first day of the week. They also broke bread apart from the assembly each day in their respective homes. Both were important, each with a different significance, each filling an important Christian need.

The difference between those two expressions of the breaking of the bread was the assembly. When the Christians assembled as a church, they proclaimed who they were as baptized Christians. Assembling on the first day of the week, they proclaimed the new creation in Christ. As such, the assembly was symbolic of the unity of the human race in the person of Christ.

Breaking bread each day in their homes was also significant. Those meals were also an expression of their religious life as Christians. Referring to the breaking of bread in their homes, Luke wrote that "they ate their meals with exultation and sincerity of heart, praising God and enjoying favor with all the people" (2:46–47).

Gathering as intimate family units, friends or colleagues, the Christians nourished their life as Christians. Christ was surely present with them at those meals. In some sense, therefore, they must be considered eucharistic. Unlike the meals when Christians assembled as a church on the first day of the week, those meals, however, were not a sign of the unity and universality of the church.

To avoid confusion, I do not refer to these meals as celebrations of the eucharist. Theological reflection on such Christian meals would be helpful for us today when many communities lack a priest to celebrate the eucharist. As we saw in the story of the breaking of the bread at Troas, the breaking of the bread is a matter of life (20:7–12). In the story of the breaking of the bread on the ship in the midst of a great storm, the breaking of the bread is also a matter of salvation (27:33–38).

Breaking bread in our homes or among friends, we should pray and recall the meals Jesus shared as part of his ministry. We should also recall the meals the early Christians shared at home when they did not assemble as a church. But we should avoid speaking the eucharistic prayer with its liturgical formula for the Lord's Supper. Breaking bread each day in our homes should make us hungry to break bread on the first day of the week.

For the church, the assembly fulfilled many purposes. Assembling as a church, the Christians prayed (12:12; 13:1–3), collected money (Acts 11:29; 12:25; 1 Corinthians 16:1–2) and distributed money, food and other necessities to those in need (Acts 6:1). The assembly was also an opportunity for preaching and teaching, as Paul did at Troas before the breaking of the bread (20:7–12). Some assemblies were very special, as when a noted apostle, prophet or teacher came (20:7–12), or when the church assembled to address a major issue (1:15–26; 6:1–7; 15:1–29).

The high point of the assembly was the breaking of the bread, when the Christians took bread, gave thanks to God, broke the bread and ate. After eating, they shared the word in light of their breaking of the bread. As such, what we call the liturgy of the word and the homily took place after the eucharistic liturgy, not before. In that setting, the homily could take the form of discourse, discussion, dialogue or conversation.

Special Roles in the Breaking of the Bread

In Luke's Gospel, Jesus is the only one who takes bread, blesses God or gives thanks, breaks the bread and gives it to those assembled (9:16; 22:19; 24:30). From the Gospel, we learn very little of what the communities did after Jesus' passion and resurrection.

From elsewhere in the New Testament, including the summary of the life of the church in Acts (2:42–47), we learn that the communities broke the bread. But just about every reference to the breaking of the bread leaves us with a question. Who actually broke the bread? In our terms, who was the presider or celebrant at the breaking of the bread?

We assume that, at least at the very beginning, those who welcomed the community to their home must have been those who did what Jesus did. As Jesus did in the Gospel, the host must have taken bread, blessed God or given thanks, broken the bread and given it to the participants. In our terms, the host was the presider or celebrant.

We assume that later, those who were appointed elders (see 14:23) acted as the host for the church. Acts does not distinguish between the elders *(presbyteroi)* and the overseers *(episkopoi)* of the church (see Acts 20:17–28). One of the elders must have been the presider or celebrant when the Christians assembled as a church for the breaking of the bread.

Fortunately, three stories in the Acts of the Apostles open a window on the early development of special roles at the breaking of the bread. First, there is the story of the Seven in Acts 6:1–7. There is also the story of Paul at Troas (20:7–12). Finally, there is the story of Paul breaking bread on the ship at the height of the storm (27:33–38).

The story of the Seven (6:1–7) shows how the Seven were chosen to serve *(diakonein)* at tables. The Seven were selected by the community, which presented them to the apostles. The apostles then "prayed and laid hands on them," (6:6) conferring on them the ministry they themselves fulfilled. According to Luke, Jesus served at table at the Last Supper (22:27) and he told the apostles to do the same (22:26). That is how they would fulfill his command, "do this in memory of me" (22:19). In the story of the Seven, the apostles shared that responsibility with the Seven.

The apostles would attend to the ministry of the word, the proclamation of the gospel, and to prayer. Sharing in the mission of Twelve, the Seven would serve at tables. The story of the Seven tells about the beginning of specialization in the ministry of the church. It also shows that the ministry of the word together with prayer is the primary ministry, the one on which all the other ministries depend to be effective.

Luke-Acts does not distinguish between the various orders that the church has today. In modern terms, however, the story of the Seven says more about the origin of the priesthood than about the diaconate. Chosen by the community, the Seven served at table as the Twelve did. They served at the breaking of the bread. We have to conclude that, according to Acts, the Seven must have fulfilled the role that the presider or celebrant fulfills today.

The two references to the breaking of the bread in Paul's great journey to Rome shed light on the development of liturgical roles in the early church. Both say explicitly that Paul broke the bread (20:11; 27:35).

Paul was not a member of the local community at Troas. As the one who first preached the word at Troas and visited the community several times, Paul was a special guest. In 20:7–12, he came to address the community for the last time. He did that when the community assembled to break bread on the first day of the week. As such, he came to the church in Troas as a prophet and teacher (see 13:1–3). He also acted as prophet and teacher when he broke the bread on the ship in the midst of the storm (27:33–38).

The stories show that an itinerant prophet was expected to break the bread for the community. In our terms, the elder who hosted the community may have presided at the assembly but he was not the celebrant. Paul, the itinerant prophet, was the celebrant.

The practice of having a Christian prophet break bread must have been fairly widespread. The section on the eucharist in the *Didache* includes this instruction: "But permit the prophets to give thanks as much as they desire" (*Didache* 10:7). In the *Didache*, the name for the Lord's Supper is "the eucharist," that is, giving thanks. If in the *Didache* the name had been "the breaking of the bread," the instruction would have referred to breaking bread instead of giving thanks.

Notes

Chapter 1

1. See Eugene LaVerdiere, *Dining in the Kingdom of God: The Origins of the Eucharist According to Luke* (Chicago: Liturgy Training Publications, 1994) (hereafter cited as *Dining in the Kingdom of God*).

2. In Mark, the women's visit to the tomb (Mark 16:1–8) forms the conclusion of the Gospel. Luke transformed Mark's conclusion into an introduction (Luke 24:1–12) for the story of Emmaus (24:13–35) and Jesus' appearance to the community in Jerusalem (24:36–53).

3. For Luke 24, see Richard J. Dillon, *From Eye-Witnesses to Ministers of the Word: Tradition and Composition in Luke 24* (Rome: Biblical Institute Press, 1978); Joseph A. Fitzmyer, *The Gospel According to Luke X–XXIV,* The Anchor Bible, 28A (Garden City, New York: Doubleday, 1985), 1532–1593; *Dining in the Kingdom of God,* 150–186.

For the story of Emmaus, see also Arthur A. Just, Jr., *The Ongoing Feast: Table Fellowship and Eschatology at Emmaus,* A Pueblo Book (Collegeville: The Liturgical Press, 1993).

4. Like John, Luke tells of two visits to the tomb: that of the women (Luke 24:1–11) and that of Peter (Luke 24:12; see John 20:1–2, 11–18 and 20:3–10). Later, on the way to Emmaus, Cleopas refers to both visits (Luke 24:22–23 and 24).

5. For commentaries in English on the Acts of the Apostles, see F. F. Bruce, *The Book of the Acts,* rev. ed. (Grand Rapids: William B. Eerdmans, 1988), and *The Acts of the Apostles: Greek Text with Introduction and Commentary,* 3rd ed. (Grand Rapids: William B. Eerdmans, 1990) (hereafter cited as *Acts of the Apostles, Greek Text*); Ernst Haenchen, *The Acts of the Apostles: A Commentary* (Philadelphia: Westminster Press, 1971); Robert C. Tannehill, *The Narrative Unity of Luke-Acts: A Literary Interpretation,* vol. 2, *The Acts of the Apostles* (Minneapolis: Fortress Press, 1990); Luke Timothy Johnson, *The Acts of the Apostles,* Sacra Pagina 5 (Collegeville: The Liturgical Press, 1992).

6. Bruce describes "the acts of the apostles" as "for Luke the acts of the ascended Christ"; As such, "they have their place among the events which herald the passing away of the old age and the inauguration of the new"; *Acts of the Apostles, Greek Text,* 99.

7. The *Catechism of the Catholic Church* (1994) refers to this verse (Acts 2:42) seven times, more than any other verse of Acts (quoting directly in 949, 1342, 2624, and referring indirectly in 3, 857, 1329, 2178). Luke's description of the apostolic church in Jerusalem remains very significant for the church today.

8. For a general study of the eucharist in the New Testament, see Xavier Leon-Dufour, *Sharing the Eucharistic Bread: The Witness of the New Testament,* trans. Matthew J. O'Connell (New York: Paulist Press, 1987). For shorter studies, see J. Delorme et al., *The Eucharist in the New Testament: A Symposium,* trans. E. M. Stewart (Bethlehem: Helicon Press, 1965); *The Breaking of Bread, Concilium* 40, ed. Pierre Benoit, OP,

Roland Murphy, oCarm, and Bastiaan Van Iersel, smm (New York: Paulist Press, 1969); and Jerome Kodell, *The Eucharist in the New Testament,* Zacchaeus Studies: New Testament (Collegeville: The Liturgical Press, 1991).

9. *Dining in the Kingdom of God,* 1–30.

10. For the eucharist in the Acts of the Apostles, see Eugene LaVerdiere, "The Breaking of the Bread: The Eucharist in the Acts of the Apostles," *Emmanuel* 100 (July–August 1994): 324–335; Philippe H. Menoud, "The Acts of the Apostles and the Eucharist," in *Jesus Christ and the Faith,* trans. Eunice M. Paul (Pittsburgh: The Pickwick Press, 1978), 84–106.

11. See also Isaiah 58:7, where the LXX's expression is *diathryptein ton arton,* instead of *klon ton arton.*

12. For early rabbinical positions regarding blessings at a meal, see *The Mishnah,* First Division, *Zeraim* ("Seeds"), First Tractate, *Berakoth* ("Blessings"), 8:1, 5–8.

13. For the Jewish ritual, see Joachim Jeremias, *The Eucharistic Words of Jesus,* trans. Norman Perrin (Philadelphia: Fortress Press, 1966), 108–111, 119–120. "Breaking bread" was basically a domestic rite: "Among the Jews the action of 'breaking bread' was the central one in a 'domestic' rite that marked the beginning of a family meal, whether ordinary or festive" (Leon-Dufour, *Sharing the Eucharistic Bread,* 22).

14. For the practice of "breaking bread" in Jewish usage and in the early church, I am indebted to Rene Pothier, sss, a Canadian colleague, who made available to me his unpublished essay, *La Fraction du Pain,* which he submitted to the Institut Catholique de Paris for his master's degree in theology (October 1993).

15. The term "companion" comes from the Latin words *cum* (with) and *panis* (bread). Etymologically, a companion is one who eats "bread with" someone.

16. A number of early Christian blessing prayers have been preserved in chapters 9 and 10 of the *Didache.* For these, see Jean-Paul Audet, *La Didache: instructions des apôtres* (Paris: J. Gabalda, 1958), 372–433; Enrico Mazza, *The Origins of the Eucharistic Prayer* (Collegeville: The Liturgical Press, 1995), 12–41; Eugene LaVerdiere, "On the Lord's Day: The Eucharist in the *Didache,*" *Emmanuel* 100 (October 1994): 452–465, revised and published as part of Eugene LaVerdiere, *The Eucharist in the New Testament and the Early Church* (Collegeville: The Liturgical Press, 1996), 128–147.

17. For the eucharistic symposium and the cultural background, see *Dining in the Kingdom of God,* 16–18.

18. I first learned that in the Philippines, where Tagalog and the other Filipino languages have no word for "community." It is the same in many other languages. For the Filipinos, community is simply part of human life.

19. As we read in an instruction from the Congregation for Divine Worship and the Discipline of the Sacraments, *Inculturation and the Roman Liturgy,* issued January 25, 1994, "The nature of the liturgy is intimately linked up with the nature of the church; indeed, it is above all in the liturgy that the nature of the church is manifested (*Sacrosanctum Concilium,* 2; *Vicesimus Quintus Annus,* 9). Now the church has specific characteristics which distinguish it from every other assembly and community.

"It is not gathered together by a human decision, but is called by God in the Holy Spirit and responds in faith to his gratuitous call (*ekklesia* derives from *klesis,* "call") (#2).

20. As we read in *Inculturation and the Roman Liturgy,* "Because it is catholic, the church overcomes the barriers which divide humanity: By baptism all become children of God and form in Christ Jesus one people where 'there is neither Jew nor Greek, neither slave nor free, neither male nor female' (Galatians 3:28). Thus church is called to gather all peoples, to speak the languages, to penetrate all cultures" (#2).

21. See K. L. Schmidt, *ekklesia,* in Kittel's *Theological Dictionary of the New Testament* (Grand Rapids: William B. Eerdmans, 1965), III: 501–536.

22. In the Septuagint, *ekklesia* is the ordinary rendering of the Hebrew term *qahal.*

23. For the background of *koinonia* and related words, see Friedrich Hauck, *koinos,* in Kittel's *Theological Dictionary of the New Testament* III: 789–809, especially 804–809.

24. Besides Acts 2:42, *koinonia* appears 17 times in the New Testament. Of those, 13 are in the letters of Paul: Romans 15:26; 1 Corinthians 1:9; 10:16 (2); 2 Corinthians 6:14; 8:4; 9:13; 13:13; Galatians 2:9; Philippians 1:5; 2:1; 3:10; Philemon 6. Apart from these, the term appears in Hebrews 13:16 and 1 John 1:3, 6, 7.

25. *Sic apparet universa Ecclesia sicuti "de unitate Patris et Filii et Spiritus Sancti adunata"* (Saint Cyprian, *De Orat. Dom.* 23). For the English translation of the documents of Vatican II, see Austin Flannery, OP, general editor, *Vatican Council II: The Conciliar and Post Conciliar Documents,* Vatican Collection, I (Northport, New York: Costello, 1975).

26. The word "joy" *(chara)* is a favorite word in Luke-Acts, appearing 8 times in Luke (1:14; 2:10; 8:13; 10:17; 15:7, 10; 24:41, 52) and 4 times in Acts (8:8; 12:14; 13:52; 15:3).

27. *Communicando enim Spiritum suum, fratres suos, ex omnibus gentibus convocatos, tamqum corpus suum mystice constituit.*

28. *Sicut vero omnia corporis humani membra, licet multa sint, unum tamen corpus efformant, ita fideles in Christo* (see also 1 Corinthians 12, 12).

29. *In fractione panis eucharistici de Corpore Domini realiter participantes, ad communionem cum Eo ac inter nos elevamur. "Quoniam unus panis, unum corpus multi sumus, omne qui de uno pane participamus"* (1 Corinthians 10:17). *Ita nos omnes membra illius Corporis efficimur* (see also 1 Corinthians 12:27), *"singuli autem alter alterius membra"* (Romans 12:5).

30. 2 Corinthians 13:13 is Paul's closing greeting at the end of the letter. Very likely, Paul's opening and closing greetings are based on traditional Christian greetings used when a church assembled for the Lord's Supper.

31. For the Second Eucharistic Prayer and its relationship to the anaphora of Hippolytus, see Enrico Mazza, *The Eucharistic Prayers of the Roman Rite,* trans. Matthew J. O'Connell (New York: Pueblo, 1986, now from The Liturgical Press), 88–122; for the translation of the beginning of the preface and of the epiclesis, see pages 95 and 118. See also David N. Power, *The Eucharistic Mystery: Revitalizing the Tradition* (New York: Crossroad, 1992), 89–93.

32. See Jerome Murphy-O'Connor, "The First Letter to the Corinthians," in *The New Jerome Biblical Commentary* (Englewood Cliffs, New Jersey: Prentice-Hall, 1990), 808.

33. See *Dining in the Kingdom of God.*

34. See *Dining in the Kingdom of God.*

Chapter 2

1. As a secondary preface, Acts 1:1–2 recalls Luke 1:1–4, a preface for the whole of Luke-Acts. Both prefaces address Theophilus, who was very likely a patron who saw to the copying and dissemination of Luke's two-volume work.

2. Luke's summary of the gospel as "all that Jesus began to do and teach" (1:1) is reminiscent of the title for the Gospel of Mark, "The beginning of the gospel of Jesus Christ [the Son of God]." Like Mark, who wrote "the beginning of the gospel," Luke wrote what "Jesus began to do and teach." Unlike Mark, however, Luke wrote a second volume, the Acts of the Apostles, dealing with what Jesus continued to do and teach.

3. Regarding the Hellenistic symposium, see *Dining in the Kindom of God,* 16–18.

4. The aorist passive form, *anelemphthe* (see also *analemphtheis* in 1:11), of the verb *analambano,* is related to the noun *analempsis,* used when Jesus began his journey to the ascension (Luke 9:51).

5. Concerning the expression *synalizomenos,* Hans Conzelmann commented, "The setting for the incident described here is not clear, nor is the sense of the verb *synalizesthai.* Does it mean 'assemble' (this is the sense of the active in Josephus), or 'eat (salt) together' (cf. 10:41!)?"

6. See William F. Arndt and F. Wilbur Gingrich, *A Greek-English Lexicon of the New Testament and Other Early Christian Literature* (Chicago: University of Chicago Press, 1957), 791.

7. Besides *halas* (salt), *halizo* (to salt) and *synalizo* (in the passive, to share salt with), the New Testament vocabulary related to salt includes *halykos* (salty), *analos* (salt-less, insipid), *artyo* (to season as with salt) and *moraino* (in the passive, to become tasteless, insipid).

8. See James E. Latham, *The Religious Symbolism of Salt,* Theologie Historique 64 (Paris: Beauchesne, 1982), 221–225. See also Eugene LaVerdiere, "Salted with Fire," *Emmanuel* 97 (September 1991): 394–400.

9. For an analysis, see Latham, *The Religious Symbolism of Salt,* 212–220.

10. For an analysis, see Latham, *The Religious Symbolism of Salt,* 203–211.

11. For a literal reference to salt in the New Testament, see James 3:12, referring to salty *(halikos)* water *(hydor),* in the sense of a salt spring.

12. Lexicographers distinguish between the literal and the figurative meanings of a word. When someone fails to recognize or refuses to accept the figurative meaning, we call that person's interpretation not literal, but literalistic.

13. See Arndt, Gingrich, *A Greek Lexicon,* 791.

14. For an example of the verb *synalizo* (long *a*) in the active voice, see *Jewish Antiquities:* "And all the other vessels he [Solomon] collected *(synalisas)* and deposited within the temple" (VIII. 105).

15. For an example of the verb *synalizo* (long *a*) in the passive voice, see *Jewish War:* "Vespasian, in order to prevent the pirates from congregating *(synalistheien)* there again, established a camp on the acropolis and left in it the cavalry with a small body of infantry" (III. 429).

16. Arndt, Gingrich, *A Greek-English Lexicon, loc. cit.,* 791. See also Bruce, *Acts of the Apostles, Greek Text,* 101.

17. For a comprehensive and insightful treatment, see Latham, *The Religious Symbolism of Salt;* see also his entry *"Sel"* in *Dictionnaire de Spiritualité* (Paris: Beauchesne, 1990), XIV, cc. 544–549.

18. For a good analysis of Job 6:2–7, see Norman C. Habel, *The Book of Job: A Commentary* (Philadelphia: Westminster Press, 1985), 137–151.

19. See Jerome Carcopino, *Daily Life in Ancient Rome,* trans. E. O. Lorimer (New Haven: Yale University Press, 1959), chap. 2, "Houses and Streets," 22–51.

20. *"ibi maxime usurpanda observatione quae totis corporibus nihil esse utilius sale et sole dixit"* Pliny the Elder, *Natural History,* Book XXXI, xlv, 102.

21. For a reevaluation of the place of salt in the modern diet, see Suzanne Hamlin, "Salt Is Regaining Favor and Savor," *The New York Times* (Wednesday, June 5, 1996), C 1.

22. Pliny, *Natural History,* Book XXXI, xli, 87.

23. Pliny, *Natural History,* Book XXXI, xli, 87.

24. *"ergo, Hercules, vita humanior sine sale non quit degere, adeoque necessarium elementum est uti transierit intellectus ad voluptates animi quoque nimias. Sales appellantur, omnisque vitae lepos et summa hilaritas laborumque requies non alio magis vocabulo constat"* (Pliny, *Natural History,* Book XXXI, xli, 88).
See also Cicero, the orator, who taught that every oration should be salted with humor and wit: *"libandus est etiam ex omni genere urbanitatis facetiarum quidam lepos, quo tamquam sale perspergatur omnis oratio"* (De Oratore I. 34).

25. *"et salem cum pane esitasse eos proverbio apparent"* (Pliny, *Natural History,* Book XXXI, xli, 89).

26. "The *mola salsa* of the Romans was a carefully ground meal mixed with salt. It was offered to the gods at the beginning of each meal and sometimes thrown on victims to be immolated in the name of the State" (Latham, *The Religious Symbolism of Salt,* 31).

27. Plutarch's Moralia VIII, "Table-Talk," *Quaestiones Convivales,* trans. Herbert B. Hoffleit (Cambridge: Harvard University Press, 1969), Question 4, #3, 344–349.

28. Concerning meals of hospitality, see *Dining in the Kingdom of God,* 19–21.

29. Aristotle, *Nicomachean Ethics,* VIII, iii, 8.

30. Aristotle, *Eudemian Ethics,* VII, ii.

31. Cicero, *De Amicitia* XIX, 67.

32. Pliny, *Natural History,* XXXI, xli, 89.

33. Virgil, *The Aeneid,* II, 133. The translation is from Latham, *The Religious Symbolism of Salt,* 31.

34. For the various kinds of sacrifice, especially the holocaust and the communion sacrifice, and their significance, see Roland de Vaux, "Les sacrifices de l'Ancient Testament," *Les Cahiers de la Revue Biblique* 1 (Paris: J. Gabalda, 1964): 29–48.

35. Exodus 25–31, presenting the divine command to build and maintain God's Dwelling (LXX, *skene,* tent), is attributed to the priestly author and redactor.

36. The preserving and purifying functions of salt were closely associated. That may help explain why Elisha purified bad water by throwing salt into it (2 Kings 2:19–22).

37. Philo, *The Special Laws (De Specialibus Legibus),* trans. F. H. Colson, The Loeb Classical Library, Book VII (Cambridge: Harvard University Press, 1958) Book I, 289.

38. Philo, *The Special Laws,* Book I, 285.

39. Philo, *The Special Laws,* Book I, 290.

40. Much of the Book of Numbers, including 1:1—10:28; 15; 17—19; 26—31, and 33—36, is from the priestly author(s). Those sections are thus attributable mainly to the 6th century, but with later additions; see Conrad L'Heureux, "Numbers," *The New Jerome Biblical Commentary* (Englewood Cliffs, New Jersey: Prentice-Hall, 1990), 80.

41. Before the work of Latham, the only extended treatment of the expression "covenant of salt" was a booklet by H. C. Trumbull, *The Covenant of Salt* (New York: Charles Scribner's Sons, 1899). Trumbull was helpful in gathering up some of the ancient material and with some of his reflections, but as Latham wrote, "Trumbull's final conclusion is so gratuitous that it cannot be taken seriously" (*The Religious Symbolism of Salt,* 41).

42. For the various forms of covenant in the ancient world and their relationship to the covenants in the Old Testament, see Dennis McCarthy, *Treaty and Covenant,* Analecta Biblica 21A, rev. ed. (Rome: Biblical Institute Press, 1981). McCarthy shows that the Sinai covenant reflects many elements from the extra-biblical covenants, but is basically quite original; see chap. 12, "Sinai," 243–276.

43. As Bruce wrote, "Luke presents one continuous story of Jesus, telling how he worked first on earth and then from heaven. *Erxato* is emphatic here, and should not be regarded merely as a semitizing auxiliary" (*Acts of the Apostles, Greek Text,* 98). See also Johnson, *The Acts of the Apostles,* 24.

44. "By many convincing ways" is my rendering of *en pollois tekmeriois.* The noun *tekmerion* may mean "sign" or "proof." In this case, "sign" seems too weak, and "proof" a bit misleading. For Aristotle, *tekmerion* meant "proof," but of an argumentative kind, whereas to signify Jesus presenting himself alive after the passion calls for some form of direct experiential evidence.

45. The city of Joppa, whose Hebrew name is Japha, is by the sea on the outskirts of present-day Tel Aviv. Early on, there must have been a flourishing community there. According to Acts, Peter stayed a long time in Joppa at the home of Simon the tanner (9:43).

46. At the time, Peter was a few miles away in Lydda (9:38). Lydda, whose Hebrew name is Lod, is at the present-day site of Israel's Ben Gurion Airport.

47. See also the story of Jesus raising the only son of the widow of Nain: "Young man, I tell you, arise!" When the young man sat up and began to speak, Jesus gave him to his mother (Luke 7:11–17). All three stories (Acts 9:36–43; Luke 8:40–42, 49–56; Luke 7:11–17) were very likely handed down in a baptismal, catechetical or liturgical context.

48. The relationship between eating and being alive is also highlighted in the story of Eutychus (20:7–12). When the community at Troas assembled for the breaking of the bread on the eve of Paul's departure, Eutychus fell from the fourth story to his death. Raised to life, the boy returned upstairs with Paul and joined the community in breaking the bread. At daybreak, "they took the boy alive *(zonta)* and were immeasurably comforted" (20:12).

49. In Mark, however, Jesus did not fast. While he was among wild beasts, angels ministered *(diakonoun)* to him (Mark 1:13).

50. Mount Horeb, like Mount Sinai, is a name for the mountain of God.

Chapter 3

1. For the implications of "eating with" someone in the context of Luke-Acts, see Robert J. Karris, OFM, *Luke: Artist and Theologian* (New York: Paulist Press, 1985), 57–65.

2. See Murphy-O'Connor, "The First Letter to the Corinthians," in *The New Jerome Biblical Commentary,* 808.

3. The expression "golden age" is from Hesiod's *Works and Days,* written to show how to live in a difficult world. Hesiod divided the history of the world into five ages, beginning with the golden age (lines 110–120), which was followed by a silver age, a bronze age, a heroic age and an iron age (Loeb Classical Library; Cambridge: Harvard University Press, 1936). Presenting the founding years of a community or city in terms of a "golden age" was widespread in Hellenistic literature (see Johnson, *The Acts of the Apostles,* 62).

4. This is the first time (5:11) the term "church" *(ekklesia)* appears in Luke-Acts.

5. See Jeremias, *The Eucharistic Words of Jesus,* 120–121, n. 3.

6. In the preparations for the Last Supper in Luke, the term for "upper room" was *anagaion* (Luke 22:12) instead of *hyperoon* (1:13).

7. See Johnson, *The Acts of the Apostles,* 43–44.

8. With the exception of "Judas Iscariot, who became a traitor" (Luke 6:14), the names of the apostles given in Acts 1:13 are the same as in Luke when Jesus "called his disciples to himself and from them he chose Twelve, whom he also named apostles" (Luke 6:13). The names, however, are not given in exactly the same order.

9. Peter's inaugural discourse in Jerusalem (2:14–41) is to Acts what Jesus' inaugural discourse at Nazareth (Luke 4:16–30) is to the Gospel. Just as Jesus' discourse defined and announced his mission, Peter's discourse defines and announces that of the church. For a short synopsis of the speeches in Acts, see Eduard Schweizer, "Concerning the Speeches in Acts," in *Studies in Luke-Acts,* ed. Leander E. Keck and J. Louis Martyn (Philadelphia: Fortress Press, 1980), 208–216.

For a study of tradition and Lukan reinterpretation in the speeches of Peter in Acts 2 and 3, see Richard F. Zehnle, *Peter's Pentecost Discourse,* Society of Biblical Literature Monograph Series 15 (New York: Abingdon Press, 1971). Borrowing a phrase from Henry J. Cadbury (*The Making of Luke-Acts,* 1927; 188), Zehnle described Peter's first discourse as a "keynote address" (17). Cadbury had used this expression to describe Jesus' address in the synagogue at Nazareth (Luke 4:17–28). Regarding Peter's Pentecost discourse, Zehnle concluded that it is to be regarded "as a theological synthesis of Luke, placed at the head of the book of Acts to give the theological perspectives from which the mission of the community is to be understood" (136).

10. Regarding Peter's second discourse, Zehnle concluded that "Luke has reproduced in it traditions which reflect the preaching of the apostles in the period that preceded the beginning of the break with the synagogue" (*Peter's Pentecost Disourse,* 136).

11. Peter's discourses in the first section of Acts, along with his discourse at the home of Cornelius (10:34–49) and Paul's discourse in 13:16–41, contain the basic preaching *(kerygma)* and teaching *(didache)* of the apostles. For this reason, the discourses are often referred to as "kerygmatic." In 1 Corinthians 15:1, Paul refers to the same preaching or teaching (see 1 Corinthians 15:3b–5) as "the gospel" *(to euggelion)* he preached *(ho euaggelisamen)* when he first came to Corinth (1 Corinthians 15:1–3a).

12. The first part of Acts (1:15—5:42) thus includes three major summaries of life in the community (2:42–47; 4:32–35; 5:12–16). The three summaries are thematically related. These summaries move the story forward and fill it in when further stories would distract from the greater picture. The summaries not only describe the community in Jerusalem at its origins, but constitute an appropriate challenge for the other communities. Ultimately, the summaries are about the church as such, not only the church in Jerusalem.

13. For the brief concluding summaries, see 2:41; 4:4, 31; 5:11, 42; see also 1:14 at the end of the prologue. Each unit in the first part of Acts (2:1–41; 3:1—4:31; 4:32—5:11; 5:12–42) concludes with a summary.

14. This last summary recalls a theme from the first major summary (2:42–47), with its reference to the teaching and proclaiming the Messiah, Jesus, "both at the temple and in their homes" (5:42).

15. For the literary history of the summaries, see Pierre Benoit, "Some Notes on the 'Summaries' in Acts 2, 4 and 5," in *Jesus and the Gospel,* II (New York: Crossroad, 1974), 94–103.

16. The summaries regarding the growth of the church (see 2:47b; 5:14; 6:7; 9:31; 11:21, 24; 16:5) and the growth of the Word (6:7; 12:24; 19:20) form an important refrain in the Book of Acts.

17. Some read Acts 2:42 as a concluding summary for the Pentecost unit (2:1–42) or for the unit beginning with the assembly to replace Judas (1:15—2:42). But since 2:41 is already a summary and since 2:42 is developed in 2:43–47, it seems best to read it as a transitional summary.

18. For a good commentary on the parables in Luke, see John R. Donahue, sj, *The Gospel in Parable: Metaphor, Narrative, and Theology in the Synoptic Gospels*

(Philadelphia: Fortress Press, 1988), 126–193. For Donahue, the parables "offer a Gospel in miniature and at the same time give shape, direction, and meaning to the Gospels in which they are found," ix.

19. The plural for "magus" is "magi." Magi, originally associated with the ancient Iranian religion of Zarathustra (Zoroaster), had spread through much of the Roman world by the first century AD.

20. Like Peter's discourse on Pentecost, Paul's discourse at the synagogue in Antioch of Pisidia can be considered his inaugural discourse, giving the keynote for all his later discourses.

21. For the verb *kerysso* in Acts, see 8:5; 9:20; 10:37, 42; 15:21; 19:13; 20:25; 28:31.

22. See Luke Timothy Johnson, *Sharing Possessions: Mandate and Symbol of Faith* (Philadelphia: Fortress Press, 1981).

23. The origins of the Essenes can be best seen in the document catalogued as 1QSa, where we see them as part of a revolutionary movement, probably related to the revolt of the Maccabees. See D. Barthelemy, "Annexes à la Règle de la Communauté," in *Discoveries in the Judaean Desert* I (Oxford: Clarendon Press, 1955), 107–118. After a few years, they seem to have broken with the mainstream of the movement but retained a quasi-military form of community life, referring to themselves as living in "camps." By the last quarter of the second century BC they had gravitated to the towns and villages of Judea and lived alongside other Jewish groups. Their life in "camps" as well as in towns and villages is best seen from the Damascus Document. See G. Vermes, *The Dead Sea Scrolls in English* (Baltimore: Penguin Books, 1962), 97–117.

24. See Vermes, *The Dead Sea Scrolls in English,* 110.

25. See A. R. C. Leaney, *The Rule of Qumran and Its Meaning* (Philadelphia: The Westminster Press, 1966), 115, 122–123. For other references to property in the *Rule of the Community,* see 3:2; 5:1–3, 14–20; 6:13b–23, 24–25; 9:7–11.

26. See Karris, *Luke: Artist and Theologian,* 23–46, as well as his earlier article, "Poor and Rich: The Lukan *Sitz im Leben,*" in *Perspectives on Luke-Acts,* ed. Charles H. Talbert (Danville, VA: Association of Baptist Professors of Religion, 1978), 112–125.

27. For a good analysis of the background and meaning of the expression, *epi to auto,* see Max Wilcox, *The Semitisms of Acts* (Oxford: Clarendon Press, 1965), 93–100; James Hope, J. H. Moulton, Wilbert Francis Howard, *A Grammar of New Testament Greek* II (Edinburgh: T. & T. Clark, 1920), 473; Matthew Black, *An Aramaic Approach to the Gospels and Acts,* 2d. ed. (Oxford: Clarendon Press, 1954), 9–10.

28. See Matthew 22:34; Luke 17:35; Acts 1:15; 2:1, 44, 47; 1 Corinthians 7:5; 11:20; 14:23. It also appears in Acts 4:26 in a quotation from the Septuagint, Psalm 2:2.

29. The ordinary meaning of *epi to auto* persisted outside Christian circles. In the Acts of the martyrdom of Justin and his companions (circa AD 165), "Rusticus the prefect said, 'Where do you assemble?' Justin said, 'Where each one chooses and can; for do you fancy that we all meet in the very same place *(epi to auto)*? Not so; because the God of the Christians is not circumscribed by place; but being invisible, fills heaven and earth, and everywhere is worshipped and glorified by the faithful.'" See *The Ante-Nicene Fathers* I (Grand Rapids: William B. Eerdmans, 1981); for a critical text in Greek and a translation in French, see Andre Wartelle, *Saint Justin: Apologies* (Paris: Études Augustiniennes, 1987): 226–233.

30. See *Dining in the Kingdom of God,* 33–70.

31. In Mark, Jesus gave orders to the Twelve to have the crowd recline by symposia. The people then took their places by symposia of hundreds and fifties (Mark 6:39–40). In Mark, the communities numbered between fifty and one hundred.

32. See *Dining in the Kingdom of God,* 121–148.

33. See *Dining in the Kingdom of God,* 153–174.

34. For the upper room in relation to the life of the community, see Bradley Blue, "Acts and the House Church," in *The Book of Acts in Its Graeco-Roman Setting* (Grand Rapids: William B. Eerdmans, 1994), 130–138.

35. See Eugene LaVerdiere, "Mary's Son, God's Firstborn," *Church* (Winter 1994): 5–9.

36. For an excellent historical and archeological study concerning "the upper room," see Jerome Murphy-O'Connor, OP, "The Cenacle — Topographical Setting for Acts 2:44–45," in *The Book of Acts in Its Palestinian Setting,* ed. Richard Bauckham (Grand Rapids: William B. Eerdmans, 1994), 303–321. Murphy-O'Connor's thesis is "that the determination of the strong Christian community in Aelia Capitolina to maintain contact with the site, despite severe obstacles, betrays an attachment to the place which is explicable only in terms of the importance the site had in the 1st century, when the quarter was the home of the most affluent residents of the city" (305). For a short archeological report on wealthy homes in the same quarter of Jerusalem, see Nachman Avigad, "How the Wealthy Lived in Herodian Jerusalem," *The Biblical Archaeology Review* 2 (December 1976): 21–32.

37. In Galatians, Paul associates James the brother of the Lord (1:19) with Cephas and John as one of the pillars of the church in Jerusalem (2:9). Later, he tells that until "some people came from James" Cephas used to eat with Gentiles, that is, Christians of Gentile origin, but when they came he withdrew from them (2:12). In 1 Corinthians, Paul speaks of Jesus' appearance to James and the apostles (15:7).

38. See John Koenig, *New Testament Hospitality* (Philadelphia: Fortress Press, 1985), 85–123. Koenig suggests that "the Acts of the Apostles may be read structurally as a collection of guest and host stories about the missionary ventures generated in the Spirit-led communities of Jerusalem and Antioch" (87).

39. Besides Galatians 3:27-28, see 1 Corinthians 12:13; Romans 10:12; and Colossians 3:11.

40. For the expression "the first day of the week" and its use in the New Testament, see Eugene LaVerdiere, "The Origins of Sunday in the New Testament," in *Sunday Morning: A Time for Worship,* ed. Mark Searle (Collegeville: The Liturgical Press, 1982), 11–27.

41. Jesus "raised his hands, and blessed them" after leading "them [out] as far as Bethany" (Luke 24:50). Earlier in the Gospel, Luke had situated Bethany "at the place called the Mount of Olives" (Luke 19:9).

42. In place of an ordinal, Hebrew uses an adjective, *rishon,* formed from the noun *rosh,* meaning "head."

43. Regarding the cults, see L. Michael White, *Building God's House in the Roman World* (Baltimore: The Johns Hopkins University Press, 1990), 26–59.

44. See White, *Building God's House in the Roman World,* 1–25, 102–148. Studying the beginnings of Christianity until the fourth century, White shows how early church architecture developed out of domestic architecture in various parts of the Roman world. He also shows how cult centers and synagogue architecture had a parallel development.

45. The term comes from Adolf Harnack, *The Mission and Expansion of Christianity in the First Three Centuries,* trans. J. Moffatt, 2 vols. (London: 1908), II: 86 f; see White, *Building God's House in the Roman World,* 154, note 36.

46. See Allison A. Trites, "The Prayer Motif in Luke-Acts," in *Perspectives on Luke-Acts,* 168–186.

Chapter 4

1. The Greek verb for "scatter" is *diaspeiro,* from which the noun *diaspora* ("dispersion" or "diaspora") is derived. In the New Testament, the noun itself appears only in John 7:35 (of Jews) and 1 Peter 1:1; James 1:1 (of Christians); see D. Sanger, *"diaspora, diaspeiro," Exegetical Dictionary of the New Testament* (Grand Rapids: Eerdmans, 1990), I: 311–312.

2. Outside the list of the Twelve (Luke 6:14–16) and of the Eleven (Acts 1:13), seven of the Twelve, namely Philip, Bartholomew, Matthew, Thomas, James the son of Alphaeus, Simon who was called the Zealot and Judas the son of James, are never mentioned in Luke-Acts.

3. Luke often introduces personages well before they become major figures in the story. Later, when they do, the reader is already familiar with them. See, for example, Barnabas, who sold a property and placed the proceeds at the feet of the apostles (7:36–37). Later, he would introduce Saul to the apostles and the community in Jerusalem (9:27) and become a major personage in the history of the church at Antioch (11:22–30; 12:25) along with its missions (13:1—15:39).

4. Philip either originally came from Caesarea or later made Caesarea his home. Philip's home became a house for the church in Caesarea (see 21:8–14).

5. For a redactional study of Acts 6:1–6, see Joseph T. Lienhard, sj, "Acts 6:1–6: A Redactional View," *Catholic Biblical Quarterly* 37 (1975): 228–236. Lienhard reviews earlier positions, relating Acts 6:1–7 to an early source or tradition described as a "Stephen cycle" or an "Antioch source" and approaches the story in the context of Acts. He also makes an effort to separate traditional from redactional elements in the story. I have found many of his suggestions helpful. Unfortunately, his study did not include the story's concluding verse (6:7).

6. From the very beginning, Saul had two names: Saul, a Jewish name, and Paul, a Roman name. The same was true of John Mark (12:25) and Silas Silvanus (15:40; 1 Peter 5:12). Acts uses the name Saul until 13:9, where it introduces the name Paul: "Saul, also known as Paul." Thereafter, throughout Saul Paul's mission among the Gentiles, it uses Paul, except in the discourses where Paul recounts his conversion story (22:7; 26:14).

7. Lienhard refers to *diakonia* at tables as "one of the lowlier aspects of the work" *(diakonia)*, "the work of a servant," contrasting with the *diakonia* of the word, "a divine calling" ("Acts 6:1–6: A Redactional View," 232, 234). That may have been the case for serving at ordinary tables, but not for serving at the table of the Lord. For this, see from Jesus' discourse at the Last Supper: "For who is greater: the one seated at table or the one who serves *(ho diakonon)*? Is it not the one seated at table? I am among you as the one who serves *(ho diakonon)*" (Luke 22:27). In a different context, Jesus compares a disciple to a servant who fulfills his duties (Luke 17:7–10).

8. Such a literary frame is often referred to as an "inclusion," or, in Latin, an *inclusio*. Such inclusions are frequent in Luke's writing. For examples, see the story of Zacchaeus (Luke 19:5, 9) and the story of Emmaus (Luke 24:16, 31). It often indicates a story's general or principal theme.

9. *Dining in the Kingdom of God,* 58–70.

10. *Dining in the Kingdom of God,* 75–86.

11. See F. Scott Spencer, "Neglected Widows in Acts 6:1–7," *Catholic Biblical Quarterly* 56 (October 1994): 715–733. I found Spencer's work very helpful in its analysis of Acts 6:1, as well as for the treatment of widows in Luke-Acts; much less helpful, however, for the relationship of Acts 6:1 to 6:2–6 and 6:7. In his view, the apostles subordinated " 'menial' forms of *diakonia*, such as feeding widows, to the more 'spiritual' pursuits of teaching and preaching and of prayer." In this the apostles failed to follow the pattern set by the Lukan Jesus "of conjoining various forms of service, not of stratifying or polarizing them" (729–730). Whereas Lienhard viewed the contrast as historical ("Acts 6:1–6: A Redactional View," 228–236), Spencer attributed it to the apostles.

12. Away from Jerusalem, the early disciples also had two foci or settings for Christian life and ministry, one in the synagogue and one in their homes. After the destruction of the temple and when they became separated from the synagogue, they continued to have two foci, one in a large home open to them where they could gather as a church, the other in their respective homes.

13. Acts distinguishes between a Greek person and a Greek-speaking person. The designation, "Hellenists" *(Hellenistai,* 6:1; 9:29), a Greek-speaking person, is derived from *Hellenisti,* the word for "Greek," in the sense of the Greek language (see 21:37). The word for a Greek person, on the other hand, is *Hellen* (11:20; 14:1; 16:1, 3; 17:4; 18:4; 19:10, 17; 20:21; 21:28), which is derived from *Hellas,* the word for "Greece" (20:2). Its adjectival form is *Hellenis* (17:12).

14. Acts recognizes the distinction between a Jewish person *(Ioudaios,* 2:5, 10, 14; 9:22, 23, passim, 79 times in all) and a Hebrew-speaking person *(Ebraios,* 6:1). Not all Jews spoke Hebrew or Aramaic. In the diaspora, the language commonly spoken was Greek.

15. The designation "the Hebrews" *(hoi Ebraioi),* used only in 6:1, is derived from *Ebrais,* the word used in Acts for the Hebrew language (21:40; 22:2; 26:14). The term *Ebraisti,* a second term for the Hebrew language corresponding to *Hellenisti,* is used in the New Testament only in John 5:2; 19:13, 17, 20; 20:16; Revelation 9:11; 16:16, not in Acts.

16. Acts also uses the term *Hellenistai* with reference to Greek-speaking Jews who were not Christians (9:29).

17. See Bruce, *The Acts of the Apostles, Greek Text,* 181.

18. See Johnson, *The Acts of the Apostles,* 105–106.

19. In Luke, Jesus raises to life the only son of a widow at Nain (Luke 7:11–17). One of the examples Jesus gives while inaugurating his ministry at Nazareth is Elijah going to the widow of Zarephath (Luke 4:25–26; see 1 Kings 17:7–24). He also uses the figure of a persistent widow in one of his parables on prayer (Luke 18:1–8). While teaching in the temple, he then warns his disciples against acting like the scribes who "devour the houses of widows," exploiting them religiously (Luke 20:45–47), reinforcing the warning with the example of a poor widow, who, out of her poverty, placed two small coins into the temple treasury (Luke 21:1–4). Besides these references to widows, we also have Anna, the prophetess, in the prologue (Luke 2:36–38). In Acts, besides 6:1, the only other reference to widows is in the story of Tabitha (9:36–43).

20. The Greek word for "daily," *kathemerinos,* an adjective, appears only here in the New Testament. Ordinarily, Luke-Acts uses an adverbial phrase, *kath' hemera* (Luke 9:23; 11:3; 16:19; 19:47; Acts 2:46; 3:2; 17:11; 19:9). The adjective *kathemerinos* also appears one time in the Septuagint (Judith 12:15).

21. In both the choice of the Seven and the call of Levi, the first setting or situation introduces a basic theme to which the story returns in the conclusion. For Levi, that theme is the call to follow Jesus (Luke 5:27–28), which is then developed in the conclusion as Jesus' calling sinners to repentance (5:32). In Acts 6:1–7, the theme is the growth of the community, introduced in 6:1 and developed in the conclusion, 6:7.

22. The reference to "the word of God" in Acts 6:2 parallels the same expression in 6:7; 12:24 and 19:20. For an excellent article on the expression, see Jerome Kodell, "'The Word of God grew,' The Ecclesial Tendency of *Logos* in Acts 6, 7; 12, 24; 19, 20" *Biblica* 55 (1974): 505–519. Summarizing the article, Kodell notes, "After the resurrection, the word of God is embedded in the Christian community. It lives in the the church in a community of life with the believers. In preaching the word, the believer is preaching his own life as lived in community, and the offer and challenge of faith is an offer of community" (518).

23. See Kodell, "'The Word of God grew,' The Ecclesial Tendency of *Logos* in Acts 6, 7; 12, 24; 19, 20" 505–519.

24. Older studies of Paul's conversion in Acts focused on the similarities and the differences in the three accounts (9:1–19; 22:1–21; 26:1–23) and accounted for these by postulating different sources. More recently, the similarities and the differences have been attributed to the hand of Luke. See, for example, D.M. Stanley, "Paul's Conversion in Acts: Why the Three Accounts?" *Catholic Biblical Quarterly* 15 (1953): 315–338; Charles W. Hedrick, "Paul's Conversion/Call: A Comparative Analysis of the Three Reports in Acts," *Journal of Biblical Literature* 100 (1981) 415–432. For a contemporary approach more sensitive to literary form and context, see Beverly Roberts Gaventa, *From Darkness to Light* (Philadelphia: Fortress Press, 1986), 52–95. See also Raymond F. Collins, "Paul's Damascus Experience: Reflections on the Lukan Account," *Louvain Studies* 11 (1986): 99–118.

25. Paul himself spoke of his conversion in his letter to the Galatians: "But when [God], who from my mother's womb had set me apart and called me through his grace, was pleased to reveal his Son to me, so that I might proclaim him to the Gentiles . . . " (Galatians 1:15–16). See also 1 Corinthians 15:8: "Last of all, as to one born abnormally, he appeared to me."

26. "Before the baptism, moreover, the one who baptizes and the one being baptized must fast, and any others who can. And you must tell the one being baptized to fast for one or two days beforehand" *Didache* 7:4, *Early Christian Fathers* (New York: Macmillan Publishing Company, 1970), 174. For the date, literary form and the context, see Eugene LaVerdiere, "The Eucharist in the New Testament and the Early Church VIII; On the Lord's Day: The Eucharist in the *Didache*" *Emmanuel* 100 (October 1994): 452–465.

27. Justin Martyr's "First Apology" 61–67; see Richardson, *Early Christian Fathers,* 282–288. For the date, literary form and the context, see Eugene LaVerdiere, "The Eucharist in the New Testament and the Early Church X; The Food Called Eucharist: The Eucharist in the Writings of Justin Martyr" *Emmanuel* 100 (December 1994): 580–593.

28. See Robert Karris, OFM, *Luke: Artist and Theologian* (New York: Paulist Press, 1985), 47–78.

29. See Joseph F. Wimmer, *Fasting in the New Testament: A Study in Biblical Theology,* Theological Inquiries (New York: Paulist Press, 1982).

30. Beginning with 1:13–14 until 4:4, Acts also described the growth of the church by naming the members (1:13–14) or giving specific numbers. In 1:15, the number was 120; in 2:41, 3,000 were added; in 4:4, the number grew to some 5,000.

31. "The Way" *(he hodos)* is an early designation for the church (see also 18:26; 19:9, 23; 22:4; 24:14, 22). As "the Way," the church was not just a reform movement in Judaism. Nor was it another Jewish sect *(hairesis)* alongside those of the Pharisees, the Sadducees and the Essenes (see 14:14). As "the Way" of the Lord Jesus (18:25), it was comparable to Judaism itself, representing its authentic expression. The Essenes at Qumran and elsewhere also saw themselves as the adherents of the Way (in Hebrew, *derek*). See 1 QS 10:20 f; CD 1:13; 2:6.

32. For Paul's own account of his life as a persecutor of the church, see Galatians 1:13–14, 22–24; 1 Corinthians 15:9; Philippians 3:6; 1 Timothy 1:13.

33. For a concise presentation concerning Paul, the chronology of his life and his career, see Joseph A. Fitzmyer, SJ, "Paul," *The New Jerome Biblical Commentary* 79 (Englewood Cliffs, New Jersey: Prentice Hall, 1990), 1329–1337.

34. Later in the two discourses, Paul would refer to "light from the sky" as a "great light" (22:6, 11) and "a light from the sky, brighter than the sun" (26:13).

35. See Ronald D. Witherup, SS, "Functional Redundancy in the Acts of the Apostles: A Case Study," *Journal for the Study of the New Testament* 48 (1992): 67–86, see 67, n. 1; see also Gaventa, *From Darkness to Light* 66; Benjamin J. Hubbard, "Commissioning Stories in Luke-Acts: A Study of Their Antecedants, Form and Content," *Semeia* VIII (1977): 103–126, and "The Role of Commissioning Accounts in Acts," in *Perspectives on Luke-Acts,* 187–198.

36. For a related but somewhat different interpretation, see Dennis Hamm, SJ, "Paul's Blindness and Its Healing: Clues to Symbolic Intent (Acts 9; 22 and 26)," *Biblica* 71 (1, 90): 63–72. Hamm's conclusion is that "Luke signals to the reader that Paul has his eyes opened spiritually even while he is physically blind" (71). My interpretation suggests that Paul has his eyes opened spiritually, that is, he wants to see, but is unable to do so.

37. Ananias is the second early Christian in the Book of Acts called by that name. The first, the husband of Sapphira, belonged to the church in Jerusalem (see 5:1–11).

38. That Ananias was highly regarded by the Jews in Damascus indicates that until that time Christians had peaceful relations with the Jews, and that they had not yet been affected by the persecution in Jerusalem.

39. See Pierre Grelot, "The Resurrection of Jesus: Its Biblical and Jewish Background," *The Resurrection and Modern Biblical Thought* (New York: Corpus Books, 1970), 18–19.

40. Christianity must have come to Damascus at an extremely early date for a community to be established there before persecution broke out in Jerusalem (see 8:1–3; 9:1–2). The New Testament gives no indication how the Word and the Way came to Damascus.

41. For the story of Peter and Cornelius, see Jacques Dupont, *Études sur les Actes des Apôtres,* Lectio Divina 45 (Paris: Les Éditions du Cerf, 1967): 75–81; Robert W. Wall, "Peter, 'Son' of Jonah: The Conversion of Cornelius in the Context of the Canon," *Journal for the Study of the New Testament* 29 (1987): 79–80.

42. See also the protests by Pharisees and scribes that Jesus "welcomes sinners and eats with them" (Luke 15:1–2). In response, Jesus told them three parables, those of the lost sheep (15:3–7), the lost coin (15:8–10) and the lost son (15:11–32).

43. After the story of Cornelius, centurions figure several times in Paul's great journey to Rome (21:32; 22:25–28; 23:17, 23; 27:1–44), very often assuring Paul's safety and the continuation of his journey to Rome. As such, they are instruments of divine providence.

44. For God-fearers *(phoboumenoi ton theon)* in Acts see also 10:22; 13:16, 26. A closely related term is *sebomenoi* (Acts 13:50; 17:4, 17) and *sebemonoi ton theon* (Acts 16:14; 18:7). Josephus ascribes the wealth and influence of Jews in the diaspora in part to God-fearers: "But no one need wonder that there was so much wealth in our temple, for all the Jews throughout the habitable world (*kata ten oikoumenen;* see Luke 2:1), and those who worshipped God *(sebomenon ton theon),* even those from Asia and Europe, had been contributing to it for a very long time" (*Jewish Antiquities* XIV, 110).

45. For the close relationship between giving alms and prayer, see Matthew 6:2–6 and *Didache* 15:4.

46. For various reasons, devout Jews avoided being tanners of leather, innkeepers, tax collectors and caravaneers. See Joachim Jeremias, *Jerusalem in the Time of Jesus* (Philadelphia: Fortress Press, 1969), 5–6, 303–312.

47. The Third Letter of John describes a situation where the church met at the home of someone named Diotrephes (9–10). The letter presupposes that Christians traveling from other cities and regions would normally have received hospitality at the home of Diotrephes. In the letter, "the Presbyter" (1) accuses Diotrephes of refusing to give hospitality to "the brothers" coming from the church led by "the Presbyter." That is why the Presbyter is writing to another Christian, one named Gaius (1), requesting hospitality for "the brothers" (5–8) and asking Gaius to "help them in a way worthy of God to continue their journey" (6). The Presbyter himself intends to come quite soon and stay with Gaius (14).

48. See Mark 7:1–23.

49. For a brief synthesis concerning Jewish meal customs and the dietary laws, see Gene Schramm, "Meal Customs, Jewish Dietary Laws," *The Anchor Bible Dictionary,* IV, 648–650. The Hebrew term for the Jewish dietary laws is *kashruth,* a term that can also be applied "to any matter of ritual acceptability or appropriateness" (648). With reference to food, *kashruth* covers "the full range of biblical precept, rabbinic ordinances, evolving custom, and local practice within the Jewish community" (648).

50. The same term, *anelemphthe,* was used in Acts 1:2 for Jesus' ascension (see also Luke 9:51).

51. The situation was the same in the story of Jesus and Levi the tax collector (Luke 5:27–39). Before Jesus called Levi to follow him, Levi was a tax collector. But after Levi left everything behind and followed Jesus, he was a follower. So were the other tax collectors who accepted Levi's invitation to dine with Jesus. It was very appropriate, therefore, for Jesus and his disciples to dine with them.

52. The structure of Peter's discourse at the home of Cornelius is the same as that of his discourse on Pentecost (2:14–41), where the introduction addressed the immediate situation (2:14–21), the body gave the basic message concerning Jesus as the Messiah (2:22–36) and the conclusion showed that many Jews in Jerusalem came to be baptized (2:37–41).

53. The adjective *prosopolemptes,* which Luke coined from the expression *prosopon lambano,* literally "to raise (someone's) face," meaning preferring someone to another. For the expression see Galatians 2:6; Psalm 82:2 (LXX, 81:2), Deuteronomy 10:17. Applied to Jesus, see Luke 20:21.

54. The Greek term *logos* refers to "word" in relation to meaning and communication. As in Acts 10:36, it can be translated as "message." The Greek term *hrema* refers to "word" in relation to the reality it conveys. As in Acts 10:37, it can be translated as "what."

Chapter 5

1. Paul's missions from Antioch began *circa* 46 AD and lasted until *circa* 60 AD.

2. During the second mission, Paul returned to Antioch for a brief visit (18:22b–23a), but literarily Paul's visit to Antioch is part of the same mission from Antioch. After the visit, Paul continued the mission. Had Luke intended to present 18:23–19:20 as a new mission, he would have introduced it as he had the two previous missions (13:1–3; 15:36–41).

3. Barnabas' name is first in the list (13:1), as Peter's name is first in the list of the Twelve (Luke 6:12–16; Acts 1:13). In the first mission from Antioch, Barnabas was the leader.

4. The gospel message and the church also spread through devout Jews who came to Jerusalem on pilgrimage, met some early Christians and returned home as Christians with the gospel message. Acts presents a typical but idealized scenario of how that happened in the story of the Ethiopian eunuch (8:26–40). Although Acts is silent on the matter, this is very likely the way Christianity first came to Damascus, Alexandria and Rome.

5. For a review of traveling conditions in the first century, see Jerome Murphy-O'Connor, OP, "On the Road and on the Sea with St. Paul," *Bible Review* (Summer 1985): 38–47.

6. The apostle Paul had two names: one Jewish (Saul) and the other Gentile (Paul). Hellenized as *Paulos,* Saul's Gentile name was actually Roman: in Latin, *Paulus.*

7. They stoned Paul as they had stoned Stephen (7:58a). At the stoning of Stephen, the witnesses laid down their cloaks at the feet of Saul (7:58b). Saul had consented to Stephen's execution (8:1). Ironically, he now suffered the same fate. Unlike Stephen, however, Paul survived the stoning.

8. This is the first time that presbyters are mentioned in the Book of Acts. Although Luke attributed the appointing of presbyters to Barnabas and Paul, they themselves did not initiate the institution. When the two went to Jerusalem for the great assembly, Luke wrote, they met with the apostles and the presbyters of the church in Jerusalem.

By the writing of Luke-Acts, presbyters were already an ordinary part of the structure of the church. At the time, however, the presbyters were not distinct from the overseers *(episkopoi).* In his farewell discourse to the elders of the church at Ephesus (20:17), Paul addressed them as overseers (20:28).

9. Prayer and fasting have become part of the life of the church (see also 13:3). At the great banquet Levi gave for Jesus, Jesus defended the disciples for eating and drinking, but spoke of days to come, "when the bridegroom is taken away from them," when they would fast (Luke 5:33–35).

10. John, who was also called Mark, was introduced when Peter went to the home of his mother, Mary, after Peter's mysterious release from prison (12:12). John Mark also accompanied Barnabas and Saul after their relief mission to Judea, when they visited Jerusalem and returned to Antioch (12:25). Later, Mark left them in Perga in Pamphylia and return to Jerusalem (13:13).

11. Timothy was "the son of a Jewish woman who was a believer, but his father was a Greek" (16:1).

12. For Prisca (Priscilla) and Aquila, see also 18:2–3, 24–28; 1 Corinthians 16–19; Romans 16:3; 2 Timothy 4:19. For a study of this couple who contributed significantly to Paul's missionary work, see Jerome Murphy-O'Connor, "Prisca and Aquila," *Bible Review* (December 1992): 40–51, 62.

13. Concluding the story of the beginning of the church at Antioch (11:19–26), Luke wrote that "it was in Antioch that the disciples were first called Christians" (11:26b). Now that the church included a large number of Gentiles as well as Jews, it represented a new reality. Neither Jew nor Gentile, the new reality required a new name.

14. Tyre, a port city in Phoenicia, played an important role in Mark's Gospel. People came to Jesus from, among other places, the region of Tyre and Sidon (Mark 3:8). Jesus himself went to Tyre with his disciples. That is where he healed the daughter of a Syrophoenician woman (Mark 7:24–30). In Luke, Jesus mentioned Tyre and Sidon in relation to the misson of the seventy-two (Luke 10:1–16): "Woe to you, Chorazin! Woe to you, Bethsaida! For if the mighty deeds done in your midst had been done in Tyre and Sidon, they would long ago have repented, sitting in sackcloth and ashes. But it will be more tolerable for Tyre and Sidon at the judgment than for you" (Luke 10:13–14).

15. Like Phoenicia, Samaria has an important position in the Gospel of Luke. At first, the poeple of Samaria did not welcome Jesus because he was on his way to Jerusalem (Luke 9:52–53). Later, rebuking the disciples for wanting to call down fire from heaven on them (Luke 9:54), Jesus held up a Samaritan as a model for a scholar of the law (Luke 10:25–37). Later yet, after Jesus healed ten lepers, only one, a Samaritan, returned to thank him (Luke 17:11–19). As in the case of Phoenicia, the stories about Samaria announce the early evangelization of Samaria.

16. In the Gospel, Luke probably had such converts in mind, that is, members of the community who had come from the party of the Pharisees, when he referred to Pharisees at meals with Jesus (Luke 5:27–39; 7:36–50; 11:37–54). The Christian Pharisees in Acts (15:5) have exclusive or separatist attitudes similar to those of the Pharisees who were Jesus' host or fellow guests for a formal meal.

17. The presbyters were introduced in the story of Acts at the end of the first mission, when Paul and Barnabas "appointed presbyters for them in each church" (14:23).

18. See *Dining in the Kingdom of God,* 86–95.

19. 1 Corinthians 10:14–33, Paul describes the context; see Eugene LaVerdiere, *The Eucharist in the New Testament and the Early Church* (Collegeville: The Liturgical Press, 1996), 34–37.

20. The letter follows the order given in Leviticus 17–18.

21. See Johnson, *The Acts of the Apostles,* 267.

22. Acts 16:10–17 is the first of four "we" sections in Acts.

23. The word *proseuche,* meaning a place of prayer, is the term used in Egypt for a synagogue. At Philippi, the term could indicate the presence of Jews who had come from Alexandria.

24. The same pattern can be observed for the baptism of Cornelius and his household (10:47–49).

25. Christianity had economic implications in the world of Luke-Acts. Later, at Ephesus, those who earned their livelihood from the cult of Artemis provoked a riot.

26. For the cultural background of the story, see Johnson, *The Acts of the Apostles,* 302–304.

27. See Acts 2:40, 47; 4:9, 12; 11:14; 14:9; 15:1, 11; 16:30–31; 27:20, 31.

Chapter 6

1. See "Fate," *The Oxford Classical Dictionary,* 2nd ed. (Oxford: Clarendon Press, 1970), 430–432; John M. Dillon, "Fate, Greek Conception of," *The Anchor Bible Dictionary* (New York: Doubleday, 1992) 2: 776–778.

2. For Luke's use of *dei* in relation to salvation history, see Joseph A. Fitzmyer, *The Gospel According to Luke* I–IX, The Anchor Bible 28 (Garden City, New York: Doubleday, 1981), 179–192.

3. For the use of *dei* in the meal narratives in the gospel, see *Dining in the Kingdom of God,* 114–115, 131, 166.

4. The riot was provoked by a silversmith named Demetrius who called a meeting of workers from various crafts associated with the temple of Artemis. Many workers depended for their livelihood on the sales of miniature shrines and other religious objects (19:23–25).

5. While they were in Lystra, Timothy joined Paul and Silas. Timothy's mother was a Christian and his father was a Greek (16:1–3).

6. Asia Minor represents the western part of what is now Turkey. It included "the Phrygian and Galatian territory" as well as the Roman "province of Asia," where Paul, Silas, and Timothy were "prevented by the holy Spirit from preaching the message," that is, from speaking the word (*lalesai ton logon,* 16:6).

7. Neapolis in Macedonia was one of several cities in the Mediterranean world named Neapolis, meaning New City. Today, the most famous city named Neapolis (Naples) is in Italy.

8. The story of Acts is usually told in the third person. In Acts 16:10, the story suddenly drops the third person and continues in the first person plural: "When he had seen the vision, we sought *(ezetesamen)* passage to Macedonia at once, concluding that God had called us *(hemas)* to proclaim the good news to them." The story of Acts then continues in the first person plural until 16:17. Acts 16:10–17 is the first of four such passages told in the first person plural: 16:10–17; 20:5–15; 21:1–18; 27:1–28:16. These passages are referred to as "the we-passages."

In the great journey to Rome, both passages that refer to the eucharist (20:7–12; 27:33–38) are included in a "we-passage."

For the relationship of the "we-passages" to Luke, the author of Acts, see V. K. Robbins, "The We-Passages in Acts and Ancient Sea Voyages," *Biblical Research* 20 (1975): 5–18, who concludes that the "we-passages" reflect a conventional literary device for sea voyages in the Hellenistic world. For a nuanced response, see Joseph Fitzmyer, *Luke the Theologian: Aspects of His Teaching* (New York: Paulist Press, 1989), 1–26, esp. 16–22; also Bruce, *Acts of the Apostles, Greek Text,* 509.

9. By the beginning of the second century, Troas had a flourishing Christian community. On the way to his martyrdom at Rome, Ignatius of Antioch spent a short time at Troas, where the local community reached out to him. Three of the seven letters Ignatius wrote on the journey were written at Troas: the letter to the church at Philadelphia, the letter to the church at Smyrna and the letter to its bishop, Polycarp (see LaVerdiere, *The Eucharist in the New Testament and the Early Church,* 150, 159–163).

10. The Gaius identified as a Macedonian in the story of the riot of the Ephesian craftsmen (19:29) is someone else. Gaius was a popular name in the Greco-Roman world. See Haenchen, *The Acts of the Apostles: A Commentary,* 52–53.

11. The story of Troas (20:7–12) is included in the second (20:5–15) of the four "we-passages" in Acts.

12. In the Gospel's story of Zacchaeus, the end of the introduction is at the same time the beginning of the body, and the end of the body is at the same time the beginning of the conclusion (Luke 19:5, 9). The same thing can be observed in the story of Emmaus (Luke 24:16, 31).

13. For the expression "the first day of the week," its meaning and history, see Chapter III, 30–34; Thomas J. Talley, *The Origins of the Liturgical Year* (New York: Pueblo, 1986), 13–18; David Power, *The Eucharistic Mystery,* 74–75; E. LaVerdiere, "The

Origins of Sunday in the New Testament," *Sunday Morning: A Time for Worship,* ed. Mark Searle (Collegeville: The Liturgical Press, 1982), 11–27.

14. For the "we-passages," see the above note 8.

15. In John, as in Luke, Jesus spoke to the crowd (John 6:25–59) after giving them something to eat (6:1–15). After the Last Supper (John 13:1–38), Jesus addressed the apostles with a farewell discourse (John 14:1–17:26).

16. This is the tenth time that Luke-Acts refers to a centurion. In the Gospel, there was the centurion at Capernaum (Luke 7:1–10) and the one at the crucifixion (Luke 23:47). Both had very significant roles. The first centurion with a role in Acts was Cornelius, the first Gentile convert (10:1–11:18). In Paul's great journey to Rome, centurions have important roles in six passages, including the centurion who had custody of Paul on the journey to Rome (21:32; 22:25–26; 23:17, 23; 24:23; 27:1, 6, 11, 31, 41; 28:16). All the centurions in Luke-Acts are presented in a favorable light.

17. Bearing the name of Caesar, the Cohort Augusta was very prestigious. Giving the name in this context emphasizes the importance of Paul's journey to Rome where he would appear before Caesar.

18. See above note 8.

19. For Paul's sea journeys, in particular the journey from Asia Minor to Rome, see Jerome Murphy-O'Connor, "On the Road and on the Sea with St. Paul," *Bible Review* (Summer 1985): 38–47, in particular 45–47.

20. For the Hellenistic background regarding shipwrecks, see Gary B. Miles and Garry Trompf, "Luke and Antiphon: The Theology of Acts 27–28 in the Light of Pagan Beliefs about Divine Retribution, Pollution, and Shipwreck," *Harvard Theological Review* 69 (July–October 1976): 259–267; David Ladouceur, "Hellenistic Preconceptions of Shipwreck and Pollution as a Context for Acts 27–28," *Harvard Theological Review* 73 (July–October 1980): 435–449.

21. At Philippi, Paul's deliverance from prison also took place around midnight (*kata de to mesonyktion,* 16:25). The jailer set a table for Paul and Silas between midnight and dawn (*hemeras de yenomenes,* 16:35). At Troas, Paul spoke until around midnight (*mechri mesonyktion*). He broke the bread between midnight and daybreak (*achri auges*). Here in the storm, Paul breaks the bread between midnight (*kata meson tes nyktes,* 27:27) and when day began to dawn (*achri de hou hemera emellen ginesthai,* 27:33).

22. See Bruce, *Acts of the Apostles, Greek Text,* 526.

Conclusion

1. See Eugene LaVerdiere, "Before Ever There Was a Name," *The Eucharist in the New Testament and the Early Church* (Collegeville: The Liturgical Press, 1996), 1–11.

2. *Dining in the Kingdom of God.*

3. See Eugene LaVerdiere, sss, and William G. Thompson, sj, "New Testament Communities in Transition: A Study of Matthew and Luke," *Theological Studies* 37 (December 1976): 567–597; reprinted in *Why the Church?* ed. Walter J. Burghardt, sj, and William G. Thompson, sj, (New York: Paulist Press, 1976), 23–53.